Strategic
Leadership
and Strategic
Management

Strategic Leadership and Strategic Management

Leading and Managing Change on the Edge of Chaos

Shand Stringham

iUniverse, Inc.
Bloomington

Strategic Leadership and Strategic Management
Leading and Managing Change on the Edge of Chaos

iUniverse books may be ordered through booksellers or by contacting:

iUniverse
1663 Liberty Drive
Bloomington, IN 47403
www.iuniverse.com
1-800-Authors (1-800-288-4677)

ISBN: 978-1-4759-6431-8 (sc)
ISBN: 978-1-4759-6433-2 (hc)
ISBN: 978-1-4759-6432-5 (ebk)

Library of Congress Control Number: 2012922770

Printed in the United States of America

iUniverse rev. date: 12/06/2012

Dedication

With much love to my wife, Quin, who has accompanied me on life's journey around the world. She shared my excitement for writing this book and provided much support, encouragement, and assistance.

And with love also to our children, the Five Cs,
Carson, Cammi, Caleb, Casey and Corrie,
who are all maturing into extraordinary
people. I'm very proud of them all.

Acknowledgments

I owe a special debt to my students through the years who contributed to our classroom dialogue on strategy, leadership, management, strategic thinking and strategic planning, and who have had a profound impact on my thinking.

I express my gratitude to many colleagues for their generous support in reviewing early drafts of this book and for their comments and suggestions which I found invaluable in making revisions to the manuscript. James Ziegenfuss, Robert Stephens, Jay Mumford, James Wofford Ulrich, Byron Shaffer, Louis Sheehan, and Carson Stringham reviewed the material and provided valuable feedback and insights about the academic application of the ideas and concepts for college curricula. Bryn Marley, Scot Seitz, Robert Smith, Thomas Wonsiewicz, Brad Morgan, Tracey Jones, Kathi Becker, and Phil Becker provided important suggestions about the book's potential application for corporate and government organizational settings. Robert Turner and Shellie Stringham Harris did me the immense service of reviewing an early draft and providing editorial suggestions vital to the revision and preparation of the final manuscript draft. Their input and comments resulted in substantial changes which hopefully will contribute to greater readability and overall understanding.

And finally, I express my profound thanks to my wife, Quin, who faithfully reads and edits everything I write and who provided patient support and understanding throughout the writing and preparation of this book.

I acknowledge that I have received advice and support from many quarters, but at the same time I accept full responsibility for the final product. After all the editing suggestions proffered, the remaining thorns, burrs, and other imperfections reflect my own stubbornness and obstinacy.

Shand H. Stringham
Carlisle, Pennsylvania
October 2012

About the Author

Shand Stringham holds a Bachelor of Arts (BA) degree in Political Science and International Relations from the University of Utah (1972). He completed a multidisciplinary Masters program in History at the National Autonomous University of Mexico (UNAM) in Mexico City, Mexico, in 1981. He subsequently completed a Masters of Public Administration (MPA) at Penn State Harrisburg in 1998 and is now a doctoral candidate (Ph.D., ABD) in Penn State Harrisburg's School of Public Affairs.

Shand served twenty-six years in the United States Army retiring with the rank of Colonel. He spent his last five years on active duty on the faculty at the U.S. Army War College at Carlisle, PA, teaching National Security and Strategy. He then worked as the Chief Learning Officer for the Pennsylvania Department of Transportation (PennDOT) overseeing the activities of the agency's Transportation University with responsibility for leadership and management training throughout the agency. After leaving PennDOT, he worked at the Center for Training, Learning and Leadership Development at Penn State Hershey Medical Center developing and teaching classes in management, leadership, project management, and medical Spanish.

During the past 12 years, he has worked as an adjunct professor on the faculties of Duquesne University, Penn State Harrisburg, Shippensburg University, and Harrisburg University of Science and Technology, teaching courses on leadership, management, business and society, business strategy, strategic planning, team building and teamwork, organizational behavior, decision making and problem solving, business ethics and global ethics.

Shand now resides with his wife, Quin, on a bluff on the north edge of Carlisle, Pennsylvania, overlooking the beautiful Cumberland Valley.

Contents

Introduction

I once heard a fascinating parable concerning a team of astronauts from earth which lands on a planet in a far-off galaxy. As the astronauts disembark from their spacecraft, they are met by a group of aliens who appear to be very excited about their arrival. Through hand motions and body language, the earthlings are invited to accompany the aliens to a magnificent structure nearby. As they enter into the building, each of the astronauts is escorted by alien guides to a different room where they are seized, strapped down to long tables, and dissected. When the vivisections are completed, the alien scientists know everything there is to know about earthling physiology but little about earthlings themselves.

That pretty well summarizes the state of much leadership scholarship today. Because it was mostly produced through the auspices of scientific methodology which is based upon linear reasoning focused by a reductionist perspective, researchers and scholars have generally broken down leadership into all of its component parts for examination, but have lost sight of the essential nature of leadership *relationships* in the process. Published leadership research provides a great deal of information in segmented parcels, but the true essence of leadership generally evades its grasp. It is not that this literature is not good; it's just that it doesn't inform the reader much about how to lead people in organizational contexts.

Twenty years ago, Maxwell observed that there were very few leadership books—most were about management.[1] Fortunately, some of the shortfall in leadership literature as been rectified in recent years. But there is a very good reason behind Maxwell's observation. From their founding in the 1880s, American schools of management have long eschewed teaching leadership as a legitimate academic discipline because it could not be approached in an analytical and scientific way similar to how they approached management studies. Leadership was simply not taught in our schools of business and management and its study was left to military academies, war colleges, and schools of divinity.

It wasn't until the late 1970s and early 1980s that management schools began to take note that leadership in fact forms an important if not critical skill set in dealing with organizations and people under turbulent conditions of constant change. Management textbooks began to appear with entire chapters focused on leadership but the authors typically approached the new topic area using thinly disguised, traditional management models. The outcome was predictably confusing. Even today, many textbooks treat leadership and management as synonymous concepts or subsume leadership under the umbrella of management. Neither of these two approaches is useful or appropriate as they distort the reality of the distinction between the two functions.

In this book, I approach *leadership* and *management* as distinct but complementary organizational roles. The truth is, we suffer from an unfortunate terminology deficiency in the English language—we do not have a good, solid word in modern English that combines the concepts of *leadership* and *management* in one term. Lee Hock once sought to fix a similar problem with the terms *chaos* and *order* by creating the new word, *chaordic*.[2] The term has enjoyed only limited success in the literature although I think that Hock was probably on the right track.

I have not attempted to synthesize a word here that combines the concepts of both *leadership* and *management* although I do resort occasionally to the ungainly hyphenated term *leader-manager* to refer to people in organizations today who by default must perform both roles. And so, many sentences throughout this book may seem a little clumsy as I link both terms for completeness' sake to avoid the distortions inherent in other works where one or the other term is used to count as the same thing.

The issue is not a small problem today. In earlier years, it passed unremarkably simply because the two functions were discretely assigned to different people at different levels in organizations. Today, with the flattening of organizations and the resulting reduction of multiple layers of middle-level management, the roles and functions of leadership and management now frequently reside in the same people throughout many levels of the organization. Today, most of us wear two hats—the *leadership* hat and the *management* hat and, far from representing the same skill set, **the roles and functions of leadership and management tug us in opposite directions**. These roles are admittedly complementary, but they are indeed different. It takes an astute individual to know when to respond to the needs of the leadership role or the needs of the management role amidst the hyper-competitive, turbulent environments that most organizations experience today. An important purpose of this book is to assist students in distinguishing between the two functional needs of *leadership* and *management* and knowing when and how to apply them effectively.

Building on the seminal work of Frederick Winslow Taylor's *The Principles of Scientific Management* (1911), Henri Fayol's *Administration Industrielle et Generale* (1916), Max Weber's, *Wirtschaft und Gesellschaft* (1922) and Luther Gulick's POSDCORB model (1937), most management theory and models that populate American leadership and management textbooks today were generated in the 1950s, 60s and 70s in an industrial, manufacturing economy during a period of relative stability and predictability.[3] These models fit the conditions of their day, but they are much less useful and appropriate for the constant, rapid change of our information economy today. Unfortunately, most textbooks continue to emphasize these outdated models and approaches, even though they yield uneven and frequently unsatisfactory results.

A good example of this conceptual disconnect is the Five Forces model, which was developed during the 1970s by Harvard Professor Michael Porter. Some scholars today suggest that the model is relatively static and cannot adequately reflect the dynamics of today's rapidly-changing industrial environments.[4] In a similar vein, the Industry/Product Life-Cycle model does not fully capture the complexity and turbulence that rapid technological change creates in the marketplace today. These issues illustrate another purpose of this book—to encourage readers to reexamine and consider classical theory and models in the light of emerging insights from systems theory and the complexity sciences. Complexity and chaos have much to teach us about leading and managing organizations today. The working environment of most corporate, public, and non-profit organizations has evolved from stability and predictability to white water environments characterized by rampant change, uncertainty and hyper-competition. I attempt to provide readers here with a set of conceptual tools to not only understand the nature of these changes but to actually enjoy and thrive in the white-water work environments we experience today.

This book examines the basic concepts of *strategy, leadership* and *management*. It also addresses the numerous manifestations of *strategic planning* in the work place and the more ethereal concept of *strategic thinking,* both precursors to effective strategic leadership and strategic management. There is no shortage of texts and journal articles available in the literature today on strategy, strategic leadership, and strategic management and some are quite good. However, many of them suffer from conceptual deficiencies derived from the imprecise definition and application of terms. Another purpose of this book is to suggest a more precise understanding of the terms *strategy* and *leadership* so that the otherwise excellent ideas brought out in the literature can be broadly compared, contrasted, and synthesized into a more usable body of understanding about the topic for students and practitioners alike.

This book is especially designed for undergraduate and graduate students who are struggling to put the pieces together about leadership, management and organizational science in their college courses of study. It can also be useful to leader-manager practitioners working in corporate, government, and non-profit organizations. For many readers, the ideas introduced and discussed here will be new and unfamiliar. For them it will serve as a primer on strategic leadership and strategic management. For others, it will merely confirm ideas about strategic leadership and strategic management they might already know but can bring the concepts into sharper focus.

The book departs from the traditional practice of keeping discussion of business and public administration separate. It is purposefully cross-disciplinary, a result of my personal belief that concepts of strategic leadership, strategic management and strategic planning are equally applicable in the corporate, government, and non-profit sectors. Accordingly, I have used case examples from all three sectors to illustrate some of the ideas discussed in the text.

The genesis of this book was inspired by leadership shortcomings I have observed in my own professional organizational experience. I believe that Harvard Professor John Kotter was spot on when he observed that most organizational change efforts are over-managed and under-led.[5] This book also addresses structural deficiencies I have noted in many textbooks I have used in my university coursework to teach strategic leadership and strategic management. Although most are well written, many convey an inadequate understanding to students regarding what they need to know about leading and managing in turbulent organizational settings. Worse, some of them do students a great disservice by their frequent distortions, gaps and omissions in the organizational reality. Another purpose of this book is to clarify some of these distortions and fill in the gaps to assist students and practitioners in developing and applying more effective leadership approaches.

Whenever we talk about strategic leadership or strategic management, the conversation quickly devolves into a discussion of the pros and cons of strategic planning or the down-in-the-weeds details of the strategic planning process itself. This book attempts to set strategic leadership and strategic management in a holistic, multi-level context. It discusses each from a variety of perspectives to ensure a more adequate understanding of how they should be approached in organizational settings and how strategic planning and strategic thinking form integral parts of strategic leadership and strategic management.

Strategic planning became quite popular in the corporate world during the late 1970s and on throughout the 1980s. However, by the 1990s, it had lost much of its popularity among business practitioners and many organizations dispensed with any kind of strategic management program at all. This probably happened because corporate leaders felt that strategic planning hadn't delivered on the promises of greater organizational competitiveness and increased profits.

Some critics argue that *strategic planning* hinders or precludes *strategic thinking*.[6] Mintzberg asserts that strategies are to organizations what blinders are to horses, keeping them moving in a straight line by impeding peripheral vision.[7] Others argue that in the white water turbulence that most organizations are experiencing today, strategic planning is simply a waste of time because the process can't be cycled through quickly enough for the organization to adapt to the rapidly evolving corporate environment. The brief shelf life of a written strategic plan document simply can't justify the investment in energy and time it takes to produce it.[8]

All of these criticisms have a legitimate basis in observed practice. However, it is my contention that the majority of these concerns about deficiencies in strategic planning are directed more toward *strategic planning done poorly* rather than strategic planning per se. Although well-executed strategic leadership and strategic management efforts do not guarantee corporate success, they can be a highly effective hedge against corporate failure and demise.

In summary, this text approaches leadership and management as distinct but complementary roles. Although today we typically wear both hats at the same time, the roles tug us in opposite directions—management toward stability, certainty and predictability and leadership toward turbulence, uncertainty and change. Strategic leadership and strategic management are the application of strategy by leaders and managers in an environment of turbulence and change. The book addresses four complementary objectives: first, to assist students in the classroom and leader-managers in organizational settings to recognize the competing requirements for leading and managing during times of rampant change; second, to suggest a more precise understanding of the terms and concepts associated with *strategy, leadership* and *management*; third, to encourage students and practitioners to reexamine classical management theory, models and metaphors in the light of emerging insights from the complexity sciences to not only better understand the nature of the rapidly-evolving dominant management paradigm but to actually enjoy and thrive in the white water turbulence of today's organizational environments; and fourth, to examine strategic leadership and strategic management from a variety of perspectives to promote a more robust understanding of how to lead and manage in organizational settings today.

Chapter 1—Overview of Theory, Models, Metaphors and Paradigms

The leadership and management literature today is filled with a bewildering assortment of theories, models, metaphors and paradigms that attempt to simplify and explain leadership and management in an increasingly complex organizational environment. Such conceptual tools are fundamental to human thinking and abound in all human cognitive processes. Their use is critical to scientific research and investigation, and they are ubiquitous throughout the social sciences, particularly leadership and management studies. Through these tools, we can communicate more effectively with each other and share human knowledge.[1]

Theories, models, metaphors, and paradigms are all interrelated—different in their substance but complementary in their usage and purpose. Theories formulate explanations about observed phenomena and help us make predictions about future possibilities. Theory is frequently contrasted with practice as its opposite because theory involves no **doing** apart from itself. Metaphors are implicit comparisons and help us to extend our understanding of the world around us as well and to discover new knowledge. The widespread use of metaphors demonstrates a natural human proclivity for finding resemblances between new experiences and familiar facts.[2] In a similar manner, models provide a structured way of visualizing and explaining how things work and discovering solutions to problems.[3] Metaphors and models may be used to express theoretical formulations but, by themselves, are not considered theory.[4] Paradigms represent specific world views that attempt to link together and explain global observed phenomena. Paradigms help us to understand the world around us but they may also limit our ability to recognize the true nature of that reality.[5] In short, these conceptual tools share complementary roles in pursuing human learning and understanding. It is important to understand their uses and limitations as we begin our review of strategic leadership and strategic management.

Theory

Theory is an ambiguous term. It means different things to different people and there is little agreement even among social scientists about what *theory* is. With respect to leadership and management studies, theory can be perceived as a kind of *conceptualization*. Concepts such as *leadership*, *management*, *organization*, *power*, and *bureaucracy*, when defined and used in interpretations of empirical or observed phenomena, are frequently equated with theory in the literature. However, these terms are not generally theory but constitute ideas within theories. In a loose sense, any conceptualization or way of thinking about something can be considered theory.[6]

Theories are analytical tools for understanding, explaining, and making predictions about observed phenomena. Theory refers to an explanation of reality based on observations and information available that typically has been tested for validity although not all theories are tested or even can be tested. Theories evolve and change as new information is found and integrated into the current body of knowledge. Theory distinguishes ideas from practice and it frequently implies an idea that isn't certain or a reality that requires explanation.

According to Parson and Shils[7], there are four distinct levels of theory beginning with its simplest form and moving to the most complex: ad hoc classificatory systems; taxonomies; conceptual frameworks; and theoretical systems.

Ad Hoc Classificatory Systems are the lowest form of theorizing. They consist of identifying arbitrary categories in order to distinguish, organize and summarize empirical observations. For example, the classification of voters based on their response to a simple survey questioning whether or not they support a particular political issue would be an ad hoc classificatory system.[8]

Taxonomies consist of category systems constructed to fit empirical observations so that relationships among categories can be described. Thus, taxonomies are closely related to the empirical world—the categories reflect the reality observed. An example of a simple taxonomy is three types of organizations: corporate, public, and non-profit.[9]

Conceptual Frameworks stand above taxonomies because their propositions summarize and provide explanations and predictions for empirical observations. Conceptual frameworks are a grouping of concepts that are broadly defined and systematically organized to provide a focus, a rationale, and a tool for the integration and interpretation of information. Much of what passes for theory in the social sciences actually consists of conceptual frameworks that direct systematic empirical research. For example, de Bono's *Six Thinking Hats* provides a conceptual framework for describing the different modes of conscious thought that the human brain might process such as information seeking, instinctive reaction, pessimistic judgment, harmony seeking, creativity, and process organizing.[10]

Theoretical Systems combine taxonomies and conceptual frameworks by relating descriptions, explanations and predictions in a systematic manner. This is the most vigorous level of theory—a system of propositions that are interrelated in a way that permits some to be derived from others. Thus, a theoretical system is one that provides a structure for a more complete explanation of observed phenomena. Theories facilitate discussions about topics of interest because all participants use the same definitions. Thus, theoretical systems are the bread and butter of academic researchers. What may not be so obvious is that leader-manager practitioners also use theoretical systems of a practical sort which help them work through the complexities of the organizational environment and make future projections based on observed data. Examples of leadership-management theories abound including McGregor's Theory X and Theory Y which attempt to explain different approaches to managing employees and the anticipated results or outcomes when employing those strategies.[11]

Some leader-managers view theory as irrelevant to their practical needs in the workplace. This perception relates back to the old tension between *theory* and *praxis*. However, as Kurt Lewin once stated in a more positive vein, "There is nothing so practical as a good theory."[12] Theory is not just for academics. It can bring predictability to any field of endeavor. Businessmen and women and other practitioners frequently shy away from anything theoretical because, for them, it connotes something impractical. But, in fact, it is profoundly practical and useful for moving into an uncertain organizational future. Christensen suggests that " . . . with data or without it, every time managers take an action, and every time they look into the future, they use a theory to guide their plans and actions—because a theory is a statement of what causes what and why."[13]

Christensen and Raynor suggest a three-stage model for developing theory that works equally as well for practitioners as for academic researchers.[14] First, the phenomenon that we want to know more about must be adequately described and characterized. Second, the phenomenon is classified into categories. Categorization is essential to highlight the significant differences in the complex array of phenomena. For example, research and development, production, marketing and sales, and customer service are primary categories of the corporate value chain. Third, a theory is articulated that suggests what causes the phenomena to occur and why. Christensen and Raynor assert that the tentative theory must also demonstrate whether and why the same causal mechanism might result in different outcomes, depending on the category or situation. They also point out that theory making is iterative. As we continuously cycle through the three stages, we constantly update and refine our ability to predict what actions will result in what outcomes and under what conditions and circumstances.[15]

The utility or success of a theory is measured by the accuracy with which it can predict outcomes across the entire range of situations in which we find ourselves.[16] Theories are usually accepted and supported as long as they consistently explain the facts of empirical or observed phenomena. But, as Jules Verne observed in *Journey to the Center of the Earth*: "Facts are, as usual, very stubborn things, overruling all theories."[17] Thus when the observed reality (fact) is not explained by the currently accepted theory, then a new theory must be developed which does.

For example, in *How the Mighty Fall and Why Some Companies Never Give In,* Jim Collins addresses a commonly accepted but problematic theory: "We anticipated that most companies fall from greatness because they become complacent—they fail to stimulate innovation, they fail to initiate bold action, they fail to ignite change, they just become lazy—and watch the world pass them by. It's a plausible theory, with a problem: it doesn't square with the data."[18] In response to evidence to the contrary, Collins developed a new theory that suggests that a more likely reason that businesses fail is corporate overreach.

Bottom line: Having a theoretical framework that is coherent, informative, and grounded in actual experience about the dynamics of human action in a turbulent, organizational environment can provide a powerful tool that will have practical uses and implications for responding to complex situations in the workplace. Everyone operates with theories whether they recognize it or not. It is impossible to be without theory, even if many are unarticulated.

Models

Models are simple representations of complex realities. Models tend to increase in complexity and explanatory power as the level of detail in the model increases. Thus, models help to simplify the complexity of the world that we see around us, and facilitate prediction and thus experimentation and validation. Models are used by practitioners and academics alike. Models appear in many forms. They can be physical mockups, design plans, blueprints, flow charts, wiring diagrams or organizational charts. Anytime the lights go down in the corporate conference room and someone begins projecting PowerPoint slides on the wall, you can anticipate a run of models designed to help the meeting participants understand the complexities of the topic being discussed. Sometimes they succeed in that endeavor. Sometimes the effect can be just the opposite.

Box somewhat humorously asserted that "essentially, all models are wrong, but some are useful."[19] Models indeed have their uses and limitations. The *Bonini Paradox* explains the difficulty in constructing models or simulations that fully capture the workings of complex systems.[20] The paradox can be explained as follows—The simpler the model, the easier it is to understand, but the greater the possibilities are for omissions of important details and distortion of the reality it attempts to explain. As a model of a complex system becomes more detailed and complete, it becomes more accurate or precise in its explanatory power, but it also becomes less easily understood. It also becomes entirely unwieldy—as the model represents more and more

5

information, it moves away from representation toward total replication and we begin to drown in detail.[21] The model builder then has the responsibility to construct the model appropriate to the phenomenon being represented and appropriate to the target audience's level of understanding.[22]

Eckstein suggests that models could become conceptual traps if some inessential part is mistaken for a key feature of the theory it represents. A researcher could become distracted by extraneous issues in an attempt to make the model fit the facts (or vice versa) and thus be led into unproductive efforts, all because of the basic error of confusing the model with the theory itself or, to put it in other words, of mistaking the vehicle for the journey.[23]

We use models frequently to trying to explain organizational phenomena and predict future business and market performance. Models abound in the management, leadership, and organizational literature. An excellent example of such a model is Lewin's change model: Unfreeze-Move-Refreeze.[24] The model was developed in the late 1940s and still enjoys considerable acceptance and popularity today, strong testimony of the model's usefulness and precision. In *Leading Change*, John Kotter discusses an eight-step change model that expands on Lewin's model in explaining why many companies fail in their change initiatives.[25] In the book, *How the Mighty Fall: Why Some Companies Never Give In*, Collins introduces a five-phase model that accounts for the fall of a prestigious group of corporate giants.[26] Collins acknowledges that the model isn't perfect but it does do a good job of identifying traps that these corporations fell into. He also suggests that the model, again not perfect, can be used to predict the future demise of corporations that follow along a similar path. Based upon what Collins learned from his research in developing the model, he also asserts that "decline can be avoided" and that "whether you prevail or fail, endure or die, depends more on what you do to yourself than on what the world does to you."[27]

A *business model* is a type of model that describes how the firm will deliver value to customers to compete successfully against the competition in today's turbulent marketplace. Business models are not static affairs. To remain effective, they must evolve and keep pace with the rapid rate of change in the marketplace. Osterwalder and Pigneur suggest that in today's volatile business environment, a host of new, innovative business models are emerging as entirely new industries take shape and old ones crumble. Many firms are faced with trying to compete using dated business models and are "struggling feverishly to reinvent themselves."[28] In "Reinventing your Business Model," Johnson, Christensen and Kagermann state: ". . . truly transformative businesses are never exclusively about the discovery and commercialization of a great technology. Their success comes from enveloping the new technology in an appropriate, powerful business model."[29] They further suggest that an effective business model consists of four interlocking elements: customer value proposition (CVP), profit formula, key resources, and key operational and managerial processes.[30] These elements correspond to the components of a strategy and thus a business model is part of business strategy. We will discuss the basics of strategy in greater detail later in Chapter 3.

Metaphors

Metaphors are visual images we are familiar with that provide useful insights about complex realities. For instance, we might say that business is very much like a football game, or today's organizational environment is very much like white-water rafting. These visual images can be useful in better understanding the complexities of business but they can also distort perceptions and give us false readings about their true nature and possibilities. We throw metaphors around all the time in our conversations in organizational settings. Here are just a few examples to give you an idea—"competition is like a chess match", "traveling a rocky road", "arm wrestling," "batting ideas around", "striking out", "hitting a home run", "the ball is in your court", "white-water turbulence"—the possibilities are endless.

Organization researcher Gareth Morgan proposed the simple premise that all theories of organization and management are based on implicit images or metaphors that lead us to see, understand, and manage organizations in distinctive yet partial ways.[31] He further proposed that the use of metaphor implies ways of thinking and ways of seeing that pervade how we understand our world generally.

Morgan points out that metaphor always produces a kind of one-sided insight.[32] By highlighting certain interpretations, metaphors tend to force other views or interpretations into a background role.

Thus metaphors always create distortions. Metaphor uses suggestive images to create what Morgan describes as "constructive falsehoods" which, if taken literally, or to an extreme, become absurd.[33]

Morgan's premise that *all theory is metaphor* has far-reaching implications.[34] We need to understand that any metaphor that we bring to the study of leadership, management, organization, and strategy, while capable of creating valuable insights, will also be incomplete, biased, and potentially misleading.

To illustrate, consider the classical metaphorical notion that "the organization is a like a machine." This metaphor may create valuable insights about how an organization is structured to achieve optimal, predetermined results. But the metaphor is incomplete and biased. It ignores the human aspects of organization and elevates the importance of organizational structures. The metaphor is also misleading—the organization is **not** a machine and can never really be designed, structured, and controlled as a system of inanimate, mechanical parts. Thus, Morgan suggests that metaphor is inherently paradoxical. It can create powerful insights that also become distortions, as "**the way of seeing created through a metaphor becomes a way of not seeing.**"[35]

Acknowledging this shortcoming, we can begin to mobilize the real power of metaphor in leadership and management studies. Gaddis argues that metaphors are absolutely essential to be open to impressions or empathy—we must, of necessity, be comparative, saying that something is like something else for greater understanding. Using metaphors is in our nature for being self-reflective, feedback generating, information-exchanging entities.[36]

Paradigms and Paradigm Shifts

Paradigms are thought patterns in any discipline around which all other related concepts revolve. *World view, frames of reference*, and *normal science* are frequently-used synonyms for *paradigm* in academic and practitioner literature. Thomas Kuhn was responsible for popularizing the term *paradigm* in the early 1960s with the publication of *The Structure of Scientific Revolutions*, in which he described a paradigm as "a collection of beliefs shared by scientists, a set of agreements about how problems are to be understood."[37]

According to Kuhn, paradigms are essential to scientific inquiry, for "no natural history can be interpreted in the absence of at least some implicit body of intertwined theoretical and methodological belief that permits selection, evaluation, and criticism."[38] Because a paradigm defines the thinking and perceptions of the current world view, it tends to guide and shape the research efforts of scientific communities, and it is this criterion that most clearly identifies a field as a science.

Kuhn argued that a paradigm does not simply reflect current theory, but the entire worldview in which the theory exists, and all of the implications associated with it.[39] He cautioned that, although anomalies are inherent in all paradigms, they are typically brushed away as acceptable levels of error, or simply ignored and not dealt with. However, Kuhn suggested that when enough significant anomalies have accrued against a current paradigm, the discipline is thrown into a state of crisis. During this crisis, new ideas are tried. Eventually a new paradigm is formed, which gains its own new supporters, and an intellectual battle takes place between the followers of the new paradigm and the hold-outs of the old paradigm.

This process of change in world view and the ruling theory of science is often referred to as a *paradigm shift*. The term has become widely applied to many other realms of human experience as well. A fundamental theme of Kuhn's argument is that the typical developmental pattern of a mature science is the successive transition from one paradigm to another through a process of revolution. In part, that is what this book is all about, the paradigm shift from traditional management approaches to a new way of thinking about future-focused leadership-management in organizations today. This is a paradigm shift that has been ongoing for at least the past 20 or 30 years but is being stoutly resisted on many fronts.

Kuhn asserts that, contrary to popular belief, typical scientists are not objective and independent thinkers.[40] Rather, they are conservative individuals who accept what they have been taught and apply their knowledge to solving the problems within the framework of established theory. During periods of *normal science*, the primary task of scientists is to bring accepted theory and empirical observations into closer agreement. As a consequence, scientists tend to ignore research findings that might threaten the existing paradigm and trigger the development of a new and competing paradigm. In the pursuit of science, Kuhn observed, "novelty emerges only with difficulty, manifested by resistance, against a background provided by expectation."[41]

This same resistance to change exists in organizational life and leader-managers are also guilty of defending traditional practice and the status quo even in the face of strong counter arguments and the urgent need to change. "We've always done it this way," is a frequently heard defense against pursuing innovative change. Much of the corporate world today is operating in a traditional management paradigm that was developed and fine-tuned a century ago, and in spite of advances in new knowledge, dramatic changes in the environment, and an accelerating pace of change, many leader-managers stubbornly cling to management practices that are in desperate need of a total make-over.

This is analogical to the tactical situation at the Battle of Gettysburg during the Civil War. In attacking the Union defensive positions, Confederate forces followed the traditional Napoleonic practice of arranging soldiers and units shoulder to shoulder in echelon and marching across the battlefield until just a hundred meters away from the defensive line before breaking ranks and charging headlong into the fray. However, new technologies of rifles, rifled muskets and rifled cannon were deployed across the Union front which allowed soldiers to accurately engage enemy targets at much greater distances than in earlier wars.[42] It was a recipe for disaster and produced a tragic killing field. In retrospect, the mismatch between military unit tactics and emerging technologies clearly produced conditions that demanded a thorough examination of current practices and a paradigm shift altogether in the way wars were fought.

Paradigm shifts—complete transitions from one world view to another—occur only after a long and tumultuous gestation period. Kuhn asserts that, in academia and scientific research, they usually require young maverick scientists who are not so deeply indoctrinated and invested in accepted theory who can manage to sweep an old paradigm away.[43] The same holds true in the corporate world. One of the primary learning activities of this book is to compare the worldview of the classical management paradigm which emphasizes managerial control to the emerging leadership-management paradigm which seeks to harness and leverage the power of self-organization in turbulent business environments.

A Word of Caution on the Use of Theory, Models, and Metaphors

Theories, models and metaphors are very useful tools in helping us work our way through the clutter of many organizational complexities and conundrums. They can facilitate a useful simplification of otherwise very complex relationships. However, there is a danger that, in using these tools, we sometimes reify them; that is, we treat them not as representations of our organizational and environmental reality, but as the reality itself. *Reification* is the fallacy of treating an abstraction as if it were the real thing.

The problem with reification can be illustrated by the metaphor—business is like war. There are in fact many aspects of business that are indeed much like armed conflict. However, always treating our business relationships as armed combat will generally push us toward defeating or even annihilating our competitors, and that may in fact be decidedly unhealthy in a business environment where all stakeholders are interconnected, interrelated, and interdependent. In a similar fashion, business is frequently compared metaphorically to the game of football. It can be a very useful approach to think about business relationships and activities in this way but it could encourage organizations to think always in terms of win-lose approaches rather than look for potential win-win outcomes.

Bottom line: Use theories, models, and metaphors to advance your efforts and activities in your organizational environment, but use them cautiously. Don't get sucked into reification traps as they may lead you into potentially inappropriate or dangerous realities.

Conclusion

We are continuously bombarded by a multifaceted mix of theory, models, metaphors, and paradigms as we seek to understand more about leading and managing change in organizations in turbulent environments. Although we have examined theory, models, metaphors,

11

and paradigms sequentially here as separate and distinct elements, all of these constructs overlap a great deal and many authors frequently use the terms somewhat interchangeably.

What all four of these constructs have in common is that they provide insights which can be useful in understanding organizational and realities, even though they may not represent them in a completely objective or comprehensive way. As such, they are lenses that help us see what we might otherwise miss without them.

Chapter 2—A Systems Thinking Approach to Understanding Organizations

A system is a grouping of things—people, cells, molecules, or whatever—that are interconnected in such a way that they produce their own pattern of behavior over time.[1] Thus, an organization is a system and a systems-thinking approach can help us to better lead and manage in organizations.

Systems theory has its distant roots in Aristotle's discussion of the relationship between substance and attributes.[2] Hegel, a 17th century Prussian philosopher, proposed that systems consist of interconnected and interrelated components that display behavior patterns distinct from the behavior of its individual component parts.[3]

In its simplest form, a system is composed of three elements: *inputs*, *throughput* (or *process*), and *outputs*. In systems theory, the system takes resources or inputs, processes these resources, and returns them in a changed form as outputs. The following graphic illustrates the fundamental elements of a simple system model:

This system model is frequently referred to as a *closed, mechanical system*. It is self-contained, buffered from its environment and entirely predictable. It reflects classical Newtonian linear reasoning in that outputs are equal to inputs. It is based on a reductionist perspective in which everything is equal to the sum of its parts.

Beginning with the Industrial Revolution in Great Britain in the mid-1700s, Newtonian mechanics became the organizing principle for understanding all kinds of manmade systems: machinery, factories, manufacturing assembly lines, commerce and world economics. The metaphor for this paradigm was the machine.

Closed systems were considered essentially self-contained in that they did not interact with outside influences. A closed system is buffered or separated from any outside influences and the model assumes that there is no interaction with anything outside the system.

This approach reduces system uncertainty and makes it possible to calculate outputs and future states with precision, since all necessary information and variables are known. In modern times, this closed system model was pushed further by American mathematician, Norbert Werner, a pioneer in cybernetics, who focused on system feedback. Werner and other researchers in neuropsychology, mathematics and biophysics formed a work group which produced much of the early pioneering work in systems theory, computer science, cybernetics, robotics, computer control, automation and artificial intelligence.[4]

Because of its ability to minimize uncertainty and maximize predictability, the closed, mechanical system model view was thus dominant for almost two hundred years. However, although Newtonian physics was helpful in understanding stable, predictable mechanical systems, it was inadequate in understanding the living, dynamic systems omnipresent in nature.

Building on the work of Werner and others, biologist Ludwig von Bertalanffy developed an open, organic system model which he popularized through *General Systems Theory*, a seminal work published in 1968.[5] Bertalanffy argued that the assumption of the separation and isolation of the system from its environment was not practical in many cases and simply impossible for most phenomena, particularly those involving living systems.

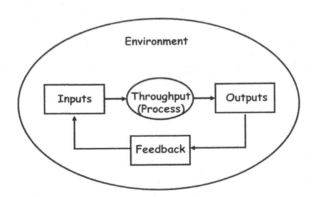

Organisms are open systems—they cannot survive without continuously exchanging matter and energy with their environment. Living systems do not exist in isolation. They interact with other systems outside themselves within their environment. Inputs enter the system from the environment and, following throughput or processing, outputs are delivered back into the environment. The open systems model suggests that systems exist within an environment and that there is a constant interaction or interchange between the system and its environment through system inputs and outputs.

The interchange between outputs and inputs is generally regulated by some kind of a feedback loop providing information about the exchange. Thus, the open or organic system model is characterized by five fundamental elements: input, throughput, output, environment, and feedback.[6]

Feedback loops generally inform the system how its outputs are being received into the environment. They can also provide the system vital information about its inputs and processes. The feedback loop is a fundamental structural element of all open, organic systems. Feedback loops are the building blocks of systems that are linked together to build more complex systems. The idea of circular feedback in systems is a basic precept of system dynamics.

Now it gets really interesting. With every feedback loop, information about the result of a transformation or a transaction is sent back and entered into the system in the form of new input data. There are essentially two types of feedback: 1) positive or amplifying feedback; and 2) negative or stabilizing feedback. In the first instance, positive feedback results in exponential growth or decline; in the second instance, negative feedback dampens change and results in the maintenance of equilibrium or status quo.

If the feedback reinforces and accelerates the transformation in the same direction as the preceding results, it is *positive feedback* and its effects are cumulative.

Positive Feedback

Explosive Increase

Beginning Point

Accelerating Decrease or Decline

Time

For example, if a person holding a microphone in a public address system steps in front of one of the system's loud speakers, the speaker's voice passes through the system amplifiers and out the loudspeakers where it is picked up by the microphone again and recirculated through the amplifier and so on. The sound is quickly amplified out of control into a high-pitched shriek that we typically refer to as "feedback."

Positive feedback leads to divergent behavior—a rapid expansion or explosive movement away from the initial stimulus. Each plus generates additional pluses creating a rapidly expanding snowball effect. Examples of systems reacting to positive feedback in this manner include: cattle stampedes, snow avalanches, epidemics, capital invested at compound interest, and inflation. However, when a minus leads to another minus and so on, it moves in the direction of a shutdown of activities and events eventually come to a standstill. Typical examples of this are bankruptcy or economic depression.

In contrast to positive feedback, if the feedback system produces a result in the opposite direction to previous results, it is referred to as negative feedback and its effects tend to stabilize or dampen the system, moving it toward some predetermined goal or status quo.

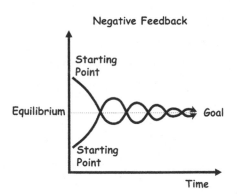

Negative feedback tends to sustain the system at the same level, temperature, concentration, speed, direction or other criteria. In a negative loop, every variation in one direction triggers a correction moving in the opposite direction. The system oscillates around an ideal equilibrium or status quo which it hovers about but never quite attains.

For example, in a building's heating and air conditioning system, the thermostat measures room temperatures and provides feedback to the central system signaling the need to provide hot air or cold air when the room temperature varies from the thermostat's preset temperature. Thus, the thermostat provides negative feedback in the heating and air conditioning system to keep the temperature of the rooms in the building at a fairly constant, comfortable level. When you set the cruise control on your car, it automatically monitors the vehicle's speed and maintains the car at the speed you set. The Fed monitors activity data from the financial markets and attempts to stabilize the economy at a set level by controlling inflation within certain bounds using the prime interest rate as a negative feedback tool. All of these are examples of regulation by negative feedback.

How does this systems-thinking approach play out in leading and managing organizations? The open systems model can be used to describe an endless assortment of systems including business firms, government agencies, and non-profit organizations. Moreover, it allows us to describe the behavior of organizations both internally within the organizational system and externally between other organizations in the environment. When we examine the environment of any system, we find that it also contains many other systems interacting with and within the environment. For example, the environment of a human being is full of other human beings. A group of interacting people may form a variety of larger, extended systems such as families, business firms and corporations, communities, cities or nations.

The mutual interactions of people and organizational systems hold these components together in a composite whole. If these component parts did not interact, the whole would not be more than the sum of its components. But because they do interact, something additional is added with the relationships and the whole is greater than the sum of its parts. This is one of the primary characteristics of Bertalanffy's open systems model which differentiates it from the classical Newtonian closed system model.

With respect to the whole, system parts are seen as *subsystems*; with respect to the parts, the whole is seen as a *suprasystem*. Thus, systems exist in hierarchies, that is, a subsystem exists within a system which in turn exists as part of a suprasystem and so on in nested fashion. For example, an employee works for a business firm which is part of a company which in turn is part of a global corporation. At the same time, the employee is a human system which is made up of a variety of subsystems like the circulatory system, nervous system, digestive system, and so on, which in turn are made up of component subsystems. Thus, a systems approach to understanding organizations allows us to shift scale up or down to focus on that which we think is really important in understanding the organization and how it functions as we zoom in and out between microscopic and macroscopic levels of analysis.[7] An emphasis on discrete, microscopic detail is referred to *reductionism*. An emphasis on macroscopic generalities and interconnections is referred to as *holism*.

The concept of an organization as a system which is part of a larger system reaffirms the importance of feedback. The organization is dependent on the other systems within the environment not only for its inputs but also for the acceptance of its outputs. More importantly perhaps, is the idea that the outputs from one system constitute the inputs for other systems.

Thus, business firms do not exist alone within their corporate environment. A business organization shares its environment with many other different kinds of systems including: customers, competitors and collaborators, suppliers and vendors, stockholders, finance and banking interests, employees and labor, government regulators, special interest and lobbyist groups, the media, and the community or society as a whole. Each of these types of systemic entities interact with each other and with the environment itself and are referred to as *stakeholders*.

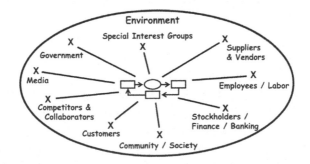

The number of systems operating within a given environment depends upon the ability of those systems to interact and affect each other. As the capabilities of transportation, communication, and information technologies continue to evolve and improve, the ability of systems to interact with other systems grows proportionately. Thus, with the advance of new technologies, the envelope or boundary for a given business environment continues to grow and include additional systemic entities or stakeholders. That is the essential nature of *globalization*. The number of players or stakeholders in the global marketplace is multiplying rapidly and the relationships between them are increasing exponentially.

Today, business firms participate in a global market environment which literally includes hundreds of millions of other systems—individuals, business firms, and nations. These systems are all interconnected, interrelated and interdependent—interacting together in a vast global network. This networked connectivity and system interdependence suggests that every part of the system has an effect, however minute, on every other part of the system. That is, a change in one system in the environment will result in adaptations and change in other systems throughout the environment. Moreover, each of the systems in the environment interact with the environment with the potential for changing the very nature of the environment itself.

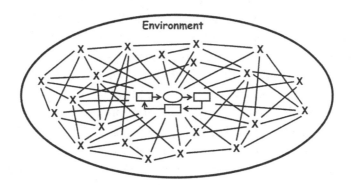

A good example of this would be the net overall effect of changing stock prices in a volatile stock market. When the net movement is positive and prices go up, we refer to the market environment as a *bull market*. When stock prices go down en masse, we call it a *bear market*. These aren't just names. The influence of a bull or bear market can affect the price movement of individual stocks themselves without regard for other more meaningful financial factors in the corporate performance.

Leaders and managers must constantly monitor the interactive system network within their corporate environment for any changes that alter the nature of the relationships within the network. As organizations sense changes in their environment, they must adapt to remain competitive with other systems or stakeholders within that environment. As any organization changes or adapts, all other systemic entities must take note and also change or adapt as appropriate. This tends to promote even more change and systemic turbulence. Failure to adapt in a changing environment will ultimately result in the inability of an organization to compete and survive. Organizations that get caught in the trap of a comfortable equilibrium or comfort zone of success are at risk of future organizational demise or death.

Stakeholder analysis has the goal of developing cooperation between stakeholders and the organization and, ultimately, assuring successful outcomes for the organization. Stakeholder analysis is a systems-thinking process of identifying the individuals or groups that interact directly with the organization that are likely to affect or be affected by a proposed change or action. It is frequently used during the preparation phase of a project to assess the attitudes of the stakeholders regarding the proposed changes. This information can be used to assess how the interests of those stakeholders should be addressed in a project plan, policy, program, or other action. Stakeholder analysis should be conducted when there is a need to clarify the consequences of envisaged changes, at the start of new projects, and in connection with organizational changes generally. Stakeholder analysis can be once and done or conducted on a regular, continuous basis to track changes in stakeholder attitudes over time.

We previously reviewed basic ideas of models and metaphors that help us to understand complex systems. *Systems thinking* is an approach for developing such models to promote our understanding of the complex interactions between stakeholders in organizational decision making and problem solving. If all subsystems in an organizational system are interrelated, interconnected and interdependent, then whenever we are interested in addressing a particular issue or situation, it is only through our understanding of the underlying systemic structure that we will be able to identify the most appropriate leverage points to effect change within the system.

A well-functioning system continuously exchanges feedback among its various parts to ensure that they remain closely aligned and focused on achieving organizational system goals. If any of the parts of the system becomes weakened or misaligned, the system must make necessary adjustments to more effectively interact with other stakeholders and achieve organizational goals.

Most organizations are set up to produce and deliver a certain set of goods and services to their customers. The outputs from one subsystem become the inputs for others within the overall organizational environment. Thus the organizational activity of any type of organization, corporate, public, or non-profit, is simply the integrated chain of systemic input-process-outputs that are linked together in a meaningful, organized way to produce and deliver organizational goods and services to their customers. An organization is made up of many administrative and management functions, products, services, groups and individuals. In business organizations, this is sometimes referred to as the *value chain*.

In an organizational system, if one part of the system is changed, the nature of the overall system is often changed, as well—by definition then, the change is *systemic*, meaning relating to, or affecting, the entire system. The word *systematic* does not mean the same thing. It merely refers to something that is methodological. Thus *methodological* thinking or *systematic* thinking does not necessarily equate to *systems* thinking.

Organizational Learning

In the late 1970s, Argyris and Schön developed a model of organizational learning through *single loop* and *double loop* learning.[8] Single-loop learning is characterized as response to changes in the internal and external environment of the organization by detecting changes or errors which could then be corrected so as to sustain the accomplishment of organizational objectives. In contrast, double-loop learning is described as organizational inquiry which resolves incompatible organizational norms by setting new priorities and weightings of norms, or by restructuring the norms themselves together with associated strategies and assumptions. Research has focused on how organizations may increase their capacity for double-loop learning.

Double-loop learning is necessary if practitioners and organizations are to make informed decisions in rapidly changing and often uncertain contexts.

Building on the earlier work of Argyris and Schön, Peter Senge published *The Fifth Discipline* in 1990, a seminal book about systems thinking in the context of learning organizations.[9] Senge identified five disciplines or component technologies that converge to support innovative learning in organizations. The first of Senge's five disciplines is systems thinking. The other four are: personal mastery, mental models, building shared vision, and team learning. Each of the five disciplines provides a vital dimension in building organizations that can truly *learn*, and that can continually enhance their capacity to adapt and realize organizational objectives.

Argyris and Schön suggested that each member of an organization constructs his or her own representation or image of the systemic whole.[10] The picture is always incomplete and thus, people, are continually working to add additional pieces of information to get a more complete view of the whole. This process is called *sense making* by Weick.[11] Individuals and teams in organizational subsystems need to know their place and purpose in the overall organization so that they can align with and support the attainment of enterprise-wide organizational objectives.

Our inquiry into organizational learning must concern itself not merely with the static nature of *organizations*, but with the dynamic process of *organizing*.[12] Individual members are continually engaged in attempting to better know and understand the organization, and to know themselves in the context of the organization. At the same time, their continuing efforts to know and to test their knowledge represent the object of their inquiry. In that context, *organizing* is an activity of reflexive inquiry.

A Systems Thinking Approach

A systems-thinking approach is fundamentally different from that of traditional forms of analysis. Traditional analysis is typically reductionist and focuses on separating complex issues or problems into their individual component elements. In fact, the word *analysis* actually comes from the root meaning "to break into constituent parts."[13]

In contrast to analysis, systems thinking focuses holistically on how issues or problems being studied are related to and interact with the other constituent parts of the overall system. This means that instead of isolating smaller and smaller parts of the system being studied, a systems-thinking approach leads leader-managers to expand their view to take into account larger and larger numbers of interconnections and interactions of the issues or problems being considered. This sometimes results in strikingly different conclusions than those generated by traditional forms of analysis, especially when what is being studied is dynamically complex or has a great deal of feedback from other sources, internal or external.[14] Thus, a systems-thinking approach can be very effective in addressing and resolving difficult kinds of problems involving complex issues, particularly those that display a considerable degree of dependence on the past or actions of other stakeholders, and those resulting from ineffective communication and coordination among those involved.

While systems thinking is an approach that can provide a very rational view of the organizational situation, it is an approach that requires a substantial investment of effort. Bellinger[15] suggests a list of indicators when a systems-thinking approach is likely warranted:

- There are multiple perspectives on just what the situation is, and how to deal with it.
- Things seem to oscillate endlessly.
- A previously applied fix has created problems elsewhere.
- Over time there is a tendency to settle for less.
- After a fix is applied the problem returns in time.
- The same fix is used repeatedly.
- There is a tendency to allow an established standard to slip.
- Growth slows over time.
- Partners for growth become adversaries.
- Limitations experienced are believed to result from insufficient capacity.
- There is more than one limit to growth.
- Limited resources are shared by others.
- Growth leads to decline elsewhere.

These criteria indicate a complex issue situation. Whenever an organization experiences one or more of these criteria, leader-managers need to consider a systems-thinking approach to deal with the issues. However, a systems-thinking approach may be unwarranted whenever the situation contains no balancing or reinforcing feedback, that is, when the action and the outcome has little or no affect on the actors.

Identifying a System's Leverage Points

A systems-thinking approach to understanding organizations helps leader-managers analyze and diagnose intervention measures to move the organization forward through change. Leverage points are those influences within a system where small interventions or changes can effect a substantial change in the system itself. At times the leverage points may be obvious, though at times they only become apparent through careful scrutiny, sensitivity analysis, and experimentation. Sensitivity analysis is a process where specific changes are made to certain influences within the model with all other components held constant to determine the impact on other elements of the structure.

Meadows provides one of the most comprehensive discussions of leverage points as places to intervene in complex, adaptive systems.[16] Her list of leverage points includes in reverse, count-down order of general effectiveness:

12. **Numbers**—Subsidies, taxes, standards.
11. **Buffers**—The size of stabilizing stocks relative to their flows.
10. **Stock-and-Flow Structures**—Physical systems and their nodes of intersection.
9. **Delays**—The length of time relative to the rates of systems changes.
8. **Balancing Feedback Loops**—The strength of the feedback relative to the impacts they are trying to correct.
7. **Reinforcing Feedback Loops**—The strength of the gain of driving loops.
6. **Information Flows**—The structure of who does and who does not have access to information.
5. **Rules**—incentives, punishment, constraints.

4. **Self-Organization**—The power to add, change, or evolve system structure.
3. **Goals**—The purpose or function of the system.
2. **Paradigms**—The mind-set out of which the system—it's goals, structures, rules, delays, parameters—arises.
1. **Transcending paradigms**—reformulating new paradigms when old paradigms no longer seem to fit.

Not all leverage points are the same. Some are easy to implement while others are more difficult. Some leverage points yield negligible results while others can yield extraordinary results in bringing about change in the organization. Meadows observes that too often we play around with numbers because they are the easiest to access and manipulate. We spend most of our time in business meetings reviewing spread sheets and crunching numbers. The problem with numbers is that they aren't particularly good leverage points for influencing systems. As we move down Meadows' list of leverage points, they become increasingly more difficult to pull off but increasingly more effective in influencing organizational systems. Negative (balancing) feedback loops and positive (reinforcing) feedback loops offer much stronger possibilities for affecting change in the system. When we reach the level of redefining the goals, structures, rules, delays, and parameters of paradigms, or even transcending existing paradigms themselves, we run the possibility of successfully bringing about extraordinary change.

Note: Because leverage points can sometimes yield extraordinary results with minimal effort, they may reflect an organization's "attack sites" which could offer antagonists and competitors vulnerable areas for attack and which organizational players should be prepared to defend.

Conclusion

In order to survive in a changing environment all component systems must be adaptable and capable of change as required to remain in balance or compete with other systems in the environment. The emerging complexity of the rapidly evolving business network environment is the engine driving change throughout our globalized world today.

Open systems are seen as highly complex and interdependent and are characterized by an expectation of change and uncertainty. An open-systems perspective views organizations as highly complex entities, facing considerable uncertainties in their operations and constantly interacting with their environment.

Systems thinking can be a powerful approach for leaders and managers to more effectively understand the nature of organizations and their environment. Systems thinking is not easy for it requires a substantial investment of effort and thought, though the results can be well worth the investment. Systems theory provides a powerful analytical tool for understanding organizations which helps leader-managers better understand internal structures and processes and the relationship between their organizations, their stakeholders, and their external environments.

Chapter 3—The Basics of Strategy: What Does It Mean and Where Does It Come From?

Before we launch into a discussion about strategic leadership and strategic management, we need to examine the basics of *strategy* first. In the literature, strategy is most frequently defined by *what it does* rather than *what it is*. And since strategy can be used to do so many different things, it falls out that there are a great many different meanings ascribed to the term.

Strategy is such an overworked term that, meaning all things to all people, it has come to mean little or nothing to anyone in the end. Builder calls *strategy* a "slippery word", like *systems analysis*, a term so widely and broadly used that its true meaning has become blurred.[1] Even as early as 1967, Wylie commented that "there are probably more kinds of strategy, and more definitions of it, than there are varieties and definitions of economics or politics—It is a loose sort of word."[2] Because there exists so much ambiguity in the use of the term, it is appropriate at this juncture to examine the word's etymology and define *strategy* more precisely.

Corporate and public organizations sometimes confuse the terms *policy* and *strategy* in their usage. Strategists, policymakers, and scholars sometimes use these terms interchangeably, but there is an important distinction between them. *Policy* refers to major goals and objectives of an organization, whether in pursuing national security interests or furthering corporate business objectives. Policy narrowly describes the things we hope to accomplish (*ends*). *Strategy*, in contrast, more broadly includes capabilities and methods (ways) and resources (means) used to accomplish those purposes. Thus, strategy describes what we want to do, how we're going to do it, and what we're going to use accomplish our goals. This, in essence, describes the nature of the relationship in strategy formulation between ends, ways and means.

Strategy formulation is characterized as balancing ends with the ways and means of accomplishing those ends. *Ends* can be expressed as organizational objectives; *means* refer to organizational resources (manpower, material, money, forces, logistics, and so forth); and *ways* are concerned with capabilities, methods, or courses of action for applying those resources to achieve organizational objectives.

Here is a simple formula for demonstrating the relationship between the three elements of strategy:

> **Strategy = Ends + Ways + Means**
>
> or
>
> **Strategy = Objectives + Capabilities + Resources**

When any of the three elements of strategy are significantly out of balance with the other two, it places the strategy at risk. This can be demonstrated by the strategy model developed by Colonel Art Lykke at the U.S. Army War College.[3] Lykke used the metaphor of a three-legged stool to describe the need for a balanced strategy. Below is a modified version of Lykke's model. One leg of the strategy stool is labeled objectives (or ends); one leg is labeled capabilities (or ways); and one leg is labeled resources (or means). When any of the three legs or elements of strategy is out of balance with the other two, it upsets the plane of the strategy represented by the seat and places the strategic agenda at risk (of falling off)—the greater the imbalance between ends, ways and means, the greater the angle from the level plane and the greater the risk.

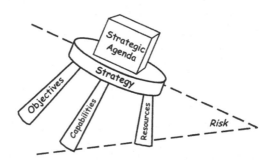

The strategy formula suggests two approaches to strategizing: *operational strategy* (based upon current resources and capabilities) and *developmental* strategy (based upon future goals and objectives). In some texts these are referred to as *strategic fit* and *strategic intent.*[4]

Strategies based upon existing organizational capabilities and resources are *operational* strategies—those that are used as a basis for formulating specific plans for action in the short-range or near-future time period. In contrast, longer-range *developmental* strategies are based not on current capabilities and resources but instead articulate objectives beyond the scope of current capabilities—such strategies provide the basis for pursuing needed adjustments in organizational workforce infrastructure, resources, and capabilities.

In short-term operational strategies, organizational resources included in the strategy formulation must already exist. In longer-range developmental strategies, the strategic objectives determine the type of organizational resources and capabilities needed for the future. Thus the balancing between ends, ways, and means to achieve a balanced strategy may be approached from either end of the strategy formula by beginning with different variables and adjusting the rest.

Management researchers Gary Hamel and C.K. Prahalad have been highly critical of the operational strategy or strategic fit model. They argue that it leads to an unhealthy focus on matching organizational objectives to current resources and environmental opportunities in the present rather than looking to building new resources and capabilities to create and exploit future opportunities.[5]

The concept of a strategic developmental strategy is well illustrated by the visionary statement of President John F. Kennedy at the beginning of the 1960s when he announced that the United States would put a man on the moon before the end of the decade. Note that JFK's vision was not yet a strategy, only a statement of national objective or policy. It remained for scientists, engineers, and political leaders to figure out what resources and capabilities we lacked to bring it all together into a solid strategy that guided our developmental efforts throughout the 60s.

Strategic fit or operational strategies tend to be more concerned with today's problems and issues rather than with tomorrow's challenges and opportunities. In contrast, Prahalad and Hamel suggest that successful companies sustain bold ambitions that outstrip existing resources and capabilities. Strategic intent or developmental strategies require the organization to build the resources and capabilities necessary to attain them. This forms the logic basis for many firms' acquisition and merger strategies—acquiring needed capabilities and resources to achieve future goals and objectives not presently attainable. If an organization is going to be successful and survive, it must balance both approaches to strategy to be competitive in the current operational environment and to remain competitive in the future environment as it unfolds.

Levels of Strategy

Strategizing takes place at all levels within an organization. From the corporate head office to the shop floor, strategy at any level is simply setting goals and objectives with consideration for the resources required and how those resources will be applied to accomplish the objectives. Most practitioners divide these levels into three tiers. It's interesting that the military and the business world generally label these three levels differently.

Levels of Organizational Strategy

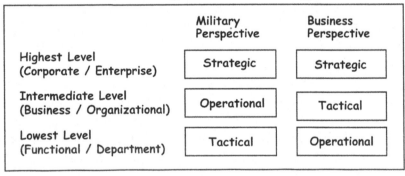

	Military Perspective	Business Perspective
Highest Level (Corporate / Enterprise)	Strategic	Strategic
Intermediate Level (Business / Organizational)	Operational	Tactical
Lowest Level (Functional / Department)	Tactical	Operational

In military parlance, the three levels of organizational engagement in descending order are the strategic level at the top, the operational level in the middle, and the tactical level at the bottom, which the military colloquially refers to as "where the rubber meets the road." As the business world adopted the strategic nomenclature it gradually coalesced in a modified descending order with the strategic level at the top, the tactical level in the middle, and the operational level at the bottom, which is sometimes referred to as the "shop floor." Thus, when reading about strategy in the literature, students and practitioners are well advised to pay attention to the source—military or business authors—for they are apt to be based upon different structural models.

In multi-leveled organizations, strategies developed at the lowest level support strategies at the next higher level which in turn support strategies at the next higher level and so on. Everyone in the organization is thus pulling in the same direction supporting the accomplishment of the overall enterprise strategy. This is sometimes referred to as *alignment*. Subordinate units within an organization build their strategies on the basis of strategies developed at higher levels.

In this alignment scheme, employees should understand what their own personal or individual strategies are in support of department, organizational and enterprise strategies. This can be effectively accomplished during performance appraisal time as supervisors and employees agree upon individual goals and objectives for the next time period and supervisors make sure that employees have the right combination of resources and capabilities to accomplish whatever goals are agreed upon.

Bottom line: the members of leadership and management teams at all levels are *all* concerned with ***ways*** to employ ***means*** to achieve ***ends*** to accomplish the overall enterprise strategic agenda.

The Three Tests of Strategy

To be effective, a strategy should meet the three tests of suitability, feasibility, and acceptability.

- Suitability—Will attainment of the strategy accomplish the effect desired?—Relates to objective (ends).

- Feasibility—Can the strategy be accomplished by the capabilities and resources available?—Relates to the course of action selected (ways).

- Acceptability—Are the consequences of cost justified by the importance of the effect desired?—Relates to resources (means).

By examining strategy in terms of ends, ways, and means, Lykke and Yarger argue that any strategy can be examined for suitability, feasibility, and acceptability, and that an effective assessment can be made of the proper balance among the three component parts.[6]

The Military Roots of Strategy

Where does the idea of strategy come from? It's a concept that has been developing over thousands of years. Strategy has its roots in military history. We will examine here a broad sampling of the writings of soldiers and military leaders, military theorists and historians, and political writers and national security analysts, all experts in the fields from whence the term *strategy* and its derivatives originate.

Strategy has its roots in two Greek words, *stratos* meaning army and *agein* meaning to lead. These words combined to form the word *strategus* which meant military commander. From these roots, the Romans later developed the Latin word *strategia* for the territories under the control of a *strategus*. In the 1740s, the French introduced the word *strateguique* which was used in the modern sense to describe the thinking behind the campaigns of Frederick the Great. Almost a hundred years later, Clausewitz extended the meaning by developing the concept of strategy itself. The U.S. military adopted the term *strategy* and the concept of *strategy* early on and it came into common usage during World War II.[7]

The term *strategy* originally pertained to the art of generalship or high command. Alexander's success in leading his relatively small Macedonian army of conquest was to a great extent attributable to his mastery of strategy formulation and execution. He was unequalled in the application of limited resources in achieving high strategic objectives. British military historian J.F.C. Fuller (1960) summarized Alexander's strategic approach with just one word—***genius***.

> Genius is a baffling word. It is neither high talent, nor outstanding intelligence, nor is it the product of learning, or of discipline or training. It is, so it would seem, a creative gift, intuitive and spontaneous in its manifestations, that endows its possessor with a god-like power to achieve ends which reason can seldom fathom. It is neither capable of

analysis nor explicable, it is solely demonstrative, and from the very opening of Alexander's reign we are brought face to face with genius in its highest flights . . . . Should there be an ingredient which affirms his genius, it is the startling rapidity with which he always acted: no situation caused him to pause; all difficulties were immediately stormed; although risks were immense, to him success seemed foreordained. Time was his constant ally; he capitalized every moment, never pondered on it, and thereby achieved his *end* before others had settled on their *means*. [my italics][8]

The Napoleonic wars spawned two extraordinary military strategist-historians, a Prussian, Carl von Clausewitz, and a Frenchman, Baron Antoine Henri de Jomini. Each had considerable experience on the battlefield, although both served mostly in the role of senior staff officers rather than as commanders of large troop units.

Clausewitz' magnus opus, *On War*, was published posthumously in 1832.[9] Jomini's *The Art of War* was published six years later in 1838.[10] Jomini was translated into English at an early date and American officers who fought on both sides during the Civil War were well familiar with his writings. Clausewitz was not translated into English until 1874 but has found great subsequent popularity in the curricula of American military academies and war colleges. Even today, there is sustained discussion of whether American military strategy is primarily Clausewitzian or Jominian. Notwithstanding their original focus on politics, war and battle, Clausewitz' and Jomini's observations on strategy and strategic planning have considerable cross-disciplinary application to strategic leadership and strategic management in corporate, government, and non-profit organizations today.

While serving as the director of the *Kriegsacademie*, Clausewitz frequently lectured that war was the extension of politics by other means and that strategy comprised the use of engagement to bring about its purposes. He acknowledged that to be successful, strategy had to define the war's central political purpose or aim so that war planners and generals could execute operational campaigns that would support those objectives. He also counseled that the "fog of war" made it very difficult to comprehend the conditions of battle as it unfolded and advised that since the prior assumptions made in military planning may not prove to be correct, military leaders and strategists had to be present on the battlefield to make continuous adjustments throughout:

> Strategy is the use of the engagement for the purpose of the war. The strategist must therefore define an aim for the entire operational side of the war that will be in accordance with its purpose. In other words, he will draft the plan of the war, and the aim will determine the series of actions intended to achieve it: he will, in fact, shape the individual campaigns and, within these, decide on the individual engagements. Since most of these matters have to be based on assumptions that may not prove correct, while other, more detailed orders cannot be determined in advance at all, it follows that the strategist must go on campaign himself. Detailed orders can then be given on the spot, allowing the general plan to be adjusted to the modifications that are continuously required. The strategist, in short must maintain control throughout.[11]

In describing the distinction between strategy and tactics, another Prussian strategist of that era, Heinrich Dietrich von Bülow defined strategy as "all military movements out of the enemy's cannon range or range of vision," and tactics as "all movements within this range."[12] Paret, Craig, and Gilbert (1986) point out that Clausewitz took exception to this approach:

> Clausewitz rejected this distinction as superficial, time bound—because it would be affected by technological change—and irrelevant, because the purpose of the two concepts was left unstated. Instead he proposed definitions that were functional and applied to every war, past, present, and future: "Tactics constitute the theory of the use of armed forces in battle; strategy forms the theory of using battle for the purposes of the war." . . . . Furthermore, Clausewitz also insisted that strategy and a theory of war must address not only elements "that are susceptible to

mathematical analysis," distances and angles of approach, for instance, but also such imponderables as the soldiers' morale and the commanders' psychology.[13]

In contrast, Jomini defined strategy in terms of level of interest and distinguished between strategy and tactical considerations. For Jomini, strategy was:

> . . . the order of the procedure of a general when war is first declared, who commences with the points of the highest importance as a plan of campaign, and afterward descends to the necessary details. Tactics, on the contrary, begins with details and ascends to combinations and generalization necessary for the formation and handling of a great army.[14]

Strategy has a similar military derivation and connotation in the eastern cultures as well. Throughout the Chinese classic, *The Art of War* (a compiled work begun around 512 B.C.)[15], Sun-Tzu's approach is thoroughly analytical, mandating careful planning and the formulation of an overall strategy before commencing a campaign. Sun-Tzu constantly stressed the need for rationality and self-control in war and preparations for war and the criticality of avoiding all engagements not based upon comprehensive, concrete analysis of the over-all situation, including combat options and one's own capabilities and weaknesses.

Heiho is a word of Chinese derivation adopted by the Japanese meaning *military strategy. Hei* means "soldier" and *Ho* means "method" or "form."[16] In the Japanese classic, *A Book of Five Rings: The Classic Guide to Strategy* (written around 1645 and later translated and published in English in 1974), Miyamoto Musashi states: "Strategy is the craft of the warrior. Commanders must enact the craft, and troopers should know this Way."[17] Musashi's seminal work is not precisely a thesis on strategy per se; it is, in Musashi's own words, "a guide for men who want to learn strategy."[18]

It is important for American business students and practitioners to note that Chinese and Japanese business men and women religiously study Sun Tzu and Musashi as part of their business management courses of instruction. **Chinese and Japanese business approaches** are thus much influenced by military strategy insights and business is frequently approached through the metaphor of *war*.

There are several important threads of thought that are interlaced through the writings of these classical military strategists and historians:

First, strategy is a balance between ways and means to achieve war's or politics' ends.

Second, strategy—the balance between ends, ways, and means—occurs not only at the highest levels of state, the strategic level, but also at the lower operational level of individual campaigns and tactical level of individual engagements.

Third, strategy is more than a quantitative analysis of friendly and enemy strengths and weaknesses. It includes a great number of variables "not susceptible to mathematical analysis."[19] Because of this, there must also be a balance constantly sought between rationally-produced, comprehensive plans and improvisational, intuitive creativity in strategic leadership.

Fourth, all of these strategists and soldiers acknowledge the difficulties presented by complexity and ambiguity in formulating strategy and laying out war plans and insist that the situation must be constantly monitored and plans continuously adjusted and updated.

Each of these ideas is fundamental to any discussion of strategy today.

The Emergence of Strategy in the Modern Corporate World

Although the study of strategy has long been a fundamental element of military studies, it was basically ignored by American schools of business management from the founding of America's first graduate management school, the Wharton School of Business at the University of Pennsylvania, for over seventy years. Then, in the intellectual aftermath of the Second World War in the mid-1950s, business management scholars began publishing pioneer work in strategy and strategic planning. Early major contributors included Peter Drucker, Philip Selznick, Alfred Chandler, Igor Ansoff, Russell Ackoff, George Steiner, and Michael Porter.

In *The Practice of Management* (1954)[20] Drucker introduced the theory that evolved into management by objectives (MBO) which was to become a fundamental part of business strategy. According to Drucker, setting objectives and monitoring progress toward achieving them should be understood and supported throughout the organization at all levels.

In *Leadership in Administration: A Sociological Interpretation* (1957)[21], Selznick introduced the idea of matching the organization's internal factors with external environmental circumstances which gave birth to the idea of Strengths-Weaknesses-Opportunities-Threats (SWOT) analysis.

In *Strategy and Structure* (1962)[22], Chandler argued for developing a long-term coordinating strategy to give the firm structure, direction and focus and made the case for the dictum that "structure follows strategy." Shortly thereafter, Ansoff published *Corporate Strategy* (1965)[23], in which he built on Chandler's work and introduced the notion of gap analysis—that we must understand the gap between where we currently are and where the firm needs to be, and then develop strategies to reduce that gap.

In *A Concept of Corporate Planning* (1970)[24], Ackoff established a preliminary systems-oriented premise for corporate planning. Two years later in *On Purposeful Systems: An Interdisciplinary Analysis of Individual and Social Behavior as a System of Purposeful Events* (1972)[25], Ackoff and Emery linked systems thinking to human behavior and ultimately to a basis for strategic planning in organizations.

In *Strategic Planning* (1979)[26], Steiner gathered together all of the ideas that had percolated up about strategic planning and laid them out in a systematic process. This was supported the following year with Porter's *Competitive Strategy* (1980)[27], which argued that the purpose of business strategy was to strengthen a firm's competitive position.

By the 1980s some business and management scholars belatedly realized that there was a vast knowledge base in military strategy and strategic planning stretching back thousands of years that they had ignored and they began turning to the great military strategists like

Thucydides, Alexander, Clausewitz, Jomini, Sun-Tzu, and Musashi for further insights. An example of this trend is the publication of *Clausewitz on Strategy* (2001), by von Ghyczy, von Oetinger, and Bassford, a book on strategic leadership and management that compiles and applies the ideas of the 19th Century Prussian strategist to contemporary corporate challenges.[28] In *Clausewitz on Strategy*, the authors thoughtfully acknowledge:

> Business is a latecomer to strategy and there is no strategic discipline comparable in seniority with war. Much can still be learned.[29]

Two more recent works that seek to apply ancient military strategy approaches to modern business practices are McNeilly's *Sun Tzu and the Art of Business: Six Strategic Principles for Managers,* and Krause's *The Art of War for Executives: Ancient Knowledge for Today's Business Professional.*[30] These authors present practical ideas about how to put ideas from Sun Tzu into practice. Based on Sun Tzu's classical approach to strategy and war fighting, they explore how to gain market share without inciting competitive retaliation, how to attack competitors' weak points and vulnerabilities, and how to maximize market information for competitive advantage. They discuss the importance of agility, speed and preparation in throwing the competition off-balance and the employment of strategy to gain competitive advantage and best the competition.

Conclusion

Strategy describes the things that we want to do (objectives or ends), how we're going to do it (capabilities or ways), and what we're going to use to do it (resources or means). Strategy formulation is characterized as the balancing between ends and the ways and means of accomplishing those ends. When these three elements of strategy are out of balance, it places the strategic agenda at risk.

Strategies based upon existing organizational resources and capabilities are *operational* or *strategic fit* strategies—strategies used as a basis for formulating specific action plans in the short-range or near future time period. In contrast, longer-range *developmental* strategies focus on *strategic intent* and are based not on current capabilities but take into consideration estimates of the future environment and requirements. Such strategies provide the basis for planning needed fixes in organizational workforce infrastructure, resources, and capabilities to adjust to the needs of a changing organizational environment.

Strategizing takes place at all levels within an organization: strategic, tactical and operational. From the corporate head office to the shop floor, strategy at any level is simply setting goals and objectives with consideration for the resources required and how those resources will be applied to accomplish the objectives.

Strategy has its roots in military history. There are several important ideas from the classical military strategists that have application in the organizational world today. First, strategy is a balance between ways and means to achieve the ends of war or politics. Second, strategy—the balance between ends, ways, and means—occurs at the highest levels of state, the strategic level, but also at the lower operational level of individual campaigns and tactical level of individual engagements. Third, strategy is more than a quantitative analysis of friendly and enemy strengths and weaknesses. It includes a great number of variables not susceptible to mathematical analysis. Because of this, there must also be a balance constantly sought between rationally-produced, comprehensive plans and improvisational, intuitive creativity in strategic leadership. Fourth, all of these strategists and soldiers acknowledge the difficulties presented by complexity and ambiguity in formulating strategy and laying out war plans and insist that the situation must be constantly monitored and plans continuously adjusted and updated. Each of these ideas is key to any discussion of strategy.

In the 1950s, business management scholars began publishing pioneer work in strategy and strategic planning. Out of this seminal work emerged concepts of management by objectives (MBO), SWOT analysis, gap analysis, and strategic planning to achieve corporate competitiveness. Today, business and management scholars in the United States and abroad are beginning to turn to the great military strategists like Thucydides, Alexander, Clausewitz, Jomini, Sun-Tzu, and Musashi for further insights in improving the development and implementation of corporate strategies.

Chapter 4—The Relationship between Organizational Environment and Strategy

During the late-1950s, as social scientists transitioned from the traditional paradigm of a closed, mechanical system to an open, organic system, they now had to consider the interconnectivity of organizational systems to their environment through feedback loops. In a journal article published in 1965, "The Causal Texture of Organizational Environments,"[1] two organizational researchers, Fred Emery and Eric Trist, described a model of four different types of environments and suggested that as organizations interconnect with their environment, there is a causal relationship that develops specific to each.

This causal relationship between the environment and the organizational systems it contains grows progressively more complex as numerous variables progress along a continuum—stability moving toward turbulence; certainty moving toward uncertainty; and market dominance moving toward hyper-competition. The model provides important insights about organizations today because this movement or evolution is changing at an increasing rate, that is, it appears to be accelerating.

Emery and Trist argued that open systems do not exist in a static equilibrium. On the contrary, they are dynamic, evolving entities and our main challenge in understanding organizations and organizational change is that the environmental contexts in which organizations exist are themselves changing, at an increasing rate, and towards increasing complexity.

Emery and Trist proposed that organizations, like all open systems, respond to changes in their environments and thus there is a condition of causality in the interaction of the system with its environment. Their model of organizational environments progresses in four steps or types from a simple, placid situation of predictable equilibrium to a highly volatile, rapidly-changing situation of hyper-turbulence. The four types are described here in a somewhat abbreviated format using the same terminology used by the authors in the original.

Type One—The Placid, Randomized Environment

At its simplest level, an environment is composed of *goals* (beneficial elements) and *noxiants* (harmful elements) which are randomly distributed throughout the environment and relatively unchanging and basically non-interactive. In this kind of environment, the organizational task is simple and straightforward: "to do one's best on a purely local basis." In such a nonchallenging environment, there isn't any distinction between *tactics* and *strategy* and the best tactic can be learned only by trial and error in the context of the local environmental variances. Emery and Trist suggested that the economist's *classical market* corresponds to this type of environment.

Type Two—The Placid, Clustered Environment

As we move away from stability, predictability, and market dominance, beneficial and harmful elements in the environment are not randomly distributed but clump together in certain patterns. This environment corresponds to what economists refer to as *imperfect competition*.

Emery and Trist argue that competition and survival in such an environment becomes precarious if an organization attempts to deal tactically with each environmental variance as it occurs. Survival becomes critically linked with what an organization knows of its environment. Now the need arises for *strategy* separate and distinct from *tactics*.

Under these conditions organizations grow in size with many distinctive parts and tending towards centralized control and coordination. In the clustered environment, an organization's objective becomes that of optimal location in which some locations are perceived as potentially richer and more rewarding than others.

In such a situation, an organization must come to know its environment well as there are twin dangers ahead: one, pursuing high-risk goals or objectives fraught with traps, or two, avoiding immediately difficult issues which may lead organizations away from potentially rewarding opportunities. To overcome these challenges, Emery and Trist suggest that organizations need to focus on the main objective, concentrate resources, and develop distinctive competencies or capabilities. These are the essential elements of strategy.

Under the conditions of a Type 2 environment, organizations tend to grow in size, developing hierarchical layering and adopting a management pattern of centralized control and coordination.

Type Three—The Disturbed-Reactive Environment

In contrast to the first two types, the third environmental type is dynamic rather than static. It consists of a clustered environment in which there is more than one system of the same kind in direct competition with each other. Competitors seek to improve their own chances by hindering each other—each knowing that others are playing the same game. Between *strategy* and *tactics* there emerges an intermediate type of organizational response—what military theorists refer to as *operations*.

Control becomes more decentralized to allow operations to be conducted. An *operation* consists of a campaign involving a planned series of tactical initiatives, calculated reactions by others, and counteractions. One has now not only to make sequential choices, but to choose actions that will draw off the other organizations. The new element is that of deciding which of someone else's possible tactics one wishes to take place, while ensuring that others of them do not. The flexibility required encourages decentralization and also puts a premium on quality and speed of decision at various peripheral points.

It now becomes necessary to define the organizational objective in terms not so much of location as of capacity or power to move more or less at will, i.e., to be able to make and meet competitive challenges. This gives rise to situations in which stability can be obtained only by a certain coming-to-terms and collaboration between competitors, whether enterprises, interest groups, or governments. One has to know when not to fight to the death.

Type Four—Turbulent Fields

The fourth environmental type is dynamic in a second respect, the dynamic properties arising not simply from the interaction of identifiable component systems but from the field itself—in other words, the ground itself is in motion. Emery and Trist referred to these environments as *turbulent fields*, a term that came into more popular use years later with the emergence of chaos theory.

The turbulence results from the complex character of the causal interconnections. Individual organizations, however large, cannot adapt successfully simply through their direct interactions. Emery and Trist assert that in such turbulent environments and its attendant uncertainty, organizational *values* take on great significance and importance as a control mechanism for their stabilizing influence.

Emery and Trist posit a number of factors that lead to the emergence of these dynamic field forces. First, economic organizations are increasingly enmeshed in legislation and public regulation, and second, there is increasing reliance on technological research and development to achieve capacity to meet the competitive challenge. These combine to result in a change gradient that is continuously present in the environmental field.

For organizations, this means an increase in relevant uncertainty. The consequences which flow from organizational actions result in outcomes that become increasingly unpredictable and which at any point may be amplified beyond all expectation.

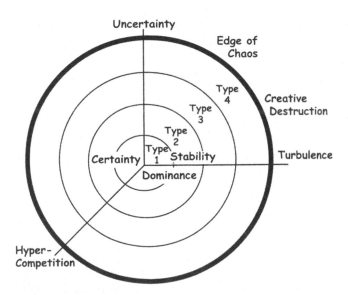

This graphic is a representation of Emery and Trist's environmental types model. It is a three dimensional model with x (stability—turbulence), y (certainty—uncertainty), and z (market dominance—hyper-competition) axes. Although necessarily depicted two-dimensionally, the z-axis comes out of the page at a 90 degree angle and the arcs depicting the boundaries between environmental types are actually three dimensional shells.

The darkened band at the outer boundary of the Type 4 environment is not a thin line but a boundary region. Because of the highly competitive, turbulent and uncertain nature of this boundary realm, it is the breeding ground of innovation and new ideas that rarely appear in more stable environments. British author Ralph Stacey calls this the "zone of creativity at the edge of disintegration."[2] This is a very similar notion to "the edge of chaos" cited by many other authors and is related to Schumpeter's "creative destruction."[3] Lindberg, Herzog, Merry and Goldstein point out that the terms refer to the way systems become fertile breeding ground for an emerging order when they are no longer bound to the requirement for maintaining the status quo or equilibrium, a state in which things are done in the same old way.[4]

Emery and Trist's model was twenty or thirty years ahead of its time and prescient of the sciences of complexity and chaos that didn't really emerge until the 1980s. The vocabulary they used in describing the four environmental ideal types sounds dated today, but the concepts they introduced in this seminal article on a systems approach to understanding organizations laid the intellectual groundwork for most of the innovative research that followed. Because of the somewhat arcane vocabulary, students today frequently have difficulty in understanding and appreciating the richness of Emery and Trist's model. I struggled with some of their vocabulary and concepts until I hit upon this fishing trip metaphor.

In a Type I environment, which Emery and Trist called a *placid, randomized environment*, it is similar to going fishing on a beautiful, pristine, placid lake. Fish abound everywhere and it doesn't matter where you drop anchor with your fishing boat, or what type of fishing gear or bait you use, you still catch fish, almost effortlessly. Because it doesn't matter where you drop anchor, there are fishing boats anchored all over the lake in random patterns. It doesn't take any special thought process or strategy to catch fish. The fishing tactic is just to get out on the lake and get fishing—strategy doesn't matter, the fishing is great. Thus, "the optimal strategy is just the simple tactic of attempting to do one's best on a purely local basis."[5]

In a Type II environment, which Emery and Trist called a *placid, clustered environment*, fishermen are beginning to notice that there are some spots on the lake that are hotter than others for catching fish. The fish seem to be gathering in deep holes. Fishermen who aren't getting many bites are watching other fishermen from a distance who are reeling them in as fast as they can cast. Soon, everyone is picking up anchor and moving toward these hot spots or optimal locations and clusters of boats begin to converge together. To be successful in this environment, the fishermen are dependent on their knowledge of the lake's topography—where the deep holes are—and they now have to develop strategies of bait, and fishing tackle, and technique to improve their success.

In a Type III environment, which Emery and Trist called a *disturbed-reactive environment*, it's beginning to get crowded and competitive around the hot spots and the strategy of many of the fishermen extends to operating their boats in such a way as to deny access to the optimal locations to others. The lake is no longer placid and smooth but is beginning to get choppy with the movement of all the boats. Fishermen are beginning to react to each other's movements trying to find ways of positioning themselves better around the deep spots. Their activities now include strategizing, operating their boats, and tactical fishing in order to realize success. The fishermen who are most successful are those who are most flexible and agile in switching bait and casting into select spots. Some fishermen who get too close to others begin to exhibit competitive, even hostile behavior.

In a Type IV environment, which Emery and Trist called *turbulent fields*, the activities of the fishermen have created such turbulence on the lake's surface that the fish have left the deep holes and are moving around the lake in schools, creating great uncertainty about where the optimal fishing spots are. The competition is fierce for the good spots where the fish are biting. As one boat experiences success landing fish, all of the other boats around it move in quickly to try to pick up on their success too. Some fishermen are now casting into other fishermen's boats just to aggravate them and get them to move away. Amidst all the turbulence, uncertainty and hyper-competition, some fishermen seem unfazed, guided by an internal compass of old-timer fishing *values*. They instinctively know what to do and are guided to fishing success despite all the turbulence on the lake.

Well, that's the metaphor. It helps me to visualize and understand the progressively more complex arenas of organizational environments. Here is a practical application of the model in analyzing recent U.S. economic history.

In the aftermath of World War II, the United States emerged as the only intact economic power. The rest of the world was devastated and struggling to rebuild. In that environment, as American business shifted from war production to consumer commercial production, it was basically without peer competitors elsewhere in the world.

Toward the end of the 1940s and throughout the early 1950s, American manufacturers could make any product they wanted and could make a good profit. It didn't require any special thought or strategy to compete in the market place. There was low-hanging fruit everywhere. There was no need for strategic planning—the best strategy was the simple tactic of just making stuff to sell—buyers abounded and they would take anything they could get. There literally wasn't any significant competition and American manufactures enjoyed virtual market dominance.

In that environment, they rejected Dr. Deming's and Dr. Juran's call to arms for quality manufacturing to improve their production lines and product outputs.[6] They just didn't see it as necessary. Not finding acceptance among American manufacturers in the United States for their ideas about quality, Deming and Juran accepted invitations to travel to Japan to assist Japanese industrialists in rebuilding their country.

Both Deming and Juran had begun their professional lives years earlier working at Western Electric's Hawthorne plant in Chicago, where they were influenced by the work of Walter Shewhart, a pioneer in statistical method. During World War II, Deming worked as a mathematician and statistician in the Census Bureau and taught statistical methods to engineers and managers. Juran helped redesign critical supply processes in the Lend-Lease Administration. Following the war, Deming and Juran travelled to Japan and assisted in rebuilding Japanese industry. Deming taught statistical methods and how to view production as a system that included suppliers and consumers. He championed a new and comprehensive quality approach for managing organizations and corporate enterprises. Juran lectured about an analytical approach for managing for quality including quality planning, quality control, and quality improvement. Japanese manufacturers and industrialists enthusiastically adopted Deming's and Juran's ideas and the evolution of Japanese quality is legendary.

As we came to the end of the 1950s and moved into the 1960s, American business still enjoyed a fairly high degree of dominance in world markets. Competition in some markets began to increase as Japanese and European industry began to reestablish itself. Success in the marketplace became less assured and American businessmen began to practice a simplistic form of strategic planning to move into a less certain future. "Made in Japan" was still an indication of an inferior product, but this was beginning to change as Japanese manufacturers embraced Deming and Juran's quality management approaches and the quality of their products improved significantly. Toward the end of this period, Japanese and European manufacturers began to dominate in certain market niches, particularly in cameras, televisions, stereo equipment, and other consumer electronic products.

In the 1970s, as the United States suffered a severe gas shortage crisis, Japanese car manufacturers made great inroads in American markets with smaller, more fuel-efficient vehicles and America began to experience considerable competition in steel and automotive production. Japanese and European manufacturers were giving American manufacturers a strong run for their money across a variety of sectors. In the face of the economy heating up globally and becoming much more turbulent, American manufacturers finally began to take notice, but their response was sluggish and non-adaptive. American business slowly came to embrace strategic management and exerted a great deal of energy on tactical, operational and strategic planning. The most successful American businesses were those which were flexible and agile in adapting to the changing conditions. Some American businesses that had refused to change or had been extremely slow to adapt had already gone out of business.

By the early 1980s, American business was facing strong competition from all over the globe. Faced with enormous competitive pressures, American businessmen invited Deming and Juran back to the United States to teach them about quality management. Total Quality Management (TQM) quickly became the hot trend of the 1980s and early 1990s. When the Iron Curtain came down and former Soviet bloc countries entered into the free world competitive market, global competition continued to heat up. Globalization was fueled by rapidly evolving transportation, communication and information technologies. The emergence of the Internet facilitated the entrance of many players into the global marketplace who before were hindered by geographic limitations. Although slow to shed communism as its economic model, China began to exhibit great economic potential. By the mid-1990s, China loomed as an enormous economic world power.

Amidst all the turbulence, uncertainty and hyper-competition, many American jobs were transferred overseas to reduce costs and sustain profitability. In response, Americans embraced various forms of reinvention, reengineering, downsizing and change management approaches in an attempt to recover competitive positions. As we moved into the new millennium, globalization knocked down the barriers to entry into the global economy for virtually the entire world and hyper-competition became the rule.

Most American businesses today finally recognize that their corporate environments are extremely turbulent, uncertain and hypercompetitive and are struggling to make appropriate adjustments and changes merely to survive. Examples abound. Faced with this incredible turbulence, IBM went through a very painful change process to adapt to the rapidly changing IT marketplace. American steel companies haven't done very well at all in adapting and competing in the emerging global market and foreign competition has put many U.S. steel manufacturers out of their misery. In the face of a global financial meltdown, GM, Ford and Chrysler were hunkered down and faced with imminent corporate demise. It eventually took a federal government bailout to keep GM and Chrysler solvent and out of bankruptcy. More recently, at the time of this publication, American automobile manufacturers have made significant organizational and structural changes and appear to face much brighter prospects in the near and long-term future.

Bottom Line: With few exceptions most organizations today are competing in Type 3 or Type 4 environments. The casualty list for Fortune 500 companies is sobering.[7] We need an entirely new leadership-management style that flourishes in turbulence, uncertainty and hyper-competition.

Conclusion

As the mechanical, closed system model was replaced by the organic, open system model, the organizational environment became recognized as a critical, causal factor in an organization's success. The Emery and Trist model provides a useful way of thinking about the evolution of organizational environments from stable, predictable environments where market dominance and success is unchallenged, to turbulent environments characterized by uncertainty and hyper-competition, where even the ground is in motion. In this evolution of the organizational environment, the role of leaders and managers has also evolved and the nature of strategy in the corporate world has changed.

In dynamic turbulence, organizational leaders and managers must come to know their working environment well as they are confronted by the twin dangers of pursuing goals and objectives in high risk ventures or overlooking difficult issues which may lead the organization away from potentially rewarding opportunities. To overcome these challenges, Emery and Trist suggest that organizations need to focus on the main objective, concentrate resources, and develop distinctive competencies or capabilities. These are the essential elements of strategy. As organizational environments become more turbulent the role of values becomes more critical to achieving organizational success.

Chapter 5—Understanding Strategic Leadership and Strategic Management

The British Industrial Revolution began in the latter part of the 1700s. It was powered by the steam engine which transformed British manufacturing processes and factory systems. The American Industrial Revolution began a half century later, initiated by the invention of the cotton gin which provided a ready source of cotton for American textile manufacture, and accelerated by the invention of the steam locomotive and the telegraph. These two subsequent inventions taken together provided the technological foundation for the establishment of railroad systems. Without the telegraph, you could only run one train on a track system at a time. But with the telegraph, you could run multiple trains at the same time, monitoring the position of trains between stations and moving one to a siding track to allow an oncoming train to pass.

During the Civil War, the railroads—overwhelmingly located in the Union North and appreciably less in the Confederate South—ultimately provided a decisive logistical advantage to Union forces as they moved troops and war materiel around the Nation from battlefield to battlefield. As the Nation emerged from the Civil War, railroad systems quickly expanded as new track was laid around the country. In 1869, just four years following the conclusion of the Civil War, the railroads connected the east and west coasts of the United States as the Union and Central Pacific Railroads joined their tracks at Promontory Point, Utah.

The rapid expansion of American railroad systems furthered explosive growth in coal and iron ore mining and steel manufacturing industries. All of these industrial systems required skilled managers to oversee their complex operations. Responding to this emerging need, the Wharton School of Business was founded at the University of Pennsylvania in 1881. This was followed by the establishment of several other American schools of business and management toward the end of the century and numerous more in the early 1900s.[1]

One of the initial tasks for these new institutions was defining the core curriculum. Coincidentally, with the founding of Wharton in the 1880s, Frederick Winslow Taylor was working in the American steel industry in Pennsylvania to apply scientific methodology to improve engineering processes in optimizing plant production output. His approach became known as *scientific management* and gained great popularity among the new schools of business and management.[2] Scientific management gradually faded over time as a distinct management theory but many of its themes and practices linger on in American management practices today including analysis, rationality, empiricism, standardization of best practices, efficiency and elimination of waste. From the beginning however, leadership was not considered a legitimate academic discipline because it could not be approached in the same analytical and scientific way as the study of management. Although leadership and management are the two sides of the same coin, leadership was simply not taught in our schools of business and leadership and its study was left to military academies, war colleges, and schools of divinity.

As leadership gradually gained traction as a legitimate discipline for academic research and study in the 1970s and 80s, management schools began exploring ways to integrate leadership studies into their management curricula. During the previous 80-90 years, management scholars amassed enormous quantities of research and models to describe management but produced little useful information about leadership. And so belatedly, management scholars were forced to overcome their earlier resistance and began conducting a broad range of studies to discover and define the finer points of leadership.

These studies resulted in the publication of another large, parallel body of literature, much of which was not particularly helpful to practitioners in *understanding* leadership or knowing how to *lead* organizations. Calas and Smircich[3] reported that researchers in these early leadership studies were frustrated in their work and didn't feel like they were getting anywhere and that the majority of the early leadership literature seemed irrelevant to practitioners. Early on, Bass and Stodgill published a ponderous 900+ page work on leadership studies that by 1990 was in its third edition.[4] The cover of the book identifies it as "the most complete work on leadership of its day" and "*the* source book on the study of leadership." Rost complains that one of the problems with such compilations of leadership studies was that most of the research and analysis had been done in the context of the industrial [scientific management] paradigm which tended to view leadership as good management.[5] In fact, many of the early leadership models in the literature are merely reworked management models that had been around for some time. A more recent popular textbook on leadership, Daft's *The Leadership Experience* (2008)[6], although a significant improvement in the field, still exhibits some of these same shortcomings. Maxwell makes the sobering observation, "There are very few leadership books; most deal with management."[7]

One of the challenges that early leadership scholars faced was the lack of a common understanding of what constituted *leadership* and how it was differentiated from *management*. They simply lacked a common definition that they could all accept and work with. Defining leadership thus became the preliminary task for all leadership research and a profusion of definitions flourished. In 1991, Rost identified no less than 221 different definitions of leadership in the literature. He concluded that: " . . . neither scholars nor the practitioners have been able to define leadership with precision, accuracy, and conciseness so that people are able to label it correctly when they see it happening or when they engage in it."[8]

Ethics scholar Joanne Ciulla observed, however, that there was a common thread throughout all of these definitions—all of them addressed leadership as "some kind of process, act, or influence that in some way gets people to do something" and that "a roomful of people, each holding one of these definitions, would understand each other."[9] She further pointed out that the question is not "What is the definition of leadership?" but "What is good leadership?"

There are a few bright spots in the literature that address the issue of what constitutes good leadership. John Kotter, a Harvard professor of management, captured the essence of leadership in his best selling book, *Leading Change*.[10] What is interesting about this work is that although Kotter is a superb scholar and researcher, he didn't base this work on the outcome of scientific research. Instead, he approached it as a management consultant who had worked with numerous Fortune 500 companies and observed the successes and failures of their change transition efforts over time. The book itself has an unacademic look, touch, and feel, with no citations, no references, no index and no bibliography.

Another bright spot in leadership literature is Kouzes and Posner's *The Leadership Challenge*.[11] James Kouzes was Chairman and

CEO of Tom Peters Group/Learning Systems. His collaborator, Barry Posner, was the dean of the Leavey School of Business and Administration at Santa Clara University. The authors had collaborated earlier as management consultants and the book takes a decidedly consultant perspective rather than an academic, scientific approach in laying out five fundamental leadership practices.

The work of James McGregor Burns also stands out in sharp contrast to the standard scientific approaches of other leadership researchers and he has became one of the most accessible and quoted leadership scholars in his day.[12] What makes Burns' work compelling is that he generally tried to understand and describe leadership from a *holistic* perspective examining leadership relationships rather than the traditional academic reductionist approach examining all of its component parts.

There are also a number of excellent works on leadership written primarily by consultants specializing in leadership development. Representative of these resources are Welter and Egmon's *The Prepared Mind of a Leader*, Lencioni's *The Five Dysfunctions of a Team*, Covey's *The 7 Habits of Highly Successful People*, and Maxwell's *The 21 Irrefutable Laws of Leadership*.[13] It is interesting to note that none of these excellent books on leadership have been academic in nature—they are mostly trade books, the kind of books businessmen and businesswomen buy in the airport bookstore and read on the flight out and back. Like Kotter's *Leading Change*, they rarely include citations and references and typically don't have an index or bibliography. Authors of such books are most frequently consultants and professional speakers—rarely academics. Perhaps that reveals something about leadership scholarship. Maybe the early business and management schools were right all along—leadership doesn't really lend itself well to scientific scrutiny and examination.

What Is the Difference between Leadership and Management?

Some textbook writers today write as if leadership and management are the same skill set. Hill and Jones' *Strategic Management: An Integrated Approach* (2008) is a good example.[14] Although an otherwise excellent text, the authors use the terms *leadership* and *management* interchangeably. This is due in part to the fact that most management scholars writing about leadership today came up through traditional management curricula. Addressing leadership roles and issues, they tend to use the same models and approaches that they have long used to discuss management roles and issues.

The notion that leadership and management are the same skill set is also partly based on the reality that, with the elimination of managerial layers of hierarchy and the flattening of organizational structures, most of us wear both hats today in the workplace—our leadership hat and our management hat.

Some authors assert that traditional distinctions between leadership and management are no longer relevant in today's turbulent workplace environment and that the skills required to be effective as a leader and as a manager are essentially identical.[15] I take a different view on the matter. Although it is true that practitioners must wear both the leadership hat and the management hat today, the functions they perform in those capacities are really quite different and, although related, the skill sets required to perform those function are also different. The setup is similar metaphorically to saying that the skill sets of fielding and batting are the same skill set because in order to experience success as a professional baseball player today you have to be able to do both well. That isn't the case and it reflects faulty logic.

In *Leading Change*, Kotter proposed a model distinguishing between the two roles or functions of leadership and management.[16] According to Kotter's model, the management function plans and budgets, organizes and staffs, and controls and solves problems. This results in the preservation of the status quo and a degree of predictability that facilitates short-term results in producing and delivering goods and services to customers. On the other hand, the leadership function establishes direction, aligns people, and motivates and inspires people.

This results in the production of change, turbulence, and uncertainty that can facilitate the organization becoming more competitive in a future context.

The net outcome of the dynamic in each column is quite the opposite. Managers strive to maintain stability and predictability in order to maximize current production of goods and services. Leaders, on the other hand, generate turbulence in order to get employees out of their comfort zones and moving in support of adaptation and change. The management role tugs us in the direction of fostering stability and our leadership role tugs us in the direction of fostering turbulence. It can be said that management is the science of maintaining equilibrium and leadership is the art of disrupting the status quo and adapting to change. Here is a chart that summarizes the distinction between the two roles:

Management:	Leadership:
<ul><li>is present-oriented.</li><li>attempts to preserve the status quo to enhance organizational equilibrium and predictability.</li><li>ensures that all work gets done in a timely and efficient manner.</li><li>focuses on the current production and delivery of goods and services while implementing organizational changes to new technologies, processes, products, etc.</li><li>typically engages in problem solving to keep organizational systems operational and functioning.</li><li>thrives in stability.</li></ul>	<ul><li>is future-oriented.</li><li>envisions the future, shares that vision, and helps staff move through the turbulence of change.</li><li>motivates and inspires people through the turbulence of change.</li><li>focuses on the continued competitiveness and survivability of the organization in a future context.</li><li>typically engages in decision making to make adjustments and affect changes to help the organizational team move into an uncertain future.</li><li>thrives in turbulence.</li></ul>

Here is the way it works in practice. Leader-managers confront hundreds of problems and issues that generate decision making opportunities every day. Although some decisions can be made without much deliberation, all decisions should be examined from the perspective of your leadership and management roles. Sometimes, wearing our management hat, our decisions will lean toward stability and equilibrium in order to optimize current production and delivery processes. At other times, wearing our leadership hat, our decisions will lean toward change and turbulence in order to adapt to threats and opportunities in the corporate environment to maintain our competitive edge in an uncertain future. It is practically impossible to lean both directions at the same time, that is, to optimize current production and distribution efforts while implementing turbulent change initiatives.

Relationship between Leadership and Management in Change Transition Activities

The twin concepts of change leadership and change management are familiar ideas in most business firms today. But how businesses lead and manage change—and how successful they are at it—vary enormously depending upon the nature of the business, the change involved, and the stakeholders affected by the change. There has been much debate about the roles of change leadership and change management and which is more important for achieving a successful change transition. This is a false dichotomy—you absolutely must have both. Today's leader-managers need to be masters of both skill sets, just like today's major leaguers need to be masters of both fielding and batting skills.

Kotter asserts that most organizations are over-managed and under-led. Such an approach tends to try to eliminate the messiness of transformations. Kotter allows that *managing change* is important but argues that the greater challenge in most organizations is *leading change*. He asserts that " . . . only leadership can motivate the actions needed to alter behavior in any significant way. Only leadership can get change to stick by anchoring it in the very culture of an organization."[17]

Kotter has a point but managing change is incredibly important today as well. Wearing our management hats, we have to oversee current production and delivery of goods and services to our customers now even as we implement system changes to be able to continue delivering goods and services to our customers in the future. This stretches organizational resources thin as we attempt to perform three concomitant tasks: 1) sustain current production; 2) develop and implement new technologies and processes; and 3) train employees on the new system processes. This almost always means long hours and overtime for all personnel involved. The longer the transition process, the more challenging and exhausting the increased work effort sustained over time becomes.

Conclusion

In today's flattened organizational structures, most of us wear two hats—our leadership hat and our management hat. But they do not represent the same skill sets. Leadership and management are two sides of the same coin, complementary but distinct roles and functions. Our management role tugs us in the direction of fostering stability and our leadership role tugs us in the direction of fostering turbulence. Most organizations today are over-managed and under-led, which means that they err on the side of stability-seeking. In the turbulent environments of constant change that most organizations experience today, this is a sure-fire recipe for disaster. In the next chapter, we will examine the drivers and pace of organizational change and a number of organizational change models that leaders and managers can use to guide change efforts in a turbulent work environment.

Chapter 6—Organizational Change Models

Organizations today are in a constant state of flux as they attempt to respond to constantly changing environmental conditions in an uncertain and ambiguous world. Many organizations are torn between pressures and forces for change and pressures and forces that resist change. Some researchers assert that some level of tension between stability and change is an inevitable part of organizational life today.[1] Since forces for stability and change coexist simultaneously within an organization, it is important to understand how they interact throughout organizational change transitions.

Forces which drive an organization's pursuit of change include a need for: 1) environmental adaptability; 2) cost containment; 3) impatient capital markets; 4) consolidation of power and control; and 5) gains in competitive advantage. Forces which encourage pursuit of stability include: 1) institutionalism; 2) sustained advantage; 3) transaction costs; 4) organizational social capital; and 5) predictability and uncertainty reduction.[2] In the face of this tension, and in today's permanently turbulent environment, those organizations that are able to overcome resistance and implement appropriate responses to changes in their environment tend to be more successful over time in their productivity, service, and survival efforts.

Organizations are always under some pressure to grow, adapt, and change.[3] Pressure may come from the outside environment in the form of requests to undertake new or expanded tasks, or it may come from the inside, from members who seek a wider scope for their own activities and who see new opportunities to be developed. These pressures create the need to make strategic choices about the organization's direction and rate of growth.

Organizational Change and the Environment

Early mechanical closed system organization models generally ignored changes in the environment and the need for organizations to adapt and change in order to survive. Bertalanffy's *General System Theory*[4] provided the intellectual framework for organizational scholars to revise classical, closed-system organization models into organic, open-system approaches. With the adoption of an organic, open-system model, organizational leaders acknowledged the need to bring about some fundamental changes in the behavior of their members if the organizations were to stay effectively related to their changing environment.[5]

Contingency approaches developed in the 1960s provided for a different organizational structure when environmental change is rapid rather than those times when it is relatively stable.[6] Ecological approaches of the 1970s suggested that an organization cannot be understood apart from its environment.[7] Later scholarship of the late-1980s emphasized the importance of examining open-system organic models in their ecological setting.[8]

The relationship of an organization to its environment is central to open systems theory. An organization's technologies, processes, and structures must be well suited to each other and to the organization's environment. If they are not well matched and if there is not a good fit, organizational performance may be significantly diminished and may become insufficient to ensure organizational survival. Emery and Trist proposed that an organization's social structure must be well matched to its technological processes, structures, and capacity. Their socio-technical approach emphasized that as organizations develop over time, the social and technological systems inherent within the organization must remain in complementary balance—neither should operate at the expense of the other.[9]

The Socio-Technical Approach to Leading and Managing Change

- Employees, customers, vendors, and consultants and the community
- Human knowledge, skills, attitudes, values and needs
- Organizational culture, reward systems and authority structures

- New technologies (information, communication, transportation),
- New processes, (manufacturing and delivery)
- New products, new buildings, additions and remodeling,
- Organizational restructuring

The accelerating pace of organizational change today is frequently ascribed to a corresponding rapidly-increasing rate of evolution of technology, and in particular, information, communication and transportation technologies and the combinations of these.[10]

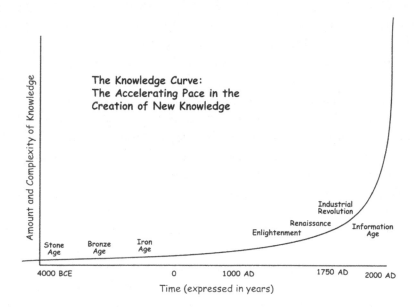

A model which illustrates the accelerating pace of the creation of new knowledge is shown as a simple Cartesian system with the passage of time reflected on the horizontal axis and the amount of total accumulated knowledge reflected on the vertical axis.[11] This graphic model has the virtue of reflecting the exponential growth of knowledge in recent years since the industrial revolution brought on by new technologies of the information age.

In practice, rampantly increasing knowledge is not the only factor feeding into environmental complexity and organizational stress and change. On a national or even global scale, the Four Horsemen of the Apocalypse—war, famine, pestilence, and natural disasters—can wreck havoc on the normal pattern of organizational environmental stability. These disruptive vectors interact with the knowledge curve to create a complex system of interactive environmental pressures for change.

Additionally, globally integrative themes such as environmental awareness, collective security, economic interdependence, technology, information, arms control, and democracy can all place further environmental pressure for change on public and corporate organizations. Disintegrative and divisive themes such as weapons proliferation, migration, religious animosity, ethnic rivalry, protectionism, rising crime, and drug trafficking can exert even stronger disruptive pressures. All of these factors can take the form of overlaying vectors that, taken together, greatly exacerbate environmental turbulence and accelerate the pace of change.

Turbulence is generally a function of an increase in the speed with which changes in organizational environment and activity take place. Rapidly evolving communication, information and transportation technologies are greatly accelerating globalization and the complexification of the organizational environment. Leader-managers today must be prepared to deal effectively with the turbulence of rapid change and increasing environmental complexity to ensure long-term organizational survival.

What is an organization to do today in the face of such environmental complexity and change? Potential strategies include: (1) adapting to the changed environment; (2) moving to a different environment; (3) managing the environment into a more compatible state; or (4) temporarily relying on slack resources, loose couplings, or other buffers.[12] Selecting from among these approaches in a rapid-paced, organizational environment places pressure on senior leadership and management decision-making processes to change.

Organizations must constantly scan the environment for nuances of change that can affect organizational well-being. Greater amounts of information must be analyzed and distributed throughout the organization. Decision making itself becomes more intensive, more frequent, and more complex. Organizational learning must be constant and consistent and leadership-management decisions arrived at must be implemented more rapidly.

The pursuit of greater understanding of the organizational environment using a traditional scientific methodology is problematic in that it typically relies upon a reductionist approach whereas a holistic approach may be much more appropriate and necessary. Reductionism's reduced focus may obfuscate the relationship and interdependence of the large number of diverse, complex, and interconnected actors in an organization's environment.

Lewin's Change Model

Change is a common thread that runs through all business organizations today regardless of size, industry or age. Our world is turbulent and rapidly changing and organizations must change quickly to survive. Organizations that handle change well will thrive, while those that do not may fail to survive. In the late 1940s, psychologist Kurt Lewin identified three stages of change that are still the basis of many change leadership and change management approaches today.[13]

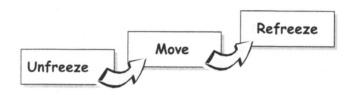

Lewin's model employs the metaphor of changing the shape of a block of ice. Lewin suggested that if you have a large block of ice, but determine that what you want is to change its shape, what do you do? First you must melt the ice to make it amenable to change (unfreeze). Then you can pour the icy water into the mold shape you want (move). Finally, you must solidify the new shape (refreeze).

The unfreezing step involves preparing the organization to accept that change is necessary, which means breaking down the existing status quo before a new way of operating can be considered and implemented. The key to this is developing a compelling message showing why the existing way of doing things is unsatisfactory and cannot continue. This is easiest to frame when you can point to problems challenging the firm such as declining sales, poor financial results, and disappointing customer satisfaction surveys. To prepare for change, you may need to challenge the beliefs, attitudes, and behaviors that currently define the organization. This is usually the most difficult and stressful part of the change process. When you start challenging the status quo by questioning the way things are done, you make everyone uneasy and put everything off balance. That can evoke strong, emotive reactions in people, which may be precisely what is needed. By forcing the organization to take a hard, objective look at itself and its shortcomings, you create a controlled crisis, which in turn can build a strong motivation for change to seek out a new equilibrium. Without this motivation, you won't get the buy-in and participation necessary to effect any meaningful change.

Lewin's "move" stage is where you begin to implement the change. This is a highly complex process because it involves continuing old patterns while new patterns are being developed and set in place. At some point in time, you have to stop doing things the old way and begin doing things the new way. During this process, people begin to resolve their uncertainty and look for new ways to do things in the new setting. People start to believe and act in ways that support the new direction.

In order to accept the change and contribute to making the change successful, employees and other stakeholders need to understand how the changes will benefit them. It's the WIIFM (*what's-in-it-for-me*) principle. Not everyone will cooperate. Even though the change is necessary, well-thought-out and well-executed, there will be some who will resist the change. Some employees may genuinely be harmed by the change, particularly those who now benefit most from the status quo. Others may take a long time to recognize the benefits that change transition brings. Effective communication and strong leader support are key to successfully bringing people through the turbulence of change. People need time to understand the changes and they also need to feel highly connected to the organization throughout the transition period. When you are leading and managing change, this can require a great deal of time and effort.

When the change transition process is completed and people have embraced the new ways of working, the organization is ready to refreeze. During the refreeze stage, the organization internalizes or institutionalizes the changes just made. In earlier years, Lewin literally meant that the organization stabilized on a new equilibrium and way of doing business. In today's highly turbulent, white-water business environment, the refreezing stage signals solidifying temporarily on the new way of doing business even as the organization looks for opportunities to accomplish even more advantageous change.

This means not falling back on old habits and ways of doing things as before. It requires managers to ensure that the new changes are used all the time and that they are incorporated into everyday business. With a new sense of stability, employees feel confident and comfortable with the new ways of working. Even though change is a constant for most organizations today, this refreezing stage is still important. Without it, employees are constantly off-balance and unsure of how things should be done and nothing ever gets done to full capacity. Moreover, in the absence of a new frozen state, it is very difficult to tackle the next change initiative effectively. Change can be perceived as change for change's sake, and the sense of urgency and motivation required to implement new changes won't be there.

Kotter's Change Model

In 1996, Kotter introduced a more sophisticated eight-step version of Lewin's three-stage change model.[14] Steps one through four are expansions on Lewin's *Unfreeze*. Steps five through seven refer to Lewin's *Move* and step eight is the equivalent of Lewin's *Refreeze*.

Kotter's Change Model

Step	Stage
1. Establish a sense of urgency.	Unfreeze
2. Create the guiding coalition.	
3. Develop a vision and strategy.	
4. Communicate the change vision.	
5. Empower broad-based action.	Move
6. Generate short-term wins.	
7. Consolidate gains and produce more change.	
8. Anchor new approaches in the culture.	Refreeze

Adapted from Kotter, 1996

Based on his experience as a consultant working with Fortune 500 companies over many years, Kotter argues that most corporate change initiatives fail because organizational leadership fails to observe all eight steps. He reminds us that managers often try to take an organization through significant change by undertaking only steps five, six and seven, or they race through the steps without ever finishing the job.

Kotter argues strongly that whenever the first four steps are ignored, you rarely achieve a solid enough base on which to proceed through the change transition, and without follow-through—the refreezing dynamic of step eight—you never can make the changes stick.

Incremental and Discontinuous Change

Change in organizations comes about in two ways. First, it can take the form of a slow, incremental, evolutionary change in which we systematically modify and improve on existing processes and practices to make them better. Although changes occur slowly and almost imperceptibly, over time, they can amount to significant differences from the way we used to do things. Second, change can take the form of rapid, discontinuous, revolutionary change in which we break completely with the past and implement something new and revolutionary that didn't exist before.

Quality management incorporates the concept of continuous quality improvement, a collaborative work effort on the part of all employees that seeks to improve organizational processes continuously through the activities of quality improvement teams. However, with the rapid acceleration of change in today's turbulent work place, some observers suggest that incremental change—merely doing the same thing but doing it better—may not produce desired results quickly enough and thus ends ultimately in failure.[15] What may be needed is radical, discontinuous change which frequently involves major shifts in organizational structure, staffing, work processes, technology, business models and corporate strategies. Discontinuous change amounts to reinventing the organization in a relatively brief period of time while continuing to operate in a complex, volatile, uncertain, and ambiguous business environment.

Conclusion

Organizations today are in a constant state of flux as they attempt to respond to constantly changing environmental conditions in an uncertain and ambiguous world. Many organizations are torn between pressures and forces for change and pressures and forces that resist change. Some level of tension between stability and change is an inevitable part of organization life today.

Organizations must be constantly scanning the environment for nuances of change that can affect organizational well-being. Trying to make sense of the organizational environment using the reductionist approach of traditional scientific methodologies is problematic. Holistic approaches may be much more appropriate and necessary in understanding the relationships between the actors and stakeholders in the organizational environment.

Lewin's simple change model—unfreeze-move-refreeze—has become the basis of most organizational change models today. Kotter's eight-step model is a good example. Change in organizations comes about in two ways: slow, incremental, evolutionary change or rapid, discontinuous, revolutionary change. Although incremental change approaches such as quality management's continuous improvement have proven effective, discontinuous change is sometimes called for. It frequently involves major shifts in organizational structure, staffing, work processes, technology, business models and corporate strategies. Discontinuous change amounts to reinventing the organization in a relatively brief period of time while continuing to operate in a complex, volatile, uncertain, and ambiguous business environment.

Chapter 7—Strategic Leadership and Strategic Management: Thinking and Planning Strategically

An organization needs to have a clear understanding of what is going on in its environment. Since all systems are interconnected, interrelated, and interdependent within an environment, an organization needs to continuously monitor its relationship with its stakeholders within the environment. As an organization observes turbulence and changes in those relationships it has two mandates: first, it must continue producing the goods and/or services it delivers to customers in order to remain viable and competitive in the present, and second, it must begin to make changes and adjustments to remain viable and competitive in the emerging, uncertain future.

Effective leaders sense changes in the direction of the organizational environment early on and "prepare the firm for the new fundamentals while continuing to operate in the old fundamentals."[1] Andy Grove, cofounder and chairman of Intel, calls these changes in direction *strategic inflection points*, and describes them as "a time in the life of business when its fundamentals are about to change."[2]

Leaders have essentially two options available as the organization undergoes a strategic change process. One, they can pursue evolutionary, incremental change, adjusting in small steps from the status quo of the present strategic agenda, or two, they can undertake revolutionary, discontinuous change, starting all over again from a clean slate. Companies that have enjoyed continued success in the marketplace seemingly have the greatest challenge with this. They become victims of their own success. In general, although most organizations are more comfortable with incremental change, given the present extremes of turbulence caused by rapidly-evolving, hyper-competitive environments, most organizations would probably benefit more in the long run from a revolutionary, quantum-change approach.

A good example of this was IBM in the 1980s. Throughout the 1960s and 70s, IBM enjoyed tremendous success in the marketplace with its main frame computer line, particularly the IBM 360. Then, in the late 1970s and early 80s, profits from the mainframes began to slack off. They continued to be highly profitable, but each quarter the profit line was less. The data reflected that mainframe computers had reached product maturity and were now in a declining market as microcomputers, servers, networks, and the Internet, began to reshape the market. IBM clearly needed to make a quantum change, but it was mired in its own success and each year corporate planners pumped out another incremental strategic plan based on main frame computers. By the early 1990s, IBM was poised on the brink of bankruptcy and it took a new CEO brought in from outside to shake the firm out of the doldrums and make the revolutionary changes necessary to keep IBM a viable, profitable firm. Today, IBM bears little resemblance to its former corporate self as it has gone through an extraordinary transformation to remain competitive in the rapidly-changing information technology market.

Strategic Leadership and Strategic Management

Early efforts by American business with strategic planning and other aspects of Strategic Leadership and Strategic Management frequently did not produce the desired results of increased profitability and business competitiveness. This was due in part because the effort was conducted sporadically and piecemeal. Like Quality Management, Strategic Leadership and Strategic Management require more than just partial or truncated implementation. They must become fundamental elements of the corporate culture.

Strategic Leadership and Strategic Management should occur seamlessly through five phases which cycle back on each other:

1) analysis; 2) planning; 3) implementation 4) measurement; and 5) adjustment.

Strategic Thinking and Analysis: Strategic practitioners today use a wide array of organizational analysis techniques including SWOT Analysis (Strengths, Weaknesses, Opportunities, and Threats), PEST Analysis (Political, Economic, Social, and Technological), STEER Analysis (Socio-cultural, Technological, Economic, Ecological, and Regulatory factors), SPEELT Analysis (Societal, Political, Economic, Environmental, Legal, and Technological) and EPISTEL Analysis (Environment, Political, Information, Social, Technological, Economic and Legal). This acronym soup reflects a concern to examine and analyze key issues of greatest importance in determining the factors at work that are shaping the corporate environment as we move into an uncertain future.

One of the primary purposes of analysis is to make sure that the organization is moving forward in the right direction. Peter Drucker once said: "There is nothing more wasteful than becoming highly efficient at doing the wrong thing."[3] One of the central activities of analysis is strategic thinking. Wooten and Horne suggest that there are three main activities in the strategic thinking process: first, making sense of information; second, formulating ideas; and third, planning action.[4] The model suggests that these authors and many others combine the activities of strategic thinking and strategic planning into a continuous whole. Other authors such as Mintzberg argue that strategic planning hinders or precludes strategic thinking entirely while others suggest that since the environment is evolving so rapidly that organizations should focus on strategic thinking and adaptation without expending any energy on a strategic planning process at all.[5] Welter and Egmon suggest that strategic thinking at its core is simply good, critical thinking about the future of the organization, a necessary ingredient for an effective strategic planning process.[6]

Some may conclude from the strategy formula that strategy making is essentially an analytical task of balancing ends, ways and means. This is an unjustified conclusion. Although Lykke's strategy model employs a mathematical formula, the formulation of strategy, in his view, is not solely a quantifying task.[7] It is not just number crunching and bean counting, although these tasks can form an integral part of the strategy formulation process. Clausewitz argued that strategy must address not only elements "that are susceptible to mathematical analysis," distances and angles of approach, for instance, but also "such imponderables as the soldiers' morale and the commanders' psychology."[8] On a more contemporary note, Drucker suggests that strategic planning is not the application of scientific methods to business decision but rather the application of thought, analysis, imagination, and judgment.[9] In other words, they all make the case for strategic thinking in combination with and indistinct from strategic analysis and planning.

Strategic planning proponents assert that analysis and synthesis are complementary activities and that, for the most part, strategic thinking and strategic planning happen simultaneously, the one feeding the other. Graetz's view is that, although strategic thinking and planning are different and distinct processes, they are interrelated and complementary in sustaining and supporting one another in an effective strategic leadership and management effort.[10] In Graetz's model, the role of strategic thinking is "to seek innovation and imagine new and very different futures that may lead the company to redefine its core strategies and even its industry." Strategic planning's role is "to realize and to support strategies developed through the strategic thinking process and to integrate these back into the business."[11]

In all fairness to Mintzberg's perspective, where an organization's strategy formulation process has depended exclusively on the quantification of variables, it has generally proved an unwieldy failure. An example of this was the Department of Defense during the Vietnam War years during which time Secretary of Defense Robert McNamara's team from Harvard and Rand Corporation attempted to turn DOD's strategy formulation process entirely into a quantifying, "bean-counting" task through the Planning, Programming, and Budgeting System (PPBS). PPBS represented a formalized attempt to couple strategic planning with programming and budgeting in a single comprehensive system.[12] As Mintzberg suggests, with its almost exclusive focus on the cold mathematical calculation of means, to the exclusion of much else, PPBS came up short on almost every count. In addition to its incredible complexity and unwieldiness, PPBS suffered from a fundamental weakness: as a strategy formulation process, it placed undo emphasis on just one element of strategy and failed to balance ends, ways, and means in a meaningful way.

This, in part, was the source of Mintzberg's overall dissatisfaction with strategic planning as commonly practiced. He believed that *strategic planning* had become more *strategic programming* and asserted that systematic approaches to planning and programming "never provided strategic thinking at all."[13] In his view, programmatic approaches stifle genuine strategic thinking and innovative genius in applying ways and means to achieve organizational ends. Mintzberg rightly points out that "when planning becomes a numbers game, so that managers pretend they are making strategy when all they are really doing is manipulating figures," then "financial management" supersedes "strategic management."[14]

Mintzberg also expresses intellectual discomfort when looking at the imbalance between *intuition* and *analysis*, which roughly corresponds to Clausewitz' terminology of *genius* and *mathematical analysis*. In Mintzberg's view, intuition and analysis are each incomplete by itself, providing only a perspective but not a complete solution to leadership/management issues and problems. For him, analysis may not be synthesis and thus planning based solely upon analysis may not be effective strategy formulation because it cripples innovation and creativity. Mintzberg concludes that the manager's strategic planning dilemma could be resolved by combining the two modes of thinking, intuition—largely represented by organizational leaders and managers, and analysis—largely represented by the organizational planners. Clausewitz and Alexander would probably agree on that point, although both would probably favor the role of leader intuition in the balance.

Strategic thinking and analysis provide critical input to the strategic planning process. Effective strategic thinking reveals potential opportunities for creating value and challenges assumptions about a company's value proposition and competitive advantage, so that when the plan is created, it targets the right set of threats and opportunities. Strategic thinking is a way of understanding the fundamental business drivers of the organization and rigorously challenges traditional thinking and approaches about them.

Strategic thinking takes many factors into account including: 1) organizational competencies and skills; 2) products and services; 3) resources and infrastructure, the organizational environment, industry and markets; and 4) organizational stakeholders including customers, competitors, suppliers, special interest groups, and government regulators. Strategic thinking moves toward strategies that are aligned, goal-oriented, fact-based, focused, engaging and adaptable.

Strategic planning is an organization's process of defining its objectives or direction, and making decisions on allocating resources to pursue that direction and determining how those resources will be used. Simply stated, strategic planning determines where an organization is going in the future and how it's going to get there. In order to determine where it is going, the organization needs to know exactly where it stands, then determine where it wants to go and how it will get there.

Done well, strategic planning can provide organizations with a number of important advantages. It can

- facilitate a systems-thinking approach to understanding the organization in the context of its stakeholders and organizational environment;
- anticipate effects of change and influences of other stakeholders.
- provide for responsiveness to change and facilitate competitive survival;
- stimulate the organization to be more responsive to customer needs;
- prepare corporate leaders to anticipate and recognize evolving changes in the organizational environment;
- provide a forum and process for setting and modifying corporate goals and objectives;
- create a basis for establishing performance measures and accountability;
- mitigate crisis management and crisis-driven decision making; and
- improve employee morale by reducing uncertainty and providing direction, communication, and inclusion.

There are many different models for strategic planning. There is no one right way to do it. There are, however, essential elements of a strategic planning process that should be included for it to achieve the desired results and be worth the opportunity cost of time, energy and organizational resources it takes to do it.

Below is a generic model for a strategic planning process adapted from a model developed by the American Society for Public Administration.[15] It is labeled "Strategic Leadership and Management Model" because it includes additional tasks beyond the planning process itself including implementation, measurement and adjustment. It is in fact a model for a full strategic leadership and management process. Let's take a more detailed look at each of the elements of the process. They are not precisely steps because they are not necessarily sequential and may occur simultaneously with other elements in the process.

Strategic Leadership and Management Model

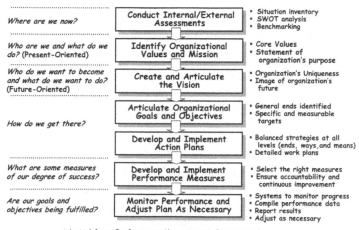

Adapted from *Performance Measurement Concepts and Techniques*, American Society for Public Administration (ASPA)

Internal/External Assessment

Much as strategic thinking, internal and external scans should be a continuous activity. Although they are reflected in the model as the initial step, they are not once-and-done events in the strategic planning process. Internal and external scans are driven by strategic thinking initiating the strategic planning process and subsequent scans provide valuable feedback to drive the plan into the future.

From a systems thinking perspective, the external scan provides feedback assessment on the external environment and reveals threats that the organization may have to protect itself against and opportunities that the organization may want to pursue and leverage. The internal scan provides feedback that lets us know how we are doing within the organizational system itself with our inputs, processes and outputs. These internal considerations are typically considered as strengths and weaknesses. If you are strong in these areas, then you can develop and pursue robust *operational strategies* in the present. If you are weak in any of these areas, you can use this information to develop and implement *developmental strategies* to pursue and develop the capabilities and resources you might need to accomplish more ambitious strategies than you may be able to consider at present.

Once you have initiated external and internal scans and begun to analyze the feedback data, you can evaluate the organization's *strategic competencies*. Strategic competencies answer four specific questions. First, do organizational capabilities reflect a combination of unique skills, processes and knowledge? Second, do these capabilities and competencies differentiate the company sufficiently from the competition? Third, do they create exceptional value for the customer? And fourth, are they difficult for potential competitors to replicate or copy?

Identify Organizational Values and Mission

The Emery and Trist model demonstrates the importance of values in turbulent, rapidly-changing organizational environments.[16] Where change is the only constant, organizational values can provide a certain degree of stability and reduce uncertainty for employees. Identifying corporate values provides an important participative activity for employees to contribute to the guidelines for how the organization will operate.

Some organizations focus on statements of *moral values* that suggest overall priorities in how people ought to interact with each other within the organization and with external stakeholders. Statements of values frequently include such things as personal integrity, mutual respect, quality of life, customer focus and service, and quality products and performance.

The mission statement defines the fundamental purpose of an organization or an enterprise, succinctly describing why it exists—its *reason for being*. The mission statement is present-oriented and is articulated using present tense verbs. It provides employees and other stakeholders with a clear understanding of precisely what the organization does and reveals how their daily work effort contributes to its accomplishment. Thus, the mission statement can galvanize employee efforts to achieve stated organizational objectives.

Create and Articulate the Vision

A vision statement is a picture of the organization set in the future. It is generally articulated using future tense verbs. The vision statement should provide employees and stakeholders with a clear picture of the direction the organization is taking into the future.

There are essentially two ways of thinking about a vision: First, it can serve as a *future goal or objective*—a goal to be accomplished or target to shoot at. That fairly well describes the role and function of John F. Kennedy's vision for putting a man on the moon before the end of the 1960s. We hit that target. Second, a vision can serve as a *force field* that moves people in a desirable direction. Martin Luther King's "I Have a Dream" speech provided such a vision. He visualized and articulated his dream painting a picture of children of different races and colors playing together and it not coming up on anyone's scope as being unusual. We aren't there yet. But the field effect of Dr. King's vision has galvanized America and we have come a long way in the right direction.

Vision expresses a long-term view. It is aligned with organizational values and culture and provides the framework for the hard work of strategic planning. An effective vision statement is a brief and vivid picture of an intended future, expressed in memorable and engaging wording that makes it possible for employees to literally **see future possibilities**. A long, complex, multi-paged vision statement is not only meaningless to employees but it fails to inspire them to make the sacrifices necessary to move in a new direction.

To be truly effective and useful, a vision statement should become part of the organizational culture. Organizational leaders must constantly and consistently communicate the vision to employees and to other stakeholders. Kotter suggests that most organizations under-communicate the vision to employees by an order of magnitude.[17] Leaders must also serve as role models, embodying the vision and encouraging others in the organization to create their own adaptation of the vision on a personal level that is compatible with and supportive of the organization's overall vision.

Many organizations confuse the vision statement with the mission statement. In some organizations, the mission statement and vision statement are combined into one statement while in others, one is simply a longer version of the other. A quick test for effective mission and vision statements is to cover up the titles and see if employees can discern which is which. I once taught a course in a training room at the Harley Davidson motorcycle manufacturing facility in York, PA. On the wall were posted Harley Davidson's mission and vision statements. One evening before class, I sat there and looked back and forth at the two statements on the wall and realized that they said virtually the same thing. I ran an experiment with my students later when they arrived for class. I had covered up the titles "Mission Statement" and "Vision Statement" and asked the students to identify which was which. They couldn't do it. The mission statement should tell you where you are and what you do **now** while the vision statement should tell you where you are going and what you want to be able to do **in the future**. When the two statements both read the same, it suggests to employees that either the organization doesn't know where it's at or where it's going.

The question might be asked: Which comes first in the strategic planning process—the mission statement or the vision statement? The answer is dependent upon the organization and its environment. If the organization is a new start-up business or if it is undergoing major reorganization, then the vision will most likely guide the development of the mission statement and the rest of the strategic plan. In the case of an established organization where the mission is already in place, then the mission most frequently guides the vision statement and subsequently the rest of the strategic agenda. The bottom line is that although the mission and vision statements are distinct and serve different purposes, they are very strongly correlated and unquestionably work stronger together than apart.

Articulate Organizational Goals and Objectives

Organizations should identify strategic focus areas from which high-level goals and objectives can be developed. These goals should be **SMART goals**—Specific, Measurable, Aligned, Realistic, and Time Bound.

Specific. A specific goal has a much greater chance of being accomplished than a general goal. To set a specific goal you must answer the six "W" questions:

Who?	Who is involved?
What?	What do I want to accomplish?
Where?	Identify a location.
When?	Establish a deadline or time frame for the goal to be accomplished.
Which?	Identify requirements and constraints.
Why?	Specific reasons, purpose or benefits of accomplishing the goal.

Example: A general goal for a student might be, "Get better grades." But a specific goal would provide greater detail, "Attend all classes, complete and turn-in all homework on time, and study a minimum of three hours a week to prepare for quizzes and exams." A general goal for a retail store manager might be, "improve store profitability." A more specific goal might read "improve store profitability by 5% by the end of the fiscal year by targeting key market segments, attracting a larger customer base, improving customer service and return customer rate, and increasing inventory turnover rate 10%.

Measurable. If you can't measure it, you can't manage it. In the broadest sense, the whole goal statement is a measure for the project; if the goal is accomplished, the project or activity is a success. However, there are usually several short-term or small measurements that can be built into the goal. Choose a goal with measurable progress, so you can see the change occur. Establish concrete criteria for measuring progress toward the attainment of each goal you set. When you measure your progress, you stay on track, reach your target dates, and experience the exhilaration of achievement that spurs you on to continued effort required to reach your goals.

Aligned. To get the greatest impact with goal setting, you need to ensure that all individual and team goals align with organizational and enterprise goals. That way, attainment of an individual or team goal furthers the organization's progress in achieving overall organizational goals and ultimately enterprise or corporate goals and objectives.

Another way of thinking about alignment is the metaphor of rowers on a raft on white water rapids. If everyone isn't rowing in the same direction, the raft will go around in circles or move aimlessly through the wash. Everyone needs to be rowing in the same direction to move the organization forward toward its envisioned objectives. Just one rower out of sync can throw the organization into disarray and put the objectives at risk.

Using one goal as a stepping-stone to the next involves **goal sequencing**. A person or group starts by attaining the easy short-term goals, then steps up to the medium-term goals, then move on to the long-term goals. Goal sequencing can create a "goal stairway." In an organizational setting, the organization may coordinate goals so that they do not conflict with each other. The goals of one part of the organization should mesh compatibly with those of other parts of the organization.

Realistic. To be realistic, a goal must represent an objective toward which you are both *willing* and *able* to work. To be truly useful, a goal needs to be a stretch goal. That is, it needs to represent a significant effort to accomplish. A goal can be both challenging and realistic; leader-managers must carefully decide just how high goals should be. But be sure that every goal represents substantial progress. A difficult goal is a better choice than an easy one because an easy goal exerts little or no motivational force. A stretch goal is more strategic and emotionally compelling. Some consultants recommend that organizations set **Big Hairy Audacious Goals** (BHAGs) in this context.[18]

Time Bound. Putting an end point or a deadline on a goal gives you a clear target to work towards. If you don't set a deadline for the goal, the commitment is too vague and the goal is never-ending. It tends not to happen because you feel you can start at any time and procrastination sets in. Without a time limit, there's no urgency to start taking action now. Usually the best goals have deadlines and milestone timelines to guide the organization toward goal accomplishment.

Implementation

Too often, organizations invest a great deal of time and energy conducting a strategic planning session and producing a ponderous, strategic plan document only to have it sit on the shelf unopened and gathering dust. Unless a strategic plan is used to guide an organization's short-term efforts, strategic planning is for the most part a big waste of time.

A fellow professor at the U.S. Army War College once told me a fascinating story about a strategic planning process that he had participated in during a previous posting overseas. My colleague was an experienced, hard-line Marine colonel who had been assigned as the Defense Attaché at one of our embassies in Latin America. Shortly after his arrival in country, the ambassador led the country team through a comprehensive strategic planning process and a detailed strategic plan was subsequently published and shipped off to the State Department in Washington, D.C. Later, a major situation erupted in country involving violent, insurgent forces. My colleague told me that they had anticipated just such a scenario and had included a contingency plan within the overall strategic plan. When the colonel approached the ambassador about next steps as outlined in the plan, the ambassador patiently explained to him that the strategic plan wasn't really used that way in the State Department and that they would now approach the emerging situation ad hoc as it developed. From the ambassador's perspective, the purpose of the strategic planning process was not so much to produce a strategic plan but to energize his country team staff in thinking about future possibilities.

When my friend related this anecdote, at first I was astounded that they would waste time developing a strategic plan that they didn't intend to use. But, I eventually came to understand their perspective that for them it was the strategic planning process itself that was important, not the written plan that the process produced. This perspective parallels a comment once made by Eisenhower: "In preparing for battle, I have always found that plans are useless but planning is indispensable."[19] However, it seems that it was a colossal missed opportunity not to follow the strategic planning process at the embassy level with similar action planning at lower levels within the various sections of the country team staff to support the overall strategic agenda developed during the planning process. It is fundamental to achieving overall organizational alignment and failure to do so places the organization at risk of becoming reactive rather than proactive in rapidly-developing situations.

Strategic planning should be closely followed by action planning efforts at lower organizational levels that break down the central components of the strategic agenda into short-range plans. Thus, *action planning* is carefully describing in detail how the strategic goals will be accomplished. Lower level objectives are associated with tactics or methods that will be used to reach each objective.

Most organizations commonly develop an *annual plan*—sometimes called the *operational plan* or *management plan*—which delineates the strategic goals, strategies, objectives, responsibilities and timelines that should be addressed in the coming year. These plans are frequently developed during the budget process and *budgets* are usually included in the annual plan and organizational work unit plans. Budgets specify the money and other resources that are necessary to implement the annual plan and how the money and resources will be used.

There is a dictum in public administration that policy is what gets budgeted. However, some organizations exhibit a disconcerting disconnect between the strategic planning process and the annual budgeting process which dictates what the organization actually does. That just doesn't make sense. You go through the strategic planning process precisely to guide your budgeting efforts—not just the budgeting of money and capital resources—but budgeting time and work effort throughout the organization as well. I once consulted with a large organization and assisted them in a small way with a comprehensive strategic planning process. The planning effort took over half a year until finally a plan was produced and distributed. Then, shortly thereafter, the organization went through their annual budgeting cycle and I was astounded to note that they paid little attention to their strategic plan in budgeting for the coming year. There appeared to be a total disconnect between the two activities.

Bottom line: The enterprise strategic plan provides the overall direction and objectives that the organization wants to accomplish. The budgeting process provides lower level leaders and managers their marching orders for how to prioritize their work effort in support of those objectives. In a constricted economic environment, firms simply cannot afford to budget resources and spend money on activities or investments that don't contribute to the accomplishment of the overall enterprise strategic agenda. For maximum economy and efficiency, strategic thinking, strategic planning, and the budget process must be tightly linked. The message should be clear and straightforward for leader-managers at all levels of the organization—if it doesn't support the enterprise strategic objectives, it shouldn't be budgeted.

Measurement

A **metric** is any type of measurement used to gauge some quantifiable component of a company's performance. There is a common business adage that *if you don't measure it, you can't manage it*. Kaplan and Norton assert that, "What you measure is what you get."[20]

Because the public and non-profit sectors usually do not generate profits in the same sense as corporate entities, these organizations must apply strategic principles to a different bottom line. That bottom line for most agencies typically relates to achieving their mission within the context of the satisfaction of their customers, stakeholders, and employees.

Metrics are a standardized measurement used to assess performance in a particular area. Metrics are at the heart of any good, customer-focused process management systems and any program directed at continuous improvement. The focus on customers and performance standards show up in the form of metrics that assess your ability to meet customers' needs and business objectives.

Metrics generally fall into two categories:

- **Performance Metrics** are high-level measures of *what* you are doing and how well you are doing it. They assess your overall performance in the areas you are measuring. They are generally external in nature and are most closely tied to outputs, customer requirements, and business needs for the process.

- **Diagnostic Metrics** are measures that ascertain *why* a process may not be performing up to expectations. They tend to be internally-focused and are usually associated with internal process steps and inputs received from suppliers.

A common mistake for organizations is to start first with diagnostic measures—measuring the organization internally—rather than beginning with an external focus on customer needs.

Metrics Best Practices

Here are a few guidelines for leaders and managers to select and put effective metrics into place:

- It's important not to have too many metrics. Concentrate on only a handful of metrics that are necessary.
- Choose the right frequency of measurement. If you only measure a metric once a year, you may not get the information in time to take the necessary corrective actions.
- Periodically reevaluate your metrics. Your core process priorities change over time, and your metrics will need to be modified accordingly.

Notwithstanding differences between the corporate world and public and non-profit sectors, the need for measuring performance against goals and objectives remains the same. Here is a simple model for how to go about setting up a metric system.

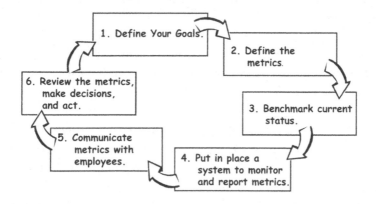

1. **Define your goals**. Make a list of your organizational goals. Goals might include sales objectives, target profit margins, or success at signing up new customers.

2. **Define the metrics**. For each organizational goal on your list, write down a metric that will help you track your progress to success. For example, if your goal is signing up new customers, your metric might involve stating the number of meetings you will have per week with prospective customers.

3. **Benchmark current status**. Now that you've established your metrics, you need to measure them. You must determine exactly how your business is doing, even if the truth is hard to swallow. By establishing the current value of each metric, you will be able to track your improvements into the future.

4. **Put in place a system to monitor and report metrics.** You may need to add new business processes that will help you calculate and report your metrics. For example, if your metric is the number of your customers who view your customer service as being "excellent," then you may want to survey your customers every month and ask them how you are doing.

5. **Communicate metrics with employees**. Once you've defined the key metrics that are important to your business, be sure to let your staff know. Then, everyone can make decisions that help improve metric results.

6. **Review the metrics, make decisions, and act**. With your metrics in place, you have greater insight into which strategies work and which don't. Review the metrics and take steps to improve your results.

I once heard this anecdote that illustrates the point of selecting metrics not for their ease of measurement but for what you need to know about your organization and its environment. One night on his way through a parking lot to his car, a man came upon a young woman down on her hands and knees looking for something. The girl told him that she had dropped her car keys and was trying to find them. The girl was searching near a car under a large light pole and the area was well illuminated so the man thought that this wouldn't be too difficult and got down on his hands and knees to help. After ten minutes of searching and turning up nothing, the man asked the young woman where she thought she had dropped the keys. The girl pointed to another area of the parking lot that was shrouded in darkness because the light on the pole there was burned out. The man was surprised and asked in exasperation, "Well if you dropped your keys over there, why are you looking for them over here?" "Duh." the young woman replied. "The light's better over here." The anecdote is illustrative of the measurement trap that many organizations fall into.

Bottom Line: Organizations tend to focus too much on things that are easy to measure rather than things that are meaningful in tracking organizational performance. Don't waste time tracking metrics that don't provide leaders and managers useful information in moving the organization into the future.

Dashboards and Scorecards

Dashboards and scorecards are frequently used by leaders and managers to provide graphical information about business performance metrics. Their virtue is that they convey critical performance information at a glance, graphical snapshots of strategic and operational data. Dashboards and scorecards are simply different types of visual display mechanisms within a performance management system.

Although the terms are sometimes used interchangeably, there are important distinctions between them. Dashboards are typically used to monitor and display data about lower level operational processes while scorecards track higher level strategic goals and objectives in much greater detail.

A dashboard is analogous to the dashboard on a car with its attendant gauges and warning lights. At a glance, the driver can ascertain the operational status of the car's systems and make adjustments as appropriate. For example, if the fuel gauge indicates that the vehicle is low on gas, the driver can pull into a service station to fill it up. If the check engine light comes on, the driver should have the vehicle checked by a mechanic to see which of the vehicle's systems are malfunctioning and in need of attention. The driver need only respond to those systems needing attention as indicated by the gauges and warning lights.

A scorecard is more analogous to the scorecards that are kept on baseball team performance. Those scorecards are detailed grids of data, set in rows and columns, reflecting specific performance data over time on the individual players and the team as a whole. A good coach or manager can review the scorecard at a glance and understand intuitively which elements of team performance need to be addressed.

Kaplan and Norton, developed the Balanced Scorecard strategic planning model in 1992.[21] More than half of the Fortune 500 corporations in the United States and a growing number of governmental agencies at all levels use this model today. The Balanced Scorecard model directs the organization's strategic focus to perspectives that frame its critical success factors. Strategic management translates performance measures and targets into action initiatives. The model provides fields for objectives, measures or metrics, targets, and initiatives.

When such scorecards for various functional areas or core processes are brought together, they provide leaders and managers with a useful tool for translating vision and strategy into actionable tasks and for tracking progress toward achieving project goals and objectives. Kaplan and Norton suggest that as a minimum, the scorecard tool be used to assess customer relationships ("To achieve our vision, how should we appear to our customers?"), financial issues ("To succeed financially, how should we appear with our shareholders?"), internal business forecasts ("To satisfy our shareholders and customers, what business processes must we excel at?"), and learning and growth opportunities ("To achieve our vision, how will we sustain our ability to change and improve?").[22]

The Pennsylvania Department of Transportation (PennDOT) used an adaptation of this model quite successfully in the early 2000s. Although the small print is hard to read at this level of resolution, the structure of the scorecard is fairly understandable and provides insight as to how PennDOT's Strategic Management Team used the scorecard to drive their strategic plan into the future. Building on a foundation of seven strategic focus areas, they developed corresponding high level goals, measurements and metrics, and specific short-term and long-term targets.

PENNDOT Scorecard of Measures

Strategic Focus Areas	High-Level Goals	How Success Will Be Measured	Measurement Tool	Target 2002	Target 2005
Maintenance First	System Preservation	Better ride conditions on major National Highway System (NHS) highways	International Roughness Index (IRI)	104 for NHS roads	99 for NHS roads
	Cost effective investment of funds on assets in all areas	Reduction in outstanding maintenance needs	Condition assessment for highways and bridges	Complete asset management system	Meet target established in 2002
Quality Of Life	Balance social, economic and environmental concerns	Timely decisions based on public and technical input on project impacts	Highway project environmental approvals meeting target dates	75% meeting target dates	90% meeting target dates
	Demonstrate sound environmental practices	Attaining world-class environmental status	ISO 14001 environmental criteria	Implement a pilot program	Meet ISO standards
Mobility And Access	Delivery of transportation products and services	Honoring commitments on scheduled transportation projects	Dollar value of 12-year program construction contracts initiated	$1.3 billion per year	$1.4 billion per year
	Efficient and effective movement of people and goods	Reduced travel delays	2002-peak period work zone lane restrictions 2005-travel delays on selected corridors	Set baseline in 2000 for reduced 2002 lane restrictions	Meet target set in 2002 to reduce corridor travel delays
Customer Focus	Improve customer satisfaction	Competitiveness on the Malcolm Baldrige Criteria for Excellence	Baldrige Organizational Review scores customer criteria	80 Department average	100 Department average
			Answer rate of calls to the Customer Call Center	94% of calls answered	94% of calls answered
Innovation and Technology	Apply technology to assure efficiency and cost savings	Efficiency, cost savings and conformance with Commonwealth standards	Baldrige Organizational Review Package scores customer criteria	500 level met by lead organizations	600 level met by lead organizations
Safety and Security	Reduce number of fatalities & severity of crashes on all Commonwealth roadways	Fewer fatalities from highway crashes	Number of fatalities per year	5% reduction in fatalities	10% reduction in fatalities
	Safer working conditions	Fewer work-related injuries	Injury rate per 100 employees working one year	8.25% injury rate	7.5% injury rate
Maximize Organizational Performance	Improve organizational and workforce performance	Positive trends in employee feedback on job-related factors	Organizational Climate Survey selected items	48% positive rating	54% positive rating

Adjustment

As strategic plans are developed and subordinate actions plans are developed and implemented, success of the plan is measured using performance metrics. At the same time, external and internal scans continue to check for any significant changes in the environment or within the organization that will require adjustments to the strategic plan as it unfolds in its implementation. **The strategic plan document is not set in cement.** It should be **constantly monitored and adjusted** as organizational leaders and managers literally "drive" the plan into an uncertain and changing future.

A **learning organization** is one that facilitates the learning of its members and continuously transforms itself, driving the strategic plan into the future. Senge suggests that employees of learning organizations are continually learning by examining feedback in the context of the whole organization, and adjusting the plan as appropriate.[23] Thus, although the organizational strategic planning meeting may take place only at yearly intervals, strategic planning is not a once-and-done effort. It should be a **continuous process** as organizations continually monitor progress and make adjustments as necessary.

Conclusion

Strategic planning is a highly complex process involving many people from within an organization and sometimes external stakeholders as well. The success of the process is much dependent upon how well the strategic planning team works together collaboratively and their combined ability to think creatively about prospects for an uncertain future. The goal of developing a clear vision of the future on which to overlay a strategic plan is daunting. Organizational environments are fluid and changing even as the planning process is conducted, and it is hard to capture the essence of that dynamic in a written document.

Many organizations respond to the issue of a complex process by producing a thick, complex, strategic plan document. This will probably not produce the desired results. If the plan is overly complex, it will prove too difficult and unwieldy in galvanizing the efforts of the members of the organization. On the other hand, if the plan is overly simplistic it will not prove useful in moving the organization forward. The strategic planning team needs to produce a plan that balances the needs for complexity and simplicity. This will facilitate greater understanding among organizational members and make it possible to effectively modify and adjust the plan as the future unfolds.

Even overcoming these challenges, the strategic planning process may not produce the desired results simply because it tends to hinder strategic thinking. As Mintzberg suggests, strategic planning and strategic thinking may become competing processes. Strategic thinking is about *creative thinking*, synthesis and understanding the many variables that provide indicators about the future's potential direction. In contrast, strategic planning is about *analytical thinking*, the breaking down of organizational goals into steps and formulating the requirements for how the steps in accomplishing the goals might be implemented.

Strategic planning proponents assert that analysis and synthesis are mutually complementary and that, for the most part, strategic thinking and strategic planning happen simultaneously, the one feeding the other. Although strategic thinking and planning are different and distinct processes, they are interrelated and complementary in sustaining and supporting one another in an effective strategic leadership and management effort.

For a strategic leadership and management program to be effective, strategic planners must integrate strategic thinking fully into the planning process, combining right-brain creativity and synthesis with left-brain analytical rationality and logic.[20] In the rapidly-changing organizational environments of today, innovation underwrites the only formula for sustained success. This reflects the duality of strategic management and strategic leadership discussed earlier. An effective strategic management program must balance the need to create value in the present while building resources and capabilities for future value creation and competitive success. Once strategic thinking has informed the creation of a viable plan, it must be considered a living document and modified as necessary as the future unfolds. Strategic planning is not a once-and-done event, but a continual ongoing, dynamic process of an effective strategic leadership and strategic management organizational culture.

Chapter 8—Leading Employees through the Psychological Challenges of Change

Many people today, particularly those of the Veteran and Baby Boomer generations, consider the normalcy of life to be relatively stable punctuated by occasional periods of turbulence or disequilibrium.[1] This model or perception is sometimes referred to as *punctuated equilibrium*.

For example, the life experience of the Veteran generation typically includes having lived through the Great Depression, World War II, and the Korean War. These great calamities tend to show up on their perceptions of life as temporary periods of turbulence in an otherwise stable and predictable world. When World War II ended, American servicemen and women deployed around the world could think of nothing else but to return home and resume their normal lives, establishing a home, raising a family, getting some schooling, getting a job and embarking on a career. Although there are not many of the Veteran generation left in the workforce today, many of their children in the early Boomer generation share those same values and perceptions.[2]

However, this image does not reflect the turbulent reality of today's workplace. On the contrary, most organizational environments today are extremely volatile, ambiguous, and uncertain and there are only occasional brief periods of stability.

The challenge this presents for leader-managers today is that we encounter many people within organizations whose idea of normalcy is a stable equilibrium in which they know basically from day to day what they will be doing in predictable ways. These folks are typically upset or dismayed by the uncertainty and turbulence produced by constant change in the workplace. It is a critical task for strategic leaders to work with people in their organizations providing them with encouragement and support to bring them successfully through the psychological challenges of change transitions.

Welter and Egmon suggest that to get any system to change in a business ecology, you must first start with the people or stakeholders within the system. Successful leader-managers strive to understand what is on the minds and in the hearts of the stakeholders of their business ecology, and they design strategy and change from that understanding.[3]

Foster's Organizational Transition Cycle Model[4] focuses on people, primarily the employees in the organization:

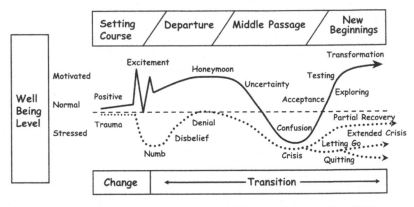

Charles Foster (2004) adapted from Dai Williams (1999)

This model incorporates an ocean navigation metaphor. At the top of the model are the four stages of navigation: setting course, departure, middle passage, and new beginning. The curved lines on the model indicate the common reactions by people in organizations to the announcement of impending change. Some are quite positive and enthusiastic while others display trauma, with some individuals beginning to go through the same psychological response they would have to the loss of a loved one. Along the two paths, the different reactions to change are indicated, and vary greatly from excitement to despair and quitting.

Not everyone follows these paths exactly nor spends the same amount of time passing though each of the stages. Generally, however, people experiencing positive or traumatic change transition through a similar cycle. One of the important points of the model is that, notwithstanding the initial reaction to the change, positive or traumatic, both paths eventually converge at some crisis point where the employees becomes discouraged and demotivated. This crisis point is where strategic leadership becomes most critical.

This model illustrates the importance of the fifth fundamental leadership practice of the Kouzes and Posner model—Encouraging the Heart.[5] Without encouragement, many otherwise excellent employees simply won't make it through the change transition. Using the ocean voyage metaphor of the model, some employees who are experiencing trauma from the change turbulence will be standing on the ship's deck at the rail, throwing up and generally feeling wretched. Some may become so unhappy and despondent from all of the turbulence that they may throw themselves overboard (metaphorically) to end it all—that is, they quit and walk away from the organization. It doesn't have to be that way. Caring leaders who take the time to talk with discouraged employees and encourage them onward is frequently all it takes to see them through the crisis. Effective strategic leaders listen to their employees empathetically and help them see better days ahead. When employees sense the genuine concern of their leader-managers, they begin to feel encouraged to hang on and stay the course of the journey.

Without that caring support, employees may continue downward from the crisis point and remain in a distressed state, quitting, letting go, or experiencing only a partial recovery. But with caring strategic leadership and support, they can turn upward headed for eventual transformation. The path toward transformation begins with acceptance, which leads to exploring and testing.

Bridges proposed a similar model about leading people through change but the Bridges model illustrates the value of leaders sharing information to assist people through the transition.[6] According to the model, leading and managing the change transition involves the process of helping people through the turbulence by simply keeping them informed and reducing disquieting uncertainty. Admittedly, it isn't always possible for leader-managers to share everything they know, but most could share more information than they typically do. Sharing information reduces uncertainty and discomfort during the turbulence of change and it can help reduce or even eliminate gossip and speculation about the unknown.

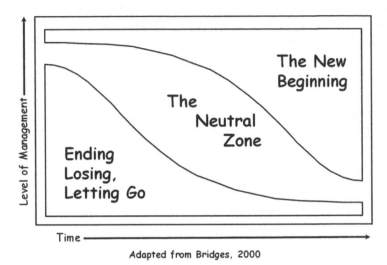

Adapted from Bridges, 2000

The Bridges model illustrates three important phases through the change transition process:

- Letting go of the old ways and the identities people had. This first phase of transition is an ending, and the time when you need to help people deal with their losses.
- Going through an in-between time when the old is gone but the new isn't fully operational. This is when the critical psychological realignments and repatternings take place.
- Coming out of the transition and making a new beginning. This is when people develop new identities, experience the new energy, and discover the new sense of purpose that make the change begin to work.

The model suggests that when people have adequate information about the turbulence and change they are experiencing, it removes some of the uncertainty and doubt and allows them to function effectively in supporting the transition. Both the Foster model and the Bridges model have an end state goal of a **new beginning** for the participants. Bridges points out that "because transition is a process by which people unplug from an old world and plug into a new world, we can say that transition starts with an ending and finishes with a beginning."[7]

Bottom line: When people find themselves in an organizational change crisis, positive leadership interventions can make all the difference in the world. This is when leaders should be most visible inspiring the heart and motivating the spirit.

Leadership and Management by Walking Around

Some leader-managers have difficulty in translating the lessons from the Foster and Bridges models into practical activities that will support employees during turbulent change transitions. An effective technique for accomplishing this is Leadership and Management by Walking Around. Too often, leader-managers at all levels hole up in their offices and don't get out among their employees. This isolation creates a barrier of uncertainty and distrust. Effective leader-managers get out among their employees as often as practicable. Here are some simple rules or ideas about how to get started on the practice of Leadership and Management by Walking Around.

1. **Get up from your desk often and get out among your people.**
   You might be tempted to think that you don't have time to do this but it is actually a great time saver in the long run.

2. **Go out of your way to catch them in the act of doing something right.**
   Any competent leader-manager can catch employees doing something wrong and many go out of their way to do so. But it's a bad approach. People will begin to dread seeing you coming and they will attempt to hide from you. In contrast, when you catch them doing something right, you can congratulate them on doing a good job as part of verbal reward and recognition system. And your employees will begin looking forward to having you drop by their work area.

3. **Never walk by anyone doing something wrong without stopping and making a correction.**

Whenever you see someone doing something wrong and you ignore it, you just set a new, lower performance standard. If you by chance see employees doing something wrong, you don't need to get angry and fly off the handle. Instead, first determine if they know how to do the task correctly. If not, conduct immediate onsite training to make sure they know how to do it correctly and then observe while they do it. When they do it right, congratulate them and move on. If they already know how to do the task correctly but were taking a shortcut, commit them to always doing it correctly. Then, down the road if you observe them doing it wrong again, it's time for a private disciplinary conversation in your office.

4. **Make it a positive experience.**

Mix your conversation about formal organizational tasks and other matters with informal, social chat. Get to know your employees. Learn about their families and pastimes, their likes and dislikes. This is fundamental in knowing what truly motivates your employees. If most encounters with the boss produce a positive experience, employees will communicate more freely and share concerns and ideas that can benefit the organization.

5. **Project the image of coach and mentor, not an inspector.**

Leader-managers are first and foremost trainers, mentors, and coaches. Their job is to bring out the best work performance in their employees possible. You can't help that happen if they are trying to hide stuff from their inspector-manager.

6. **Walk in their shoes.**

Learn something about the work tasks and work experience of your employees. Some leader-managers actually take the time for a **Shoes Program** and spend a day or half-day every so often working with employees in various locations in the organization to see how the work gets done. This practice creates incredible relationships and the leader-manager gains a detailed understanding of the practices and processes of the organization overall.

7. Ask lots of questions.

Some leader-managers don't ask questions because they are afraid that it will reveal ignorance. Get over it. Leader-managers are not expected to know everything. Practically everyone in the organization will know more than you about something. Moreover, when you ask questions, it conveys interest in what the employees know or are doing and creates a forum for positive communication and understanding.

8. Be responsive to problems and concerns.

When employees share problems or concerns, don't brush them off but attempt to investigate further and address the issue. Then, get back with them later on and tell them what you have found out and perhaps what you've done based on their input. For issues concerning the organization, this helps employees feel like they're making a positive contribution to the organization and they will be more open about matters and issues that can improve organizational performance. For personal matters, this helps employees to understand that the boss cares about their welfare and is trying to work with them in meaningful ways.

9. Share information when you can.

This is the underlying message of the Bridges model. Some leader-managers hoard important information and keep it to themselves as a supposed source of power. In today's rapidly changing, turbulent environment, this is patently a bad idea. Share information with your employees as much as possible to reduce uncertainty and enhance their ability to stay focused and work more effectively.

10. Share your vision.

Use your leadership-and-management-by-walking-around time as an opportunity to share your vision of where the organization is headed with your employees. Talk with them about their ideas on the matter and engage them in the process. As you do this, they will become more committed to whatever change initiatives that are taking place and their buy-in will make the transition just that much easier.

Communication Plan

As organizations develop strategic plans at the enterprise level and action plans at lower levels to accomplish enterprise goals and objectives, it is critical that employees and key external stakeholders be kept well informed of whatever changes in the workplace they entail.

Generally, resistance or opposition to any changes can be potentially mitigated by including employees from all levels and key stakeholders in the strategic planning process to enhance buy-in. Additionally, employees will feel much more comfortable with ongoing change turbulence if they are kept informed about what is going on. Good communication with employees and other stakeholders doesn't just happen. It needs to be well thought out and planned. A communication plan is a written document that describes all potential forms of written, spoken, and electronic interaction with employees and stakeholder groups by all means available including newspapers and magazine articles; meetings, town hall gatherings, speeches, annual reports, committee and board communiqués, legal and legislative documentation, marketing and sales tools, media relations and public relations materials, and online communications including email, Facebook and Twitter.

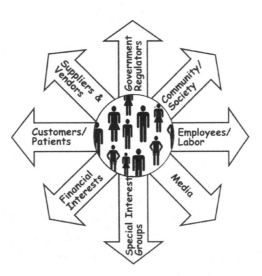

The communication plan should be developed and implemented in conjunction with the annual budgeting or organizational planning process. The communication plan should define overall communication objectives for each stakeholder group and a timetable for when particular elements of information should be shared with each group. The communication plan should outline roughly what communication activities will be accomplished and when.

There are essentially two approaches to preparing a communication plan: one, a stakeholder-based communication plan or two, an event/activity-based communication plan.

Stakeholder-Focused Communication Plan

Stakeholder Group	Messages/ Concerns	Timing	Forum/ Method	Status
Executive Team	Project Conflicts & Obstacles	Monthly	Executive Committee Meeting	Monthly 15-min Briefings
IT	Interface with Hardware/ Software	Daily/Weekly	Email & Intranet	On track
Contractors	Schedule/ Compliance Issues	Daily/Weekly	Phone & Email Weekly Sitdown Meeting	On track
Budget Team	Cost Overruns	Bi-weekly	Email & Sitdown Meetings as needed	Working
Community Activist Group	Green Issues	Weekly/Monthly	Internet & Town Hall Meetings	Next town hall meeting: 2/4/11
Employees and all Internal Stakeholders	Project Progress Parking & WIIFM	Weekly	Email, Intranet and Internal Town Hall Mtgs	Next Town Hall Meeting 2/6/11

A stakeholder-focused communication plan is prepared in conjunction with stakeholder analysis to determine issues and concerns of key stakeholders, particularly those stakeholders that might be resistant to the activities being planned. Each stakeholder group will likely have different interests and concerns and it is necessary to tailor the message for each group. Timing of communication to targeted stakeholder groups is critical to eliminate uncertainty and reduce potential unrest and resistance.

An event/activity-based communication plan focuses on planned events and activities in the milestone calendar, scheduled meetings and forums, and accomplishments and setbacks as the change initiative moves forward.

Event/Activity-Focused Communication Plan

Event/ Activity	Forum/ Method	Frequency/ Timing	Target Stakeholders	Status
Executive Team Briefing	Readahead Package & PowerPoint	Monthly	Executive Committee & Key Stakeholders	Exec Conference Room Reserved
Team Briefing	Intranet & 10-Minute Standup Meeting	Daily at 9:00 am	Team and Sponsor	Meetings running over
Weekly Intranet Bulletin	Intranet	Weekly	Team, Sponsor, & Executive Committee	Coordinated with IT
Budget and Schedule Detail	Spreadsheets & Gantt Chart By Email	Bi-weekly	Sponsor and Executive Committee	Working/Positive Feedback
Accomplishments and Setbacks	Email and Intranet	Weekly	All Internal Stakeholders	As required
Schedule Milestones	Email and Intranet	Weekly	All Internal Stakeholders	As met

Long-term change initiatives are typically divided into phases which become key milestones in the accomplishment of the overall corporate objectives. It is important to identify and celebrate reaching intermediate milestones so that all employees can feel a sense of accomplishment and catch a breather from the long-term commitment to the ongoing strategic change. Briefings, team meetings, and town hall forums should be scheduled on a regular basis to keep all stakeholders with an interest in the change initiative informed and supportive.

The communication plan should have a built-in process for measuring and evaluating results. This could take the form of a monthly report, formalized departmental reports for presentation at periodic staff meetings, briefings to the senior executive team, and a year-end summary for the annual organization report. Kotter points out that most organizations under-communicate change initiatives, leaving employees and external stakeholders in the dark about what is really going on.[8] This tends to result in great uncertainty and lack of buy-in for the overall change initiative. Developing an effective communication plan takes time and energy but it is well worth the effort. Once in place and implemented, the communication plan supports the ongoing change initiative and brings a semblance of order to the chaos and messiness of change itself.

Conclusion

Many people in the workplace today are upset and off-balance because of the uncertainty and turbulence produced by constant change in the workplace. Strategic leaders need to work with people in their organizations to provide them encouragement and support to bring them successfully through the psychological challenges of change transitions. Successful leader-managers strive to understand what is on the minds and in the hearts of the stakeholders of their business ecology, and they design strategy and change based upon that understanding. When people find themselves in crisis, positive leadership interventions can make all the difference in the world. This is when leaders should be most visible inspiring the heart and motivating the spirit. Effective leaders and managers get out of their offices and out among their employees as often as practicable.

Employee resistance or opposition to organizational change can be mitigated by including employees from all levels and key stakeholders in the strategic planning process to enhance buy-in. Additionally, employees will feel much more comfortable with ongoing change turbulence if they are kept informed about what is going on. Good communication with employees and other stakeholders doesn't just happen. Providing employees and other stakeholders with needed information can reduce fear and uncertainty about change. An effective communication plan supports the ongoing change initiative by keeping stakeholders informed during each phase of the change transition.

Chapter 9—Leading and Managing Change on the Edge of Chaos

It is difficult to understand management science today or where management and organization theoretical work is going in the future, without first having some understanding of its historical roots and what intellectual baggage it carries with it. Stein suggests that the boundaries of our traditional disciplines are dictated as much by history as by the nature of the contemporary world we try to comprehend.[1]

There is a long list of scholars whom could be cited as major contributors to the development and deployment of classical management and organization theory. Here, we examine the work of those few who are considered by most scholars as being the seminal thinkers and most important contributors to the field.

In 1687, Sir Isaac Newton published his three laws of motion, forever changing the way men would view the physical world.[2] When combined with the prior work of Rene Descartes' *Rules for the Direction of the Mind*, published in 1628, scientists then had the philosophical foundation for developing a systematic approach to scientific discovery based upon an assumption of an orderly universe, principles of certainty and linearity, and a structured, rational process of inquiry.[3]

Descartes' concept of academic comprehensiveness was subsequently complemented and expanded upon by Adam Smith's construct of Economic Man and the underpinning notion of comprehensive rationality.[4] Although there were many other contemporary scholar-contributors of lesser renown, the work of these three men provided the seminal thinking for the development of a scientific methodology that would dominate empirical research in the physical and social sciences for over two hundred years. Some scholars add Darwin to this short list of influential, paradigmatic thinkers. Frederick Taylor subsequently provided the theoretical basis for Scientific Management and introduced pragmatic notions about time motion studies to find and measure the "one best way" to do an effective [efficient] job.[5]

This chapter reviews the evolution of management theory from its classical roots in Descartes, Newton, and Smith, and framed by Taylor's Scientific Management, to modern management approaches informed by the New Sciences—relativity, quantum physics, complexity theory, chaos theory, and fuzzy set theory.

Traditional Management Theory

Rene Descartes. In the early 1600s, a French scholar, philosopher and scientist, Rene Descartes, published *Discourse on the Method of Rightly Conducting the Reason, and seeking Truth in the Sciences,*[6] a thought-provoking treatise which broke with established religious thinking of the day and promoted a purely rational method of scientific inquiry. Descartes rejected religious tradition and authority as the guide along the path to scientific and philosophical knowledge. For him, reason was both the foundation and guide for pursuing truth and absolute certainty.

Descartes felt no need for a complex multitude of rules of inquiry and fashioned instead a set of four methodological principles or injunctions that he felt would be sufficient. These four injunctions established the pattern for scientific inquiry and investigation that would be embraced by future generations of scientists and philosophers.

Rule One established a philosophical basis for scientific empiricism.

> The first was never to accept anything for true which I did not clearly know to be such; that is to say, carefully to avoid precipitancy and prejudice, and to comprise nothing more in my judgment than what was presented to my mind so clearly and distinctly as to exclude all ground of doubt.[7]

Rule Two established a bias for a reductionist approach, examining the parts of a problem to derive knowledge about the whole.

> The second, to divide each of the difficulties under examination into as many parts as possible, and as might be necessary for its adequate solution.[8]

Rule Three suggested a start point for an examination of the most simple and elementary and then working upwards towards the more complex. It also suggested a sense of linearity, that is, that one thing leads to another in a prescribed order.

The third, to conduct my thoughts in such order that, by commencing with objects the simplest and easiest to know, I might ascend by little and little, and, as it were, step by step, to the knowledge of the more complex; assigning in thought a certain order even to those objects which in their own nature do not stand in a relation of antecedence and sequence.[9]

Rule Four suggested an examination of the reality of the thing under consideration so comprehensive as to be certain of having omitted no other possible variable or element.

And the last, in every case to make enumerations so complete, and reviews so general, that I might be assured that nothing was omitted.[10]

Each of these rules carried significant implications for the scientific community and the nature of scientific research methodology. With Descartes as the philosophical father of modern scientific inquiry, **the four underpinning pillars of the emerging scientific research method became empiricism, reductionism, linearity, and comprehensive rationality.**

Isaac Newton. Fifty years later, Sir Isaac Newton published his paradigm-breaking three laws of motion in 1687.[11]

Newton's First Law: An object at rest remains at rest until acted upon by a force. An object in motion continues moving in a straight line at constant velocity until acted upon by a force.

Newton's Second Law: Acceleration of an object is directly proportional to the net force acting on the object, and inversely proportional to its mass.

Newton's Third Law: Whenever one object exerts a force on a second object, the second object exerts an equal and opposite force on the first.

Newton's first law was not original with Newton but was built on the previous scientific research and findings of Galileo. Newton's third law however suggested a new and important idea: that forces in nature come in pairs characterized by an *action* and a *reaction*. **For every action there is an equal and opposite reaction** implies a linear arrangement in nature in which outputs are proportional to inputs and cause and effect are direct, predictable and observable. Both of these ideas had a significant impact on the developing methodology of scientific observation and research. Newton's laws also suggested that the whole is equal to the sum of its parts, an idea which reinforced Descartes' reductionist approach to scientific research and further encouraged the separation of large complex problems into smaller more manageable parts.

Adam Smith. A century later in 1776, the same year representatives from the thirteen American colonies signed the Declaration of Independence, Adam Smith, a British economist, published *An Inquiry into the Nature and Causes of the Wealth of Nations*.[12] This lengthy treatise represents the classic statement of laissez-faire economics. It is an intriguing analysis of the economic facts of global economic life as Smith saw it in his day. Several fundamental principles, many of which became axiomatic in classical economic thinking, were introduced in this work, including the division of labor, supply-and-demand, and free market capitalism.

More importantly for the scientific community in general, Smith's conceptual devices of "Economic Man"[13] and the "Invisible Hand"[14] reinforced Descartes' notion of comprehensive rationality, an idea which suggests that man is capable of routinely analyzing all of the variables of a problem in a comprehensive and rational way to make economic decisions in his own best interest. The idea understates the challenges associated with the complexities of the market place that existed even in Adam Smith's day but notwithstanding, the idea went unchallenged until the mid-20th century.

Smith also examined the nature of the emerging factory system, specifically, the economic and manufacturing advantages of a pin factory over the work output of individual pin artisans. His analysis provided the early intellectual foundation for thinking about organizations in terms of a machine metaphor, an image that would be strongly reinforced later in the United States in the early 1800s as the new nation entered the era of its own Industrial Revolution.

Frederick Taylor. Beginning in the 1880s, Frederick Taylor began to expound on his idea of Scientific Management in the United States. Based on Newtonian principles, Scientific Management suggested that systems are orderly, closed, mechanistic and clockwork-like. Taylor favored a closed-system approach in which inputs-process-and outputs were linear and predictable. His system emphasized that goals and production output could be precisely measured. It also reinforced the reductionist perspective that the component steps in a manufacturing and production assembly operation could be divided up into smaller work efforts for analysis.[15]

Taylor's Scientific Management construct suggested a dichotomy between management and leadership in organizations. The scientific foundation of the day provided intellectual tools to develop principles of *management* but found the topic of *leadership* unsuited for scholarly or scientific inquiry.

Thus, during the first few decades of the 20th century, Frederick Taylor's Scientific Management was the dominant paradigm in management and organization science. The humanistic approaches introduced by Mary Parker Follett[16] and Elton Mayo's Hawthorne studies[17] were just beginning to emerge in the 1920s. Nevertheless, they would take decades to develop and mature and mechanistic, closed-system thinking would maintain its stranglehold on management theory for another thirty years, almost to the mid-century mark.

Henri Fayol. The next major voice in the development of classical management theory was that of Henri Fayol, a French engineer, who published his *Administration Industrielle et Generale* in 1916. Generally unknown to American scholars for over three decades, an English translation, *General and Industrial Management*, was finally published in 1949.[18] Fayol's work added a significant dimension beyond Taylorism. While Taylor focused on achieving individual efficiencies, Fayol examined management practices of entire organizations. Fayol's contribution to classical organization theory is considered by most scholars every bit as important as Taylor's. His work focused on managerial and organizational principles including division of work, authority and responsibility, discipline, unity of command, unity of direction, subordination of individual interest to general interest, remuneration of personnel, centralization, scalar chains, order, equity, stability of personnel tenure, initiative, and *espirit de corps*.

Max Weber. Another foreign scholar who lived earlier in the century but wasn't appreciated by American scholars until mid-century was Max Weber. Weber was a German economist, whose *Wirtschaft und Gesellschaft*, published posthumously in 1922, was finally translated into English and published in 1946.[19] A limited number of American scholars who were aware of Weber's work studied it in the original German text before the English translation became available. Weber's work emphasized bureaucratic organization, distributed authority, orderly replacement of officials, and hierarchical supervision of lower organizational levels by competent higher management levels. Weber's work on bureaucracy has since become a classic and all subsequent research and theory on bureaucratic organization builds on his seminal work.

Luther Gulick. Apparently strongly influenced by Fayol's work, Luther Gulick introduced his now famous functions of management, remembered by its mnemonic acronym, POSDCORB, in "Notes on the Theory of Organization," which appeared in *Papers on the Science of Administration*, a collection edited by Gulick and Urwick in 1937.[8] POSDCORB stands for Planning, Organizing, Staffing, Directing, COordinating, Reporting, and Budgeting. Although rather dated today, this set of principles is still very much in evidence in the workplace among traditional management practitioners.

The Lingering Influence of Classical Management Theory

The emergence and evolution of classical management theory was strongly influenced by the societal values of the time. The major tenets of classical theory were often a reflection of the mechanical system metaphor or machine metaphor which powered the Industrial Revolution. Men in organizations were dehumanized and frequently viewed as inter-changeable parts. The factory system flourished with mass production processes and mechanical systems. Organizational structures were designed to maximize effectiveness and efficiency with the machinery, and in the process, the human element of organizations was deemphasized and ignored.

Ultimately, the rational-comprehensive component of classical theory began to lose its luster for management and organization scholars and it began to be questioned in the immediate aftermath of World War II by important American scholars like Herbert Simon[21] and Dwight Waldo[22]. Nevertheless, the seminal work by the classical management and organization scholars, which by that time spanned almost two centuries, provided a firm platform and launching pad for all subsequent organizational research. As expressed by Shafritz and Ott in 1992 :

> . . . it is tempting to denigrate the contributions of the classicalists—to view them as narrow and simplistic. In the context of their times, however, they were brilliant pioneers. Their thinking provided invaluable foundations for the field of organization theory, and their influence upon organization theory and theorists continues today.[23]

Emergence of the New Sciences

As classical organization and management theorists struggled to retain their hegemony in the intellectual debate of the day, physical scientists were uncovering a whole new way of thinking about the world that would eventually provoke a significant challenge to the classical paradigm. The five most important scientific ideas to emerge in post-Newtonian science were relativity, quantum mechanics, chaos theory, complexity, and fuzzy logic. These are frequently referred to (all or part) as the new sciences or, more simply, as the complexity sciences.[24] The emergence of the new sciences forced scientists and researchers in both the physical sciences and the social sciences to reexamine their basic premises that underpinned their theoretical approaches.

Later discoveries in chaos and complexity have required even a reexamination of the fields of relativity and quantum mechanics that were developed earlier in the century. Although basic notions of chaos and complexity have been with us for a long time, the scientific study of chaos and complexity is a relatively recent endeavor appearing in the scientific community during the past twenty or thirty years. I preface this section with the interesting observations of Henri Poincaré, a French mathematician who challenged Newtonian physics in the mid-1880s, presaging the later emergence of chaos and complexity research in the next century by 80 years.

Henri Poincaré. In 1846, the planet Neptune was discovered, primarily as a result of empirical observations of small deviations in the orbit of Uranus from the predicted orbit using Newtonian physics. Then, in a paper published in 1890, French mathematician Henri Poincaré outlined weaknesses in Newton's notions of a purely deterministic and linear universe.[25] In particular, Poincaré found that Newtonian physics did not provide sufficiently rigorous tools for analyzing the relationship between three or more astronomical bodies at a time. In his calculations, Poincaré had found that small differences in the initial conditions produce great differences in the final phenomena, and the situation defied prediction.

Poincaré's ideas were largely dismissed as only minor perturbations in the linear simplicity of Newton's model and the scientific community generally resisted acknowledging or following Poincaré's prescient intellectual lead into chaos and complexity. In other words, the close approximation to reality that Newtonian linear equations provided was preferable to the more difficult and more precise nonlinear equations. The Newtonian paradigm proved resilient and unyielding to change. That would have to wait for another eighty years.

Theory of Relativity

In the early 1900s, Albert Einstein and several other scientists were working on a theory of relativity to account for new discoveries and observations about the cosmos. Although there were many researchers whose work made a significant contribution to the field, Einstein's Special and General Theories of Relativity framed the collective work of the day and consequently have received the greatest recognition.[26] At the heart of Einstein's work was his famous formulation $E=MC^2$

which described the conservation of mass and energy. Specifically, Einstein proposed that space and time are inter-related dimensions and that space-time is curved in the area of matter.

Out of this great body of work (for the most part opaque and incomprehensible to laymen in general) comes the anti-Newtonian notion of nonlinearity. Relativity also ran in the face of Newtonian physics with respect to time. Newtonian physics takes place in three dimensional space. Relativity considers a fourth dimension—time—as a key element in defining the physical reality of space. This was the kernel of an idea that would later reemerge with chaos theory that organizations (or anything else for that matter) cannot be analyzed as static entities frozen in time but only in the context of changing, dynamic processes.

Quantum Mechanics

Whereas scientists developed specific and general theories of relativity to explain the nature of the cosmos on a macro scale, quantum mechanics research was initially pursued to explain the nature of reality on the micro, sub-atomic scale. According to the older theories of classical physics, energy was considered solely as a continuous phenomenon in the form of waves and matter was assumed to occupy a very specific region of space and to move in a continuous manner.

Quantum theory suggests that these seemingly mutually distinct concepts may both be right, and proposes a dual nature for both waves and particles, with one aspect predominating in some situations and the other predominating in other situations.[27] This concept has significant implications for management and organization theory. For example, using insights from quantum theory, Zohar published in 1998 an intriguing journal article in *Management Review*, "What Would a Quantum Organization Look Like?"[28] A decade later, Harris published *The Art of Quantum Planning*, a more lengthy treatise on the application of ideas from quantum physics to strategy and leadership. Like relativity, ideas emerging from the field of quantum theory are very much dependent upon the time factor and suggest a dynamic (moving or evolving) rather than a stable (unmoving or equilibrium) state.

Chaos, Complexity, and Fuzzy Logic

Like relativity and quantum theory, the eclectic inquiry into chaos and complexity has had many contributors. No one single individual can be credited with having invented or discovered the field. Henri Poincaré certainly was one of the first in 1890 to explore ideas that entered into what we identify as chaos theory today. However, like many whose ideas are before their time, Poincaré couldn't get anyone to break with the firmly-rooted Newtonian precepts of his day and think about things in a new, very different way. Eighty years later, Edward Lorenz was probably the most influential pioneer in chaos theory among many other pioneers and popularizers breaking ground in the field during the last three decades of the past century. Among the most important of these other researchers and authors are Mandelbrot, Feigenbaum, Prigogene, and Gleick.

Edward Lorenz. Lorenz was a meteorologist at the Massachusetts Institute of Technology during the late 1950s where he experimented with computer projections of potential weather patterns.[29] At that time, computers lacked the graphic sophistication and sheer computing power of even the most modest of PCs, tablets and smart phones today. Lacking much memory, the computer Lorenz used was unable to create highly complex patterns, but it was able to reflect the interaction between major meteorological events such as tornadoes and hurricanes. A variety of weather factors could be represented or quantified by numbers. A computer run would establish the relationships between the numbers and Lorenz would examine computer printouts to analyze the results. After watching his "weather" systems develop on the computer, Lorenz began to see patterns emerge, and was able to predict with some degree of accuracy what would happen next.

While carrying out an experiment, Lorenz made a serendipitous discovery. He wanted to replicate a pattern from a previous run and entered some variables representing temperature and wind speed into the computer expecting the simulation to proceed the same as it had before. To his surprise, the pattern began to diverge from the previous run, and after a period of simulated time, the pattern was completely different.

Searching for the cause of the differences in the printout, Lorenz eventually isolated the cause in the way he had entered the variables. He had entered variables expressed to the nearest thousandth taken directly from the computer printout. However, the computer had actually been working with numbers expressed to the nearest millionth and the printout represented only an approximation of the computing precision being used. Such minute differences in the starting point of the run quickly produced significant deviations in the weather pattern and ultimately resulted in a completed divergent pattern.

Lorenz had discovered one of the major underpinning notions of what later came to be known as chaos theory: the behavior of a system of equations was sensitively dependent on the initial conditions of the mathematical model, or in other words, small deviations in an initial system can eventually result in large changes or differences over time. This was essentially the same idea proposed by Poincaré a century earlier. Lorenz characterized this notion as the *butterfly effect* and hypothesized that a weather variable as insignicant as the air movement caused by a butterfly's wings could later have profound effects on meteorological conditions elsewhere over time.[30] Lorenz deduced that if there were any errors in observing or precisely quantifying variables in the initial state of a system—and this is inevitable in any real system—an accurate forecasted prediction of the future state of the system would be impossible.

Lorenz also discovered another important principle—the effect in chaotic patterns of strange attractors. Lorenz was able to model the motion of a process using a series of equations and three variables. He then produced a graphical representation of these equations in space using his three variables as x, y, and z coordinates. Lorenz hypothesized that the graph would culminate or stop at a certain point, indicating that the system had reached equilibrium, or that a loop would eventually be reformed and retraced, indicating an infinite repeating pattern.

Neither occurred. Instead, the computer graph displayed a kind of infinite complexity. It always stayed within certain bounds, never running off the page but never repeating itself either. It traced a strange, distinctive shape, a kind of double spiral in three dimensions, like a butterfly with its two wings. The shape signaled pure disorder, since no point or pattern of points ever recurred. Yet it also signaled a new kind of order.[31]

Benoit Mandelbrot. Mandelbrot was a French mathematician who did much pioneering work in the area of chaos theory and is credited with having conceived, developed and applied fractal geometry. In 1979, Mandelbrot managed to apply a mathematical thought experiment to a natural occurrence. In the process, he discovered a branch of mathematics concerned with irregular patterns made of parts that are in some way similar to the whole and exhibiting a property called self-similarity or self-symmetry.[32] Unlike conventional Euclidean geometry, which is concerned with regular shapes and whole-number dimensions, such as lines (two-dimensional) and cones (three-dimensional), Mandelbrot's *fractal* geometry deals with shapes found in nature that have non-integer, or fractal, dimensions like rivers, mountains, leaves, and coastlines.

Ilya Prigogene. Prigogene observed that human societies, like models of chaos, are incredibly complex systems highly susceptible to initial starting point and subsequent fluctuations.[33] Prigogene became active in applying complexity and chaos concepts to organization theory. One of his principle questions yet to be decided is will the evolutionary change in organizational thought be continuous or discontinuous. Prigogine's 1984 monograph *Order Out of Chaos* is an intriguing historical account of the limitations of Newtonian science and the dynamics of complexity with Prigogine's characteristic emphasis on thermodynamics and dissipative structures.[34]

James Gleick. In 1987, Gleick published *Chaos: Making a New Science*, which popularized the mathematical science of chaos and complexity to the scientific community and, more importantly, to the general public.[35] Gleick traced the history of the study of chaos, covering all of the most interesting and intriguing ideas like: the butterfly effect, strange attractors, fractals, and dynamic systems. It was probably with this work that social scientists became forcibly aware of the emerging paradigm shift in the physical sciences and tentatively began to consider its potential implications for their own disciplines.

Ironically, it was its very popularity that Gleick's *Chaos* generated that turned social scientists away from chaos and complexity for being unscholarly and faddish. Although the practical value of nonlinear dynamics was repeatedly demonstrated in physics and the life sciences, rapid popularization and exaggerated claims for the universality of complexity as a new paradigm for the social and natural sciences was met by resistance and a general scholarly backlash.[36] Nevertheless, by the 1990s, management and organization researchers finally came to acknowledge the implications of chaos and complexity, frequently referring back to Gleick for a preliminary introduction to the field.[37]

Terminology of the New Sciences

Before we can attempt to assess the value of the complexity sciences in informing leadership, management and organization science, we need to define our terms. There is a whole family of related terms and concepts that are routinely used in the literature today as if they all meant the same thing. This includes chaos, complexity, dynamical systems, complex adaptive systems, quantum mechanics, self-organizing or self-forming systems, aperiodic systems lacking equilibrium, nonlinear dynamics and fuzzy logic.

Most social scientists like to think of *chaos* and *complexity* as closely related terms. Some have characterized them as close cousins. Others, more enthusiastically, think of them as siblings, even identical twins. Unfortunately, this inaccurate portrayal has tended to result in clouded thinking leading to unfounded conclusions. Although Overman[38] opined that chaos and quantum theory were the most important and relevant concepts for organization and administration science, we will consider just four concepts here: chaos, complexity, fuzzy logic, and nonlinear systems.

Chaos. The term *chaos* is actually a misnomer, in that what had previously been considered "chaotic" and without form or organization actually has an underlying order.[39] Scientific chaos does not signify randomness or lack of cause and effect. Every event in a chaotic system is strictly deterministic. A chaotic system is one in which a number of nonlinear functions (frequently a small number like three or four) interact deterministically in a manner such that the outcomes cannot be predicted by humans, even with massive computers.[40] That is the essence of chaos.

Complexity. Complexity is likewise a much misunderstood and misused word. It is a word rich with ambiguity and highly dependent on context. Like other fields in the physical and social sciences, management science has developed its own understandings of this word. Some authors suggest that complexity is a watchword for a new way of thinking about the collective behavior of many basic but interacting units . . . "complexity is the study of the behavior of macroscopic collections of such units that are endowed with the potential to evolve in time."[41] In other words, complexity theory can be described as an amalgamation of concepts and ideas developed in the natural and physical sciences that help explain the developmental and evolutionary behaviors of systems, even organizational systems.

According to Whitesides and Ismagilov[42], a complex system is one whose evolution and dynamics can be characterized in one of three ways: (1) a system very sensitive to initial conditions or to small perturbations; (2) a system in which the number of independent interacting components is very large; or (3) a system in which there are multiple options or pathways by which it can evolve. Analysis of complex systems typically require nonlinear differential equations. A second way of thinking about complexity lacks this technical formality and simply characterizes a complex system as complicated by some subjective judgment that is not amenable to exact description, analytical or otherwise.

Fuzzy Logic. An offshoot of chaos and complexity science, fuzzy logic is another term that carries an unfortunate and misleading moniker. The term *fuzzy logic* was generated in 1965 by Lofti Zadeh[43] and perhaps was ill-chosen.[44] In general, the word "fuzzy" has the connotation of being hazy, indistinct, loose, or not well founded. Fuzzy logic itself is none of these; it is a mathematical framework of axioms and propositions, a mathematical system that models the way humans originate, communicate, process, and store words.[45] It is a tool to better understand the way in which the mind produces preferences for meaning and nuances of meaning.

Fuzzy logic is not fuzzy in the traditional sense of the word, nor is it logical in the Aristotelian sense. In Aristotelian logic, everything can be divided into distinct sets with firm boundaries. Fuzzy logic suggests that the boundaries are in fact quite indistinct and that objects may at times be described by more than one set of descriptors. Computer binary logic is built upon the structure of either-or—1s or 0s. Fuzzy logic allows for the possibility of a variable exhibiting two characteristics at the same time and is at the heart of research into artificial intelligence (AI) software systems.[46]

Nonlinear Systems. The underpinning logic of chaos and complexity is the non-Newtonian principle of nonlinearity. In the dynamics of systems, this has to do with the relationship between variables. In linear systems, the relationship between relevant variables remains stable over time. In non-linear systems, there exists a potential for dynamic (changing) interactions between variables which can result in unstable, seemingly chaotic behavior. In trying to sort out the significance of this difference for management and organization scholars, Kiel observed:

> Perhaps the best way to understand the dynamics of nonlinear systems is to compare the behavior of such systems with that of linear systems. In linear systems, the relationships between relevant variables remains stable over time. This means that the dynamics of linear systems will typically show smooth, regular, and well-behaved motion. Linear systems respond to changes in their parameters, or to external shocks, in a proportionate and consistent manner . . . . Nonlinear systems are typified by a potential for dynamic relationships between variables during the life of the system. As these relationships change, the temporal behavior of the system may change from smooth to unstable and even to seeming randomness, referred to as chaos. The changing relationships between variables may consequently generate new system behaviors and structures.[47]

Implications of Chaos and Complexity

Scientific contributions to the rapidly developing fields of complexity and nonlinear dynamics are flowing in from many disciplines—from physics, to fractal geometry, to evolutionary biology, to computer science, to economics. This breadth, and the accompanying set of recommended resources on complexity, suggests that the new discoveries being made about how living systems evolve and adapt will have profound implications for our conception of organization science and the practice of leadership and management in organizations.

It is clear today that neither technology nor the Newtonian principles of linearity are sufficient to deal with the increasingly complex world in which we find ourselves.[48] Complexity theory contends that there are underlying simplicities, or patterns, if we but look for them. Chaos theory challenges the deterministic notion, the bedrock of Western science, that one can predict future events by gathering sufficient amounts of information. Chaotic systems, however, appear to have an underlying, unexpected, order—when plotted graphically, they yield elegant patterns. In other words, chaos theory can assist us in identifying past patterns leading up to the present, but it is of little assistance in moving forward and identifying future trends with any degree of certainty. Scientists have taken to the task of finding order in dynamic systems once believed to be random and applying that order in understanding complex systems such as organizations.[49]

The implications of chaos and complexity are significant. Researchers propose that all previous (classical) work in the physical sciences must be reexamined and adjusted as necessary to the theoretical exigencies of chaos and complexity.[50] Even quantum theory, which emerged before the advent of chaos theory has to be reexamined.[51] But many management and organization scholars are reluctant to undertake this task. Many discount the significance and importance of the paradigm shift in the physical sciences and its application to their work in the social sciences. Because of its rapid popularization among the masses, many scholars consider chaos and complexity as just another fad that will soon pass by. Begun suggested that these doubters must soon change their minds. Chaos and complexity theory are not fads and their contributions to organization and management science "are becoming foundational in those disciplines, not tangential."[52]

There is fundamental change wrought by applying chaos and complexity thinking to leadership, management, and organization thinking. Newtonian logic suggests an interaction between variables in two or three linear dimensions but ignores the element of time. The new sciences, relativity, quantum mechanics, chaos, complexity, and fuzzy logic, all require us to consider the time dynamic as an integral part of the analysis. It's like the difference between looking at family snapshots and family videos. Movement matters. The state of dynamic change in organizations is more important than a snapshot of them at any particular time. Thus, chaos and complexity thinking has the strong potential of moving organizational thinking away from analysis of simple, steady states of systems to chaotic or complex systems in transition over time.

There are three distinct directions in which chaos and complexity theory have been pushing traditional management and organization science.[53]

First, they focus on nonlinear relationships rather than linear ones. Since the days of Newton, scientists have employed linear reasoning to solve problems precisely because their mathematical tools allowed them to do so. But although their linear models allowed them to "solve" problems, unfortunately, they were only close approximations to reality . . . . and wrong.[54] Small deviations and variance that should have suggested something was amiss were simply ignored.

Chaos and complexity approaches teach us to look for complex relationships, not simple ones. It is not necessary to try to fit reality into simple, linear models. What chaos and complexity teach us is that most organization systems do not fit linear models and it is misleading to attempt to do so. Now this doesn't mean that we have to throw out all of our linear models and linear statistical approaches. However, it does mean that we need to approach management and organization research with greater caution and use linear notions only when they are clearly applicable. Although it appears that linear relationships in organizational systems are very rare, they can in fact play an important role in many complex organization systems.

Second, chaos and complexity focus on *dynamical systems* rather than stable ones. Chaos and complexity theory provide the intellectual tools for examining the evolution or change in systems over time. The relationship between variables in an organization system at any one point of time is uninteresting and uninformative. Cross-sectional information about organizations is much less useful than longitudinal data.

Third, although reductionism has been the hallmark of scientific methodology since the days of Descartes and Newton, chaos and complexity approaches argue for a more holistic approach. With complex systems, it is impossible to understand the whole by separately examining its various parts. Complexity and chaos theory suggests that all variables affecting a system are interrelated and interact over time. Chaos and complexity approaches suggest a focus on those *relationships* between variables rather than just single variables themselves. Begun suggests that traditional academic efforts to isolate single variables and their effects in social science research are misleading and ineffective.[55]

The new sciences of chaos and complexity do not invalidate the laws of Newtonian physics. In many cases, models derived from Newtonian principles may be sufficiently accurate and predictive to provide us with a fairly clear picture of some organizational realities. However, where issues are clearly too complex for Newtonian approaches, the new sciences will help us to see them in a different context and to reinterpret their significance through a different set of lenses.

Many traditional management and organizational scholars doggedly cling to classical notions anchored to the more stable, linear platform of Newton's physical laws of motion, Descartes' rational method of inquiry, and Adam Smith's economic comprehensive rationality. But, it has been aptly demonstrated that these principles do not consistently reflect the true nature of reality. Traditionalists ignore the fact that chaos and complexity theory, as developed in mathematics and the natural sciences, has led to major new advances in the understanding of natural phenomena previously considered too complex or unpatterned to comprehend.

Our old classical organization models were simpler to understand but they did not accurately reflect reality. The newer models, based upon notions of chaos and complexity are much more difficult to understand, but they do a much better job of reflecting the true nature of organizational reality. These advances have been slow to filter into the vernacular and working concepts of the management science community. Begun asserts that a concerted effort to overcome the built-in inertia and insulation of management and organization science is needed including investment in new learning by intellectual gatekeepers and a strengthening of theoretical ties to the natural sciences. If these efforts and initiatives are not actively pursued, Begun pessimistically postulates that organization science will remain "scientifically backward and largely irrelevant to the real organizational world".[56]

What then is the value-added of chaos and complexity to the evolution of organization science? Some of it is already quite apparent as permanent fixtures in today's leadership and management principles: participative management, self-directed teams, boundaryless organizations, empowerment, partnering relationships and alliances, whole systems thinking, and information networks.

Revolutionary, discontinuous change is sometimes described as *quantum* change. Hamel and Prahalad assert that new organization forms spawned by the New Sciences offer opportunities for more radical innovation, allowing organizations to reinvent the future.[57] Revolutionary innovations and quantum change generally require new organizational forms that can exploit new technologies and break away from established organizational structures and processes.

Lazslo asserts that society and organizations enter chaotic states from time to time—not a state of anarchy but *ultra-sensitivity*—the necessary prelude to change.[58] This generates new relationships between organizations in an environment and facilitates organizational practitioners to lead and manage radical innovation more effectively. Established organizations face far greater difficulty in overhauling what they do and how they do it since radical innovation, by definition, involves an overthrow of existing competencies.

Do the Complexity Sciences Represent a Paradigm Shift for Leadership and Management?

The work of contemporary management scholars such as Wheatley, Kiel, Overman, and Zohar suggests that the various schools of the complexity sciences represent a fundamentally new way of thinking about leadership, management, and organizations and consequently a dramatic paradigm shift. This perspective in turn suggests a number of fundamentally important questions: Is there anything really new, original, or unique about the complexity sciences? Do they in reality represent a paradigm shift in organizational thinking?

Fully a decade ago, Cohen asserted that the early work on open-systems theory is among the enduring accomplishments of the previous generation of management and organizational researchers. But there is something new and unique in the modeling of complex systems.[59] With the advent of the complexity sciences, our ideas about organizational systems and their dynamics are greatly changed from the way we used to think about them. And ongoing work in the complexity sciences offers new possibilities from thinking about organizations and revisiting earlier insights.

Conclusion

The dominant management paradigm at the beginning of the past century represents the collective intellectual output of a series of scientists, philosophers and researchers accumulated over a period of three centuries. The primary ideas embodied in the classical paradigm included: empiricism, reductionism, linearity, and comprehensive rationality. It was characterized by a mechanistic, closed-system model and was reflective in the assembly line factory approach of the industrial age.

But beginning with the research output of physical scientists into relativity and quantum mechanics in the early years of the 20th Century, the paradigm began to evolve from the simplicity of the input-process-output metaphor of the closed-system model to a much more complex open-system model which acknowledged feedback loops and the dynamic interrelationship of the organism (or organization) with its environment. Gradually, it was understood that changes in the environment evoked changes in the organization, which in turn evoked further changes in the environment, and so on, in a never-ending cycle of continuous interaction and organization/ environment adaptation.

Today, management and organization theorists do not, in general, take full advantage of the sophisticated complexity tools that have emerged during the past several decades for analyzing the behavior of organizations as complex adaptive systems. Many contemporary scholars simply choose to discount the implications of the New Sciences for their respective disciplines. But when they do get around to looking more closely at the new ideas, the past century of organization theory research will probably not be significantly threatened or rendered obsolete. The seminal intellectual contributions by Descartes, Newton, Smith, and Taylor, will undoubtedly persevere.

The advent of open-systems theory and the complexity sciences does not appear to diminish significantly the utility of Newtonian approaches. When viewing the extremes of the journey from classical organizational science to New Science approaches, it certainly appears that a scientific revolution of some sort has taken place. But in fact, we're observing differences and adjustments that have taken place over a period of a hundred years and, although there have been some dramatic blips on the change trend line, most of the observed differences have been evolutionary, incremental and moderately deliberate rather than revolutionary, dramatic and abrupt.

Management scientists are now in the process of examining which of the questions the old and new paradigms answer and checking for paradigm polarization that will ultimately signal a complete split. That has not happened yet, nor do we anticipate that it will for some while to come. Proponents of complexity approaches to management and organization science continue to anxiously point out the deficiencies of the classical science and the benefits of the New Sciences while traditionalists proceed cautiously forward.

Modern organizations are complex adaptive systems and management theorists should focus research efforts on understanding the fundamental nature of nonlinear, self-organized structures. With the linear cause and effect relationship of Newtonian thinking seriously diminished, new leadership and management thinking may become decidedly nonlinear. Chaos theory suggests that empirical research may not be the best way to plot and substantiate the implications of the New Sciences. In fact, it may be that traditional empirical research and statistical analysis may prove to be major obstacles and stumbling blocks in the development of new science application to leadership and management.

Chaos and complexity theory ought to be attractive to leadership-management students and practitioners for reasons related to the disjointed state of the discipline. The new sciences push leadership and management studies to be more holistic and integrative. Chaos and complexity approaches have the potential for enhancing our understanding of general systems theory, so that greater sharing of a theoretical base is possible both within the discipline and with other related disciplines. This is critical for both researchers and practitioners since the study of leadership, management, and organizations is so interdisciplinary in the first place. Chaos and complexity theory provide the opportunity to see organizations in a very different light and open the possibility for leader-managers to function more effectively in their respective roles within organizations.

Chapter 10—A Complexity Approach to Decision Making and Problem Solving

Decision making and problem solving are the two fundamental, concomitant tasks of leadership and management. This chapter examines the difficult task faced by leader-managers in organizations as they confront increasingly more complex decision making and problem solving situations in their work environment.

Complexity is not new. We have long been confronted by the complex nature of the human experience and we have developed a variety of simplification strategies and approaches to deal with it. By and large, these strategies have served us well in permitting us to act within a highly complex reality. Without these simplification strategies, we might find ourselves paralyzed with complexity, ambiguity and uncertainty.

Unfortunately, although simplification strategies permit us to act, they also tend to distort reality and frequently lead us into unintended and undesirable consequences. There is thus a natural tension between the complexity of the problem solving and decision making realm and the need to simplify.

Complexity in today's world is increasing at an accelerating pace as new information and knowledge doubles about every two to four years. Rapid advances in transportation, communication and information technologies are expanding the boundaries of our operational environments and increasing exponentially the number of relationships with other systemic entities—individuals and organizations—in our immediate decision vicinity that must be considered in our problem-solving processes. Complexity in the decision-making realm is thus exacerbated by both the explosive increase in the number of variables and by their increasingly interconnectedness and interdependency.

On a theoretical level, researchers are working to better understand the increasingly complex nature of our social environment. Unfortunately, this has not generally translated into a more robust and comprehensive curriculum in our institutions of higher academic learning nor into more effective decision making approaches utilized by practitioners in corporate, government, and non-profit sectors.

We continue to use simplistic, linear decision-making and problem-solving models to address complex problems that are patently nonlinear. Thus, with respect to complex problem solving and decision making, there is a significant gap between theory and practice. The central thrust of this chapter is to underline the shortcomings and risks of our continuing reliance on simplistic, linear decision-making and problem-solving models and to suggest a more effective, cyclical strategy for addressing complex problems in the social environment.

Complexity versus Simplification

Complexity has been defined or described in many ways. The nature of human reality is inherently complex. Complexity is characterized by more than just large numbers of actors and variables.[1] The infinite number of systems and subsystems that make up our reality are the result of complex, underlying nonlinear processes that involve intricate causal relationships that feed back on each other.[2]

A systems-thinking approach to understanding complexity suggests that all systems in an environment are interconnected, interrelated, and interdependent. At times, these relationships are trivial and insignificant, but frequently they are quite significant and changes in one system within an environment can have dramatic outcomes and consequences for others. The degree of complexity of our reality is thus compounded by increasingly larger numbers of components, interconnectedness and interdependency, and nonlinear relationships.

Corporate and public policy problems, like the kind that emerge with domestic crises, economic downturns and natural disasters, reflect the convergence and interdependency of cultural, economic, and political systems. Morçöl argues that they emerge from the dynamical interaction of all these systems and that, once they emerge, they take on systemic properties that cannot be reduced to solely economic, political, or cultural factors.[3]

Axelrod and Cohen argue that "complexity often results in features, called emergent properties, which are properties of the system that the separate parts do not have."[4] Kauffman adds that once emerged, a system's properties are irreducible to the properties of its components, because the laws of complexity that govern them are different from the laws that govern their constituent parts.[5]

Complex systems contain agents or populations that constantly seek to adapt to changing conditions and are sometimes referred to as *complex adaptive systems*. A complex adaptive system is one in which each agent or player acts in response to the actions of the other agents in the system.[6] In the complex corporate arena, this makes it difficult to predict consequences of actions and interventions by decision makers and problem solvers because agents are constantly adjusting their strategies and changing the context in which other agents are trying to adapt. Axelrod and Cohen point out that each change in strategy by an agent alters the context in which the next change will be tried and evaluated and that "when multiple populations of agents are adapting to each other, the result is a *coevolutionary* process. Thus, complexity is also defined as adaptive, emergent and coevolutionary."[7]

Attempting to deal with this complexity directly in decision making is problematic. Richardson suggests that, if policy makers were to attempt to approach decision making and problem solving from a complex "theory of everything" perspective of the world, it would render their perceptions so abstract and incomprehensible that they would be essentially useless, leaving them immobilized and unable to act.[8] This realization dictates the necessity of simplifying our complex reality into more manageable terms.

Simplification is a natural human trait—the need for simplicity is a deeply rooted human predisposition. Decision makers and problem solvers employ a variety of strategies and schemes to simplify complex realities which provide valuable insights for the decision making and problem solving process but are equally likely to create perspectives that are incomplete, distorted, biased, and potentially misleading.

Sabatier and Sharkansky recognize and discuss the tendency for decision makers and problem solvers to simplify in the policymaking process.[9] But the act of simplification has consequences. Citing Sharkansky, Morçöl describes the effects of simplification in policymaking thus:

> So analysts and policymakers ignore complexities, take shortcuts, and use simple routines. Because human beings cannot examine multiple problematic issues all at the same time, they use partial, incremental methods. Under the pressure of too many and conflicting demands, policymakers

cope with problems by attempting to find "good enough" solutions. However, ... using these simple methods to deal with complexities may lead to further complications. The simplifying acts of policymaking—from setting up bureaucratic rules to privatization and outsourcing—only shift responsibilities of dealing with complexities, not reduce them.[10]

Thus, decision makers and problem solvers are faced with a serious dilemma. At one extreme, attempting to deal directly with the incredibly complex nature of our reality potentially creates a stupefying, incomprehensible barrier to moving forward. At the other extreme, simplifying the complexity of our reality tends to distort the relationships between interconnecting and interdependent systemic variables, potentially causing us to ignore important factors bearing on the decision issue. **In this natural tension between complexity and simplicity, the search for simplicity typically prevails as the stronger of the two needs.**[11]

I need to make one further point about complexity before proceeding. Perrow argues that in complex systems characterized by interactive complexity and tight coupling between system components, the inevitable outcome is what he refers to as *normal accidents* or *system accidents*.[12] In his book, *Normal Accidents*, Perrow uses the Three Mile Island nuclear plant incident as an example of a normal accident. Tight coupling refers to a high degree of interconnectivity and interdependence between system components. Although infrequent, Perrow asserts that it is an inherent property of complex systems to occasionally experience system breakdowns when one or more of the component parts get out of sync with the rest of the system. He further points out that **the cause of such system failures frequently lies in the breakdown of the complex interactions of small, seemingly insignificant elements.**[13]

This phenomenon is supportive of chaos theory's assertion that small differences in initial conditions can result in large differences in outcomes over time. It is also demonstrative of one of the serious weaknesses of simplification and reductionist strategies in addressing complex system breakdowns—the decision maker and problem solver will probably miss the problem of the breakdown in the relationship between the components and will instead look for the root cause in one or more of the isolated components.[14]

Rational Decision-Making Models

Since the introduction of the construct of Adam Smith's Economic Man in *An Inquiry into the Nature and Causes of the Wealth of Nations* in 1776, men have attempted to pursue a rational comprehensive model of decision making.[15] It proved to be a durable paradigm and it wasn't until the 1940s that researchers and scholars began to seriously question the model. The main sticking point for most critics was the notion of complexity and the fact that men are ill-equipped and ill-resourced to deal with a comprehensive analysis of all variables affecting most problems.

With his *bounded rationality* model, Simon provided a counter proposal suggesting that because the decision making environment is simply too complex, decision makers and problem solvers in practice simplify their approach by limiting the number of variables and options considered.[16] With his disjointed incrementalism model, Lindblom later suggested that most decision makers further simplify the decision making process by making decisions in smaller, incremental steps, varying parameters only slightly from the status quo.[17]

These efforts at simplification reflect man's natural proclivity in understanding complex realities. The differences between rational comprehensive decision making and bounded rationality represent two extremes along a continuum.

Rational Comprehensive
Decision Making

Bounded Rationality
Decision Making

Need lots of options and
time to analyze them.

Quick concensus on
limited options.

Can result in
Analysis Paralysis.

Can result in
Groupthink.

At one end of the continuum, rational comprehensiveness requires the identification and analysis of all variables or options in the decision arena. Most observers agree that decision makers neither have that comprehensive awareness nor the time to analyze all the possibilities and their consequences even if they did. Carried to the extreme, decision makers would soon become totally bogged down in *analysis paralysis*.[18] The term *analysis paralysis* refers to over-analyzing or over-thinking an issue, so that a decision or action is never taken, in effect paralyzing the outcome. Decision makers spend an inordinate amount of time identifying potential options and never get to a decision.

At the other end of the continuum, when we attempt to truncate the process by bounding or abbreviating the number of options and their consequences in our analysis, we run the risk of becoming caught up in *groupthink*.[19] The term *groupthink* is a mode of thinking that happens when the desire for harmony and being a team player in a decision-making group overrides a realistic appraisal of alternatives. With groupthink, team members try to minimize conflict and reach a quick consensus decision without critical evaluation of alternative ideas or viewpoints. Thus, a defining characteristic of groupthink is an inadequate consideration of too few options.

Obviously, neither analysis paralysis nor groupthink are desirable outcomes and decision makers and problem solvers typically avoid gravitating to either extreme. However, due to man's propensity for simplification, we probably more frequently err on the side of simplification and boundedness rather than attempting to develop a thorough and comprehensive understanding of the complex decision arena.

A fundamental flaw in the rational comprehensive model is the limitation in attaining a complete knowledge about all the factors and variables affecting a problem. In part, this has to do with environmental uncertainty and the role of chance. There are simply too many extraneous and confounding variables that can influence most complex decision making situations. Four factors that combine to increase the complexity of a problem are: a large number of variables, multiple decision makers, multiple attributes, and relative uncertainty.[20]

Lindblom asserts that due to the complexity and uncertainty issue, the principles of the rational comprehensive model cannot be practiced except for relatively simple, perhaps trivial problems, and even then, only in a somewhat modified form.[21] The rational-comprehensive approach may be ideal for problem solving on a small scale, but simply lacks the sophistication and techniques to provide decision makers with the tools necessary to reflect the relevant complex reality. The major downside to decision making under conditions of uncertainty is that even if good decisions are made, they may have outcomes with at least some unfavorable consequences. Uncertainty reduces the possibility that the rational comprehensive model will guarantee the best outcome.

Another limitation preventing complete knowledge about a problem is the difficulty in isolating causal relationships in complex systems. As discussed earlier, the best that we have been able to achieve has been an understanding of some variable associations and correlations. A related limitation arises from our current inability to accurately assess the interrelationships among multiple variables. Most work in this field to date has involved two-dimensional analysis whereas it may be that three-dimensional or multi-dimensional analysis will be necessary to assess actual relationships among interactive multiple variables. Rapidly-advancing computer technology may provide the increased computational power necessary to examine and compare so many variables against each other in multiple dimensions, but the real challenge for researchers will be to describe formulas and models that accurately predict the reality of these interacting relations in the real world.[22]

Simon recognized the improbabilities of the rational comprehensive model and proposed in its place a theory of *bounded rationality* in which the decision maker is not held to a consideration of all courses of action and variables but only a limited number which may have a significant bearing on the issue at hand. The resulting decision, although not necessarily a *maximizing* course of action, satisfies or *satisfices* [Simon's word] the decision requirement.[23] Dunn suggested a different take. He argued that while bounded rationality may be appropriate under conditions of clearly defined and limited goals, most contemporary policy problems involve profound deficits of knowledge in the face of complexity and that the principle of bounded rationality was "obsolescent." He proposed that the principle of *bounded ignorance* provided a more compelling rationale for real-world problem structuring than *bounded rationality*.[24]

As a counter model to comprehensive rationality and bounded rationality, Lindblom proposed a model of *disjointed incrementalism*.[25] His approach seeks to correct the all-or-nothing quality of the rational comprehensive model. It also spreads the decision making event over time making it a continuous decision making process. The theory holds that decision makers can rarely conform to all of the requirements for rational comprehensiveness. Dunn asserts that the incrementalist approach allows the decision maker greater latitude in working through the rational steps than bounded rationality.[26] The decision maker need only consider those objectives that differ incrementally—that is, by small amounts—from the status quo and the number of consequences forecast for each alternative may also be limited. The decision maker can also make adjustments in goals, objectives and the alternatives and may continuously reformulate the problem statement (and hence goals, objectives, and alternatives) in the course of acquiring new information.[27] As a consequence, the model requires continuous analysis and evaluation of alternative courses of action rather than at a single point in time.

Building on this simplified approach, sociologist Amitai Etzioni proposed in 1967 a further simplification strategy he called *mixed scanning*.[28] Mixed scanning selectively combines elements of the rational comprehensive model and disjointed incrementalism, providing for choices based on both. Mixed scanning is essentially a compromise approach and the precise combination of incrementalism and comprehensive rationality will depend upon the situation and the nature of the problem. Mixed-scanning reduces the unrealistic aspects of the comprehensive rationality model by limiting the details required in fundamental decisions.

A Typical Analytical Problem-Solving Model

There is a plethora of different decision making and problem solving models in the literature, each with a varying number of steps. Variations of these linear models are almost universally taught in undergraduate coursework in our schools of business management and public administration. Although there are fine nuances of difference between them, they all share essentially the same elements as the following four-step model:

Four-Step Analytical Problem Solving Model

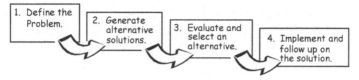

There are many problems attendant with employing such an approach in complex problem solving and decision making. The principal shortcoming is that it represents a decidedly linear, simplistic approach to what, in most cases, is a nonlinear, complex reality. The consequences of such a mismatch are frequently unsuccessful interventions and outcomes that fall short of the intended objective.

In their seminal article "Dilemmas in a General Theory of Planning," Rittel and Webber argued that there exists a set of complex problems that simply cannot be resolved with traditional analytical approaches.[29] They labeled such complex problems *wicked problems*. In wicked problem situations, requirements are volatile and constraints keep changing, stakeholders can't agree and goals and objectives are constantly evolving. It is impossible to identify the true nature of the problem without first attempting some resolution intervention. Thus, policy makers are literally shooting at a moving target that is evolving and changing throughout the problem solving/decision making process. Rittel and Webber postulated the concept of wicked problems in the context of public policy decisions. However, such decision conundrums are not just limited to the public sector. They are inherent in all open organic systems, to include all human systems.

Shortcomings with Traditional Decision Making Models

Notwithstanding the ineffectiveness of employing simple, linear strategies in addressing such complex problems, educators continue to primarily teach simplistic, linear models in our academic coursework. Due to the effects of complexity, this linear approach to decision making and problem solving is flawed from start to finish. Each of the steps in the model suffers from significant shortcomings and weaknesses. We will examine them here one by one.

Step 1. Define the Problem. The first step of the model requires an accurate identification and assessment of the problem and, in the case of collective decision making, a consensus on the problem statement. In practice, it is extremely difficult for most decision makers to precisely and accurately identify and define problems. For most collective decision making and problem solving, it proves to be the most challenging step. Bryson argues that working collectively, it is almost impossible for a group of decision makers to reach consensus on the nature of a problem.[30] Arrow suggests that even if consensus could be reached, it is impossible for decision makers in a democratic society to arrive at a collective decision that will produce a single best solution for all parties.[31]

Furthermore, because of complexity and interconnectedness of all variables, Rittel and Webber argue that it is frequently impossible to accurately describe the problem from the outset.[32] From their perspective, there is no definitive once-and-done formulation of a complex, *wicked problem*. For them, formulating the problem and the solution are essentially the same thing and occur simultaneously as each evolves over time. Each attempt at implementing a solution changes the understanding of the problem. **Thus, complex, *wicked problems* cannot be solved in a traditional linear fashion, because the problem definition evolves as new possible solutions are considered and/or implemented.** Complexity theory later referred to this phenomenon as *co-evolution*.

There are other problems incidental to problem identification. Stone disabuses us of the expectation of mathematical or economic precision at the outset in dealing with human problems asserting that " . . . there is no universal, scientific, or objective method of problem definition."[33] Edwards and Sharkansky argue that decision makers frequently will confuse symptoms of the problem with the problem itself.[34] Huber identifies three additional factors which limit our ability to identifying precisely what the problem is: 1) perceptual problems, negative information that may be totally ignored or selectively perceived in such a way so as to distort its true meaning; 2) defining the problem in terms of solutions, a dynamic Huber describes as "jumping to conclusions" but which can be related to the garbage can decision making model; and 3) mistaking symptoms of problems for the real problems themselves.[35]

Step 2. Generate Alternative Options or Courses of Action. The second step, generating alternative options or courses of action, has always been problematic. As discussed earlier, attempting to identify and evaluate too many options will result in analysis paralysis and inaction. Attempting to streamline the process by evaluating too few options results in groupthink and frequently inferior solutions. But a more challenging problem here is correctly assessing the causality between potential solutions and desired outcomes.

Since the days of Newton, scientists have employed linear reasoning to solve problems precisely because their mathematical tools allowed them to do so. But although their linear models allowed them to "solve" problems, unfortunately, they were wrong—close approximations to reality at times, but simply wrong.[36] Small deviations and variance that should have suggested something was amiss were simply ignored.

Complexity theory teaches us to look for complex relationships, not simple ones. It is not necessary to try to fit reality into simple, linear models. What chaos and complexity teaches us is that most organization systems do not fit linear models and it is misleading to attempt to do so. This doesn't mean that we have to throw out all of our linear models and linear statistical approaches. Leader-managers need to approach decision making and problem solving with great caution and use linear notions only when they are clearly applicable. Linear relationships can in fact play an important role in many complex organization systems. But, as Begun clearly asserts, linear relationships in organization systems are very rare:

> But linear relationships are rare in the more intractable natural systems, and rarer still in social and organizational relationships. The rational contingency paradigm in organization science teaches as much: Even linear bivariate relationships, such as that between centralization and effectiveness, hold only under certain conditions or in very restricted ranges. Add a third variable to the system—and a fourth and a fifth—and relationships quickly lose any resemblance to linearity.[37]

Chaos and complexity theory focus on dynamical systems rather than stable ones. *Dynamical system* is frequently used as a synonym for *chaos* in the literature.[38] Chaos and complexity theory provide the intellectual tools for examining the evolution or change in systems over time. The relationship between variables in an organization system at any singular point in time is static, uninteresting and essentially uninformative. That doesn't mean that we shouldn't pursue it; but Begun implies that it probably is of secondary importance at best:

> Again, the existence of stable systems is not denied, but study of them becomes relatively elementary. The study of simple, stable systems gets relegated to a less dominant position in the science, and it gets taught at an introductory rather than advanced level in the sequence of learning . . . . Methodologically, the new theories cast doubt on the utility of cross-sectional research except in very restrictive conditions. For complex systems, cross-sectional research reveals very little. This forces organization scientists to work harder to collect longitudinal data and to be less comfortable with settling for cross-sectional research for reasons of convenience.[39]

Newtonian science is based upon linear, predictable causality (sometimes referred to as *proportionality*). By Newtonian logic, effects should be proportional to causes. Outcomes from decisions and problem resolution should be proportional to the variables weighed and resources expended. In simplifying the problem or decision domain, Morçöl suggests that regression analysis is illustrative of this perspective.[40] Regression analysis looks for linear relationships between variables. The Newtonian logic of regression analysis excludes nonlinearities. In regression analysis, nonlinearities are treated as context or error terms and resulting uncertainty is treated as an externality. In other words, they are typically ignored. Chaos and complexity theory, on the other hand, teaches us that the reality of complex systems is nonlinear.

Step 3. Evaluate and Select an Alternative. The third step, evaluating and selecting an alternative that optimizes or satisfices the problem situation, is also extremely challenging for decision makers and problem solvers. Harmon and Meyer argue that such "administrative decisions are difficult and complex precisely because they are made and acted upon in an organizational context, a web of relationships that often confounds not only observers, but even the actors themselves."[41] The simplification schemes frequently employed at this step in buffering the problem arena from the consideration of the complete web of relationships results in outcomes based on incomplete, distorted, and biased data and analysis. The effectiveness and timeliness of the decision outcome or problem intervention is highly dependent upon where the decision maker falls along the comprehensiveness-boundedness continuum. Typically, the degree of effectiveness will be inversely related to the degree of timeliness.

Step 4. Implement and Follow up. The fourth step, implement and follow up on the solution, almost always pursues a short-term, truncated focus. Problem solvers and decision makers monitor the resolution implementation only to confirm that it is working generally to achieve immediate expectations. Due to budgetary considerations and time constraints, typically there is little effort invested in looking beyond the immediate problem arena to identify any new potential problems created by the problem resolution intervention. Project management protocols require the project leader to develop or commit to a project charter initially before beginning the project implementation and an essential element of that charter is project scope. Project leaders are typically held to a tight budget and avoid *scope creep* at all costs. In similar fashion, military planners and commanders are cautious of *mission creep.*

In Project Management, project charters typically follow the same logic as the four-step analytical problem solving model. Problem identification is fixed at the onset and commitment to the charter and leaves little allowance for an evolution in problem statement understanding over time. The simplification strategy of truncating the problem situation in time and only examining immediate or short-term effects may facilitate the immediate process but almost always exacerbates negative outcomes over the long haul. Long-term second-, third—and fourth-order effects of decisions and problem interventions are typically ignored. Later, when unfortunate outcomes from the resolution intervention emerge, problem solvers and decision makers are frequently taken by surprise.

Other Early Simplification Strategies: Thomas Aquinus and William of Ockham

We have discussed thus far the natural tension between the complexity of the decision making/problem solving realm and the need for simplification. Man has employed various simplification schemes and strategies throughout history. Prior to the 20th century, it was a commonly-held belief that nature itself was simple and that simpler theories about nature were thus more likely to be true. In earlier chapters we discussed Descartes, Newton, and Adam Smith and the simplification approaches that emerged from their work including reductionism and linearity. But even previous to these scientist-philosophers, we have the lingering influence of the theological and philosophical work of Thomas Aquinus and William of Ockham.

In the 13th Century, theologian Thomas Aquinas argued for simplicity in this manner: "If a thing can be done adequately by means of one, it is superfluous to do it by means of several; for we observe that nature does not employ two instruments where one suffices"[42]

A century later, Franciscan friar and logician William of Ockham proposed a philosophical construct that came to be known as Ockham's razor (also spelled Occam's razor). Ariew observes that the principle of Ockham's razor urges the researcher or decision maker to make as few assumptions as possible, eliminating those that make no difference in the observable predictions of the explanatory hypothesis or theory.[43] The principle is often referred to as the "law of parsimony" and is sometimes articulated as "All things being equal, the simplest solution tends to be the best one." In other words, when multiple competing theories are equal in other respects, the principle recommends selecting the theory that introduces the fewest assumptions and postulates the fewest hypothetical entities—in other words, simple explanations trump complex ones.[44]

Examples of Complex Decisions Gone Awry

Policymakers—problem solvers and decision makers—face a paradoxical choice. When confronted by a problem or opportunity in their decision environment, they can choose to intervene and do something or they can choose to do nothing. Any time that we intervene in a complex adaptive system, we change the interrelationships between the system components, frequently in unanticipated, and possibly undesirable ways. There is a parallel in physics that suggests that the mere effort of observation inevitably affects what is observed. It is possible that the outcome of an intervention may result in a less desirable future than the current situation or in the resulting future had we chosen not to act. Stacey describes this dilemma this way:

> Furthermore, when you see the world through the new lenses, you will realize that you cannot reduce your risk by simply letting the long term take care of itself. Common sense may tell you that doing nothing or doing only what seems absolutely safe is the best way of dealing with unknowable futures. Yet again, however, common sense turns out to be a poor guide. For, in complex systems, even doing nothing could have escalating consequences as could some chance aspect of something that seems to be absolutely safe. You may as well, then, take a chance and do something positive, even though you cannot know its outcome and it too could fail. If the consequences of doing something and doing nothing are both unknowable, how can you now which is safer? Instead of trying to reduce your risk, you will be more inclined to take risks and be creative when you really face up to the unknowability of the long-term future.[45]

Thus, rather than remaining hamstrung by such uncertainty and ambiguity, decision makers and problem solvers frequently charge ahead attempting to do something. Because of the attendant uncertainty, they typically focus entirely on the immediate problem at hand while ignoring potential second-, third—and fourth-order effects of their actions. The literature and newspapers are rife with examples of policy decisions gone bad, producing unanticipated and deleterious long-term effects. Sometimes, the results border on disastrous as the following examples illustrate.

The Nile River System and the Building of the Aswan Dam. In the early 1950s, Egypt was faced with two significant public issues. One was the annual flooding of the Nile River which resulted in human casualties and the other was the lack of electrical power to advance the nation into the post-war era. The policy decision was made to build a huge rock fill dam just north of the border between Egypt and Sudan. The dam was finally completed in 1970 after 18 years of work. Completion of the dam signaled the successful accomplishment of the two policy objectives. However, it signaled the beginning of a whole array of unintended and unforeseen consequences that have affected Egypt and its people in a very negative way.[46]

In the past, the annual flooding of the Nile provided deposits of rich sediments which served to fertilize the land in a natural way. With the damming of the Nile, Egyptian farmers were forced to use millions of tons of artificial fertilizer a year as a substitute for the nutrients which no longer fill the flood plain. Poor drainage of the newly irrigated lands has led to saturation and increased salinity. Whereas it was once considered one of the richest farmland deltas in the world, over half of Egypt's farmland was now rated medium to poor soils. Further downstream, the Nile delta was having problems due to the lack of sediment as well since there was no additional agglomeration of sediment to keep erosion of the delta at bay. Furthermore, the runoff of fertilizer into the delta and the decreased water flow affected the shrimp population in the Mediterranean. Following completion of the dam, the shrimp population decreased about 97% and Egyptian fishermen were unable to make a living shrimping and were forced into unemployment. Furthermore, the shrimp catch had traditionally been sold in Egyptian markets and provided a large percentage of the protein needs of the Egyptian diet. With the demise of the shrimp catch, Egypt had to import other protein sources. Furthermore, the previous annual flooding had helped to keep the population of a certain species of snail in check. Without the annual flooding, the snails multiplied out of control and the parasitic disease *schistosomiasis*, associated with the stagnant water of the fields and the snails, caused a major problem among the Egyptian population.

Brazilian Pigeons and Ethanol Production. Brazil is the leading country in the world in developing ethanol as an alternative fuel source. The primary source for ethanol production in Brazil is sugarcane. When land was cleared for sugarcane fields, the clearings eliminated Brazilian pigeons' natural habitat and they, in turn, flocked to built-up urban areas. Brazilian cities were plagued by huge flocks of pigeons which dirtied the plazas and raised the potential for spreading serious infectious diseases. In an article put out by the Associated Press April 10, 2007, it was reported that Brazilian policy makers were now faced with coming up with interventions to rid cities of tens of thousands of pigeons. Many options were being explored including broadcasting loud noises and introducing predators to scare them away—each of which violated current ordinances—and which, if implemented, could result in even more serious unintended consequences.[47]

Florida Tire Reef Disaster. Also reported by the Associated Press, February 18, 2007, was a well-intentioned attempt in 1972 by Florida planners to create artificial reefs made up of old automobile tires. A mile offshore from Fort Lauderdale, Florida, lay an underwater dump of almost two million old tires strewn across the ocean floor, a veritable ecological disaster. The original concept behind the policy decision was simple and straightforward—create new marine habitat and alternate dive sites to relieve pressure on natural reefs, while disposing of tires that were clogging landfills. But intervening in complex adaptive systems is fraught with uncertainty and peril—the plan failed miserably. As reported by the Associated Press:

> Little sea life has formed on the tires. Some of the bundles bound together with nylon and steel have broken loose and are scouring the ocean floor across a swath the size of 31 football fields. Tires are washing up on beaches. Thousands have wedged up against the nearby natural reef some 70 feet below the sea surface, blocking coral growth and devastating marine life. Similar problems have been reported at tire reefs worldwide . . . . No one can say with certainty why the idea doesn't work, but one problem is that, unlike large ships that have been sunk for reefs, tires are too light. They can be swept away with tides and currents from powerful

storms, and marine life doesn't have a chance to attach. Some scientists also believe the rubber leeches toxins.[48]

According to the Associated Press article, Federal and local groups were working together to address the problem. It was the environmental equivalent of an aquatic landfill. Cleanup promises to be extremely expensive and would require the collaborative effort of Federal, state, county and local government organizations. Corporate organizations were also joining in the effort to increase capacity to clean up the disaster. Florida Governor Charlie Crist's proposed budget included $2 million to help dispose of the tires. The full-scale salvage operation began in 2007 and was expected to run through 2010 at a cost to the state of about $3.4 million.

China's Three Gorges Dam Project. The common thread through the preceding three examples is that whenever we intervene in a complex system to solve a problem, we always create new problems. A final example of a major project fraught with 2nd, 3rd, and 4th order effects surprises is the Three Gorges Dam that spans the Yangtze River in China. When completed in July, 2012, the dam became one of the world's two largest power generation stations.[49] The dam was built to address at least four primary policy objectives: 1) stop deaths from the annual flooding of the Yangste River, 2) serve as a major hydraulic power generation station, 3) reduce greenhouse gases by not resorting to coal burning power generation, and 4) facilitate greater river traffic and shipping capacity on the Yangste River. A highly controversial project from the very beginning, as construction on the dam neared completion it apparently was well on its way to accomplishing those purposes. However, the anticipated and unanticipated 2nd, 3rd, and 4th order consequences of building the dam have been dramatic.[50]

During construction of the dam, over 1.3 million people had to be displaced from their homes, towns, and farmland and relocated to other areas. Water backing up in the reservoir behind the dam soon flooded important archaeological and cultural sites, some of which they were unable to excavate and relocate before the water submerged them. The water also soon submerged landfills and toxic waste dumps which will surely begin to leach toxins into the reservoir. Although construction of the dam was a policy catalyst for building new waste treatment plants and improving existing facilities, over one billion tons of waste water are released annually into the river which now accumulates in the reservoir whereas before the dam's construction, it was more likely to be swept away downstream. The initial net effect for the rising water behind the dam is that it looks murky and polluted.

Construction of the dam represents a huge shock to the ecology of the region and benthic sediment buildup will result in uncontrolled biological damage and potentially greatly reduce biological diversity. Much of the 40 million tons of sedimentation that used to flow down the Yangste River to the Shanghai delta will now settle on the reservoir floor above the dam.[51] The greatly reduced flow of sedimentation will make downstream riverbanks more vulnerable to flooding.[52] It is projected that Shanghai, which depended upon the sedimentation to strengthen the geologic bed on which it rests, will now be much more vulnerable to flooding.[53] Erosion caused by the reservoir's rising waters have caused numerous landslides thus far: two major incidents in May of 2009 when over 91,000 cubic yards of material plunged into the flooded gorge[54], and 97 significant landslides since 2010.[55]

Bottom Line: Although we might be inclined to believe that the negative outcomes of public interventions such as the Aswan Dam project, the Brazilian ethanol-pigeon dilemma, the Florida tire reef disaster, and the Three Gorges Dam are exceptional and occur only infrequently, the truth of the matter is that such things happen all too frequently as the unintended second-, third—and fourth-order effects of misguided decisions. They are typically the result of decision makers and problem solvers applying various simplification schemes and linear approaches to work their way expeditiously through complexity toward policy decisions and problem solving interventions. When confronted by complex realities and the urgency to act, problem solvers and decision makers almost always err on the side of simplification.

What Insights and Implications Does Complexity Theory Offer Decision Making and Problem Solving?

Kiel and Elliott point out that complexity theory calls into question many of the basic principles and tenets upon which traditional scientific and social inquiry is based.[56] Some researchers interested in emerging complexity perspectives suggest that these approaches imply a shift or major reorientation in thinking so profound as to constitute a paradigm shift.[57] Brodnick and Krafft argue that "the complexity paradigm requires a shift in thinking, although it makes more explicit what many social scientists and practitioners have long known as they recognized that human institutions are not amenable to prediction and manipulation in simple linear terms."[58] Some policy researchers of this opinion argue for an immediate and all-encompassing incorporation of the complexity sciences into policy analysis in order to overcome many of the problems besetting the field.[59]

Many social science researchers and policy studies scholars have concluded that the complexity sciences will unquestionably have an impact on their respective disciplines.[60] Overman predicted that "just as Newtonian physics profoundly influenced the growth of scientific management and of bureaucratic theory and practice nearly a century ago, so too will the post-Newtonian sciences influence the growth of the new administrative science."[61] In an article discussing disaster response systems, Comfort describes the transition from linear to nonlinear reasoning in policy design. She asserts that as that change takes place, all relationships in the policymaking process are altered. For her, the increase of complexity in policymaking results in nonlinear movement: "The problem of change involves not just wholesale elimination of old programs or the creation of totally new programs but a capacity for transition between states of performance within existing systems."[62]

Complexity theory offers a number of important insights for decision makers and problem solvers, some new and original ideas never before considered, and other ideas that confirm previous work already accomplished in the field; these insights include concepts of holism; pattern recognition; nonlinearity; sensitive dependence to initial conditions; interconnectedness and interdependency; dissipative structures, bifurcation points, and discontinuous change; strange attractors; fuzzy logic; and emergence. These concepts have been well developed in other publications and it is my purpose here only to suggest some possible applications of these insights from the complexity sciences to problem solving and decision making.

Holism.

Clearly, complexity theory argues for holistic approaches. Although reductionist approaches may tell us something about isolated parts of a system, they tell us little about how the parts are related and interact together or about how the whole system functions. Sanders argues that complexity approaches reveal relationships, connections, patterns of interactions, and subtle changes that more closely approximates the dynamics of the real world in which decisions are made.[63] Laszlo argues that the systems view of nature can be basically summarized in four propositions that amplify the principle of holism: 1) natural systems are wholes with irreducible properties; 2) natural systems maintain themselves in a changing environment; 3) natural systems create themselves in response to self-creativity in other systems; and 4) natural systems are coordinating interfaces in nature's holarchy.[64] Thus holism further defines and amplifies the basic tenets of systems theory and argues for a holistic analysis of systems to gain an understanding of the relationships among component parts.

Tasaka takes this point one step further. He argues that as the world increases in complexity, it begins to display "new properties that had never existed before."[65] This suggests that reductionist methodologies may be missing important elements visible only on a holistic scale. Following an eastern tradition of thought, Tasaka further suggests that "the world is intrinsically a living system that cannot be reduced to a collection of its living parts, because the instant it is broken down into parts it loses its life force." He concludes that this is the fundamental reason that the search is on for a way of "knowing the whole," one that "comprehends the whole in all its complexity."[66]

Visualization and Pattern Recognition.

Complexity approaches to complex issue analysis and problem solving provide the tools for scientific visualization and pattern recognition through the integration of high-speed computation and graphical modeling. The graphical printout of the Lorenz Attractor was the first picture of a nonlinear dynamical system which allowed Lorenz to see the order hidden within the disorder of the meteorological data he was observing.[67] In the same manner, graphing complex systems using the mathematics of chaos and complexity may provide social scientists and policy studies researchers the capability of seeing the otherwise hidden order in the seemingly chaotic and nonlinear relationships of the variables they are seeking to understand. The sociopolitical world is made up of complex adaptive systems that are constantly changing and adapting. Traditional, purely quantitative approaches may be inadequate to detect the changes. Christensen suggests that organizational strategists and planners must develop skill in recognizing patterns and interpreting the meaning of events as they unfold, arguing that pattern recognition is the best means of supporting decision making given our present state of knowledge.[68]

Sanders suggests seven specific advantages in visualization that researchers can take advantage of by simply modifying variables in complexity models and observing changes and differences in emerging patterns: 1) synthesis, 2) comparison or validation of data, 3) detecting changes, 4) comprehending abstract concepts, 5) seeing inaccessible or invisible phenomena and relationships, 6) communications, and 7) discovery.[69] Campbell and Mayer-Kress argue that the deterministic chaos present in many nonlinear environmental and socio-political systems imposes fundamental limitations on our ability to predict behavior, even when precisely defined mathematical models exist.[70] Sanders cautions that mathematics and numerical simulations cannot provide the insight nor the foresight needed to understand the behavior of sociopolitical systems but, she asserts, the field of scientific visualization has demonstrated how visual models can be used to stimulate insight and foresight by engaging the enormous information-processing abilities of the visual mind.[71]

Nonlinearity.

In a Newtonian linear system, change is proportionate and cause and effect relationships are predictable; in a nonlinear system, they are not. Elliott and Kiel point out that nonlinear dynamics differs from linear dynamics concerning assumptions about the nature of systemic relationships:

> In the world of linear dynamics analysts often assume
> that relationships between variables are stable over time.

In a nonlinear world, the relationships between related variables may be quite dynamic. The potential for these dynamic relations is thus seen as a primary source of the uncertainty that often dominates in nonlinear systems. When the relationships between system variables are thus both dynamic and capable of nonlinear amplification the analyst's concern for prediction and control may give way to the mere hope of improved understanding.[72]

Durlauf suggests that the effects of different policies may be highly nonlinear, rendering history a poor guide to evaluating policy effectiveness.[73] Sanders argues that nonlinear thinking is critical to recognizing clues about changes in the environment.[74]

Warren, Franklin, and Streeter discuss nonlinearity in the context of feedback and suggest that this research approach seems to provide a more intuitive depiction of the patterns one observes in certain social contexts where interactions do *not* behave in linear fashion.[75] Matthews, White and Long suggest that one of the more significant substantive implications of the complexity sciences is that dynamic, nonlinear systems may exhibit surprising and counterintuitive behavior, "making prediction and control (and possibly management as it is popularly conceived) problematic."[76] Cartwright argues that an important implication for policymakers and planners is that even if the "rules of the game" are completely known and understood at the local level, it may be impossible to predict global results and that "planning based on prediction is not merely impractical in some cases; it is logically impossible."[77]

Bendor and Hammond argue that complexity (chaos) theory has demonstrated that "if a recursive rule is nonlinear, it can create a pattern that is so complex as to appear random, even though the rule itself is completely deterministic."[78] They refute Allison's focus on the supposed linear nature of organizational behavior and argument for relatively corresponding simple process patterns. They also express some amazement in Allison's use of the metaphor of chess in discussing how bureaucratic institutions are constrained in choice of options. They point to a common estimate of 10^{120} possible options in chess, an almost infinite variety of courses of action.[79]

Sensitive Dependence to Initial Conditions.

Campbell and Meyer-Kress argue that the implications from the Lorenz Attractor (butterfly effect) discussed earlier are that the sensitivity to initial conditions of a complex system make it impossible to predict long-term behavior in the system. Two points starting very near each other on a system attractor may evolve over time in dramatically different ways.[80] Saperstein gives the contrasting examples of the 1994 shooting down of a plane in Africa that led to the massacre of hundreds of thousands of people and a similar shooting down of a plane in Korea in the 1980s that resulted only in the death of the passengers.[81] World War I provides another example of how small deviations in initial conditions can have large effects on the end result or outcome. The death of Archduke Ferdinand in Sarajevo in 1914 at the hands of Serbian nationalists was the spark that ignited the powder keg of increasingly tense European relations into a bloody world conflict. The context of the situation and the interaction among the state players in the case was extremely sensitive and ultimately dreadfully significant. The end result of a series of the seemingly unforeseen successive political and military decisions and actions that followed drew the region into a bloody conflict that became World War I which ultimately claimed over 35 million military and civilian casualties, gave birth to communism, and sowed the seeds that culminated in World War II. Because of this sensitive interdependence, prediction using complexity theory is only reliable for the very short term at best. Long term predictions are impossible.[82]

Interconnectedness and Interdependency.

Jervis suggests that within a complex adaptive system, we are dealing with a set of subunits or elements that are all interconnected and interrelated so that "changes in some elements or their relations produce changes in other parts of the system, and the entirety exhibits properties and behaviors that are different from those of the parts."[83] In a complex system, such chains of interactions may extend over time and many areas and the effects of action are always multiple. Jervis uses the example of doctors who typically refer to the undesired impact of medications as "side effects." He argues that such language is misleading, for "there are no criteria other than our desires that determine which effects are 'main' and which are 'side.'"[84] Marion and Bacon argue that in interactive networks of complex adaptive systems, actors unite in an ordered state of sorts, and the behavior of the resulting whole is more than the sum of individual behaviors.[85] They cite earlier arguments by Talcott Parsons that social structures as a whole function anthropomorphically. In their view, interacting socio-political systems not only transcend and modify the behavior of individual actors, but that interdependency significantly affects individual fitness as well.[86] If policymakers and public managers are to achieve greatest good in serving individual public needs, they need to understand and also consider the social system aggregate needs.[87]

The bottom line with interconnectedness and interrelatedness is that disturbing any point within a complex system will produce corresponding, multiple changes throughout the system. Durlauf suggests that such interdependence among various actors in a political system can, without anyone planning or intending it, generate many varieties of aggregate or emergent behavior. As a consequence, he asserts, the outcomes of policies will depend critically on the nature of the interdependencies between all actors.[88]

Strange Attractors.

A strange attractor is simply an issue, event, or new development to which a system is sensitive. It affects the system by prescribing certain boundaries within which the system tends to operate.[89] Wheatley suggests that attractors act as fields that keep systems operating within certain limits or boundaries.[90] Brodnick and Krafft point out that although variables within the boundaries of a complex adaptive system may be entirely unpredictable, attractors may make the shape and nature of the entire system extremely stable and predictable.[91] The graphing of Lorenz' meteorological equation demonstrates the unpredictability of the variables and their dynamics but the predictability of the shape and boundaries of the dynamical system. Understanding the nature of a complex social system's attractors may assist policymakers in understanding the direction a policy decision might take within a social system, even without a concise notion of the dynamics of the variables involved. It may be that the application of insights from strange attractors may broaden our understanding of policy and decision domains. Why do such dynamic systems hold together so predictably? A search for attractors may, in part, hold the answer.

Fuzzy Logic.

Zadeh introduced the notion of fuzzy sets and the mathematical definitions of inclusion, union, intersection, complement, relation and convexity as a derivative of Boolean logic.[92] Zadeh employs fuzzy logic with the purpose of modeling how people reach conclusions when the information available is imprecise, incomplete and/or not totally reliable. Kosko suggests that the notion of fuzzy logic directly challenges the fundamental precepts of positivist science.[93] For example, he asserts that "up close things are fuzzy" and "borders are inexact and things coexist with nonthings."[94] As a consequence, he argues, there is a mismatch between bivalent science and fuzzy reality. His observation is that "the world is gray but science is black and white."[95]

What distinguishes fuzzy set theory from classical set theory? Treadwell explains that

> according to classical set theory, an element either belongs to one set or it belongs to another. In fuzzy set theory an element may belong partially to a set. Fuzzy sets have gradations of set membership and blurred boundaries. Classical theory has well defined set boundaries and membership is as clear as black and white. At issue is to which set does gray belong? Classical theorists may attempt to create a new set called gray; yet the problem still persists. When does dark gray become black or conversely when does light gray become white? The fuzzy-theory approach neatly handles the assignment of gray as a partial member of both the white and black sets. The darker the gray, the more it tends to be a member of the set black and less a member of the white set. The world of perception does not have sharp edges. It is full of ambiguity and uncertainty, and it is only reasonable then to promote the use of fuzzy membership assignments. One can begin to see that classical sets, using mutual exclusivity

as the defining operative, create boundaries that are actually the zones over which conflict reigns.[96]

Kosko argues that all "human knowledge is fuzzy" and that despite all the efforts by bivalent science to make our minds function in a binary fashion, it does not work that way. He argues that our brains are full of fuzzy sets . . . . we think in fuzzy sets and we each define our fuzzy boundaries in different ways and with different examples . . . . we group things into loose fuzzy sets and then play with the groups and look for connections. Thought is set play. That is what fuzzy logic is—reasoning with fuzzy sets.[97]

Emergence.

Emergence is at the heart of the study of complexity theory. Dimitrov asserts that emergence brings forth complex patterns of order, driven by strange attractors, whose forms and dynamics are constantly evolving.[98] He concludes that the logic of contemporary decision making is held captive to linearity and choice such that even advanced approaches such as artificial intelligence, neural networks, fuzzy logic and evolutionary programming are not entirely free from this captivity. Within the construct, decision emergence does not depend upon standard rational requirements, a set of alternatives to choose from, a set of criteria to satisfy, and a goal or set of goals to focus on and accomplish. Decision emergence is thus not a function of logical analysis; it is the dynamic and continuous outcome of spontaneous combination and insight

Toward A More Effective Decision-Making and Problem Solving Model in Complex Environments

Although there is a growing appreciation of its value by academics and practitioners, the wholesale application of all of the insights and implications of complexity theory to problem solving and decision making isn't likely to happen overnight. We need first to develop solid conceptual and practical tools that will permit us to leverage these ideas to best advantage. But there are several concepts and ideas that we could immediately implement. For example, educators need to modify course curricula to complement instruction about simple, linear decision making and problem solving models with more sophisticated approaches that more effectively address the complex reality of the decision making environment.

Likewise, public and corporate practitioners need to extend their problem solving and decision making practices beyond simple linear models. The majority of the problem and opportunity situations that present themselves in our social, economic and political environment are wholly complex and nonlinear in nature. Certainly the problems we face in the realm of domestic crises and natural disasters match that description. Government, corporate, and non-profit organizational failures in addressing recent events of crisis proportions in the United States demonstrate the urgent need to change now.

Some of the things that we could implement immediately include: 1) maintain a more holistic perspective; 2) keep a long term perspective and habitually develop alternate scenarios and contingency plans; 3) use an open systems approach in evaluating potential interventions and employ a more robust stakeholder analysis in decision making and problem solving; and 4) use cyclical rather than linear, once-and-done strategies.

1. Maintain A More Holistic Perspective. Reductionism is ingrained in us. It was the central tenet of the scientific methodology for the past several hundred years and this has bled over into practically every aspect of our daily lives. In order to understand complex realities, we typically break them down into their component parts and examine each separately. But we tend to forget that the complex whole is much greater than the sum of its individual parts. The emergent properties of complex systems represent systemic properties that the separate parts simply do not have. This is not a call for the abandonment of reductionist strategies. But it is an acknowledgement that we will never understand the complex nature of our social decision environment until we remember to examine and evaluate how all of the individual parts connect together. Relationships are important, maybe the critical factor. At the conclusion of our habitual reductionist analysis, we need to address the additional holistic issue of what is there about how the component parts of the system interconnect and interrelate which are important to know and that tell us something more about the true complex nature of the system being examined.

2. Keep a long-term perspective and habitually develop alternate scenarios and contingency plans.

Americans have grown accustomed to expect instant gratification. At variance with most other cultures of the world, we generally maintain a short-term rather than a long-term perspective. As investors, we are typically more interested in quarterly earnings than long-term growth. As decision makers and problem solvers, we implement solutions to immediate problems without serious consideration for long-term consequences and second-, third—and fourth-order effects.

Decision makers and problem solvers need to move beyond the natural tendency for simplification and develop cognitive tools for understanding complexity and engaging in long-term processes. We must avoid getting caught up in the fantasy of our reified simplification strategies for a complex reality. We shouldn't be surprised by the unexpected or unanticipated. Notwithstanding our best efforts at control, elements of our reality will combine and co-evolve in ways that we can't predict.

Instead of planning for just one anticipated future, we should describe different scenarios that could possibly happen in the future and develop contingency plans for each of those scenarios. Even if the scenario that eventually does emerge doesn't precisely match any of the scenarios we developed, we will be better prepared to adapt and apply the contingency plan for the scenario that came closest to the emergent reality.

3. Employ a systems thinking approach and rely on a more robust stakeholder analysis.

Decision makers must learn to recognize interconnectivity, co-evolution, and emergence in complex system. Systems theory helps us understand the complex nature of the interconnectivity and interdependence of the various elements in a system. Interdependency is reflected by the absorption of outputs from one subsystem in an environment as the inputs for others. Due to rapidly evolving transportation, communication and information technologies, the number of stakeholders in the decision environment is expanding exponentially. Decision makers and problem solvers must move beyond a truncated review and analysis of key stakeholders to a more comprehensive understanding of how all stakeholders interrelate in the decision realm.

4. Use non-linear, cyclical approaches rather than linear, once-and-done approaches. The twin problems associated with the traditional problem solving and decision making models we teach in the university classroom and employ in the public and corporate workplace are that they: 1) use a linear approach for what is in actuality a highly complex, interactive, and nonlinear reality, and 2) employ various simplification strategies that distort the nature of the problem arena and ignore information that could prove key in problem resolution. We need to teach a modified approach to the model which intuitively guides the decision maker into a cyclical rather than a linear, once-and-done process.

For many complex problems, the revised model might be applied like this: At step 1, decision makers need to only tentatively define the problem statement with the expectation that it will evolve over time throughout the process. At step 2, decision makers need to generate potential solutions and incrementally implement possible solutions on a limited scale as a means of ferreting out additional information concerning the reality of the problem, redefining the problem, and moving the problem resolution in the right direction. The problem statement should be revised as any changes evolve or emerge in the decision area. At step 3, the selection of an appropriate overall course of action will only be made after it has been selectively tested for suitability and effectiveness. At step 4, the decision is implemented and monitored for effectiveness in resolving the revised problem. At step 5, the decision arena is surveyed for changes in the environment and any new problems or issues that have surfaced as a consequence of the problem resolution can now be addressed in a continuing cycle.

Revised Analytical Problem Solving Model

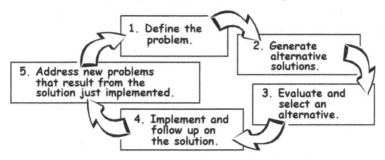

This model is somewhat similar to the Plan-Do-Check-Act Model. Originally developed by Walter Shewhart at Bell Laboratories during the 1930s, it is often referred to as the **Shewhart Cycle**. Later promoted during the 1950s by quality guru, Edward Deming, it also came to be known to many as the **Deming Wheel**.[99]

The nonlinear thought process behind this model is its strength. It conditions the decision maker to accept continuity and evolution in the decision arena and to accept responsibility and accountability for new problems created. More importantly perhaps, with the mindset that decision making and problem solving is cyclic and never-ending, decision makers are less likely to be caught by surprise by the unintended second-, third-, and fourth-order effects of their policy implementation.

Conclusion

As our understanding of the implications of complexity expands, we must correspondingly adjust our understanding of the role of rationality and comprehensiveness in decision and policymaking. The time is far overdue to reexamine traditional, classical approaches to decision making and problem solving processes.

During the past two decades, emerging complexity-based ideas and insights have complemented and reinforced many traditional ideas about complexity. They have in some cases forced social researchers and policy scientists to push their empirical methodologies harder in searching for time-series structure associated with complexity approaches. The images created by visually graphing complex relationships suggest that there may be a rich wealth of additional information on trends, changes, and dynamic structures hidden in ostensibly well-understood, linear, theoretical models. Although these may be appropriate for certain limited situations, linear analytical approaches to complex problem solving and decision making distort our perception of the actual social reality.

For most organizational environments, complexity approaches offer a more comprehensive set of tools and strategies for accurately assessing real world systems and can produce more robust decisions, fewer unintended consequences, and problem resolutions more acceptable to a broader set of stakeholders.

Chapter 11—How to Avoid Strategic Leadership and Strategic Management Failure

The goal of developing a clear vision of the future on which to overlay strategic planning is daunting. Perhaps even more challenging is implementing a strategic plan in a turbulent, rapidly-changing, organizational environment, adapting the plan as necessary to evolving conditions in the marketplace.

There are numerous examples of major organizations stumbling and falling during the past several decades—Xerox, Eastman Kodak, IBM, Sears, Kmart, Circuit City, Borders, Smith Corona, Blockbuster, Enron, Arthur Anderson—the list goes on. Some observers suggest that they fell from their lead positions in the marketplace due to complacency and lack of visionary innovation. This, in part, may be true, but it doesn't explain all of the corporate failures. Many of these fallen giants actively pursued a comprehensive strategic management regimen. It is evident that merely going through the motions of strategic leadership and strategic management does not necessarily guarantee corporate success.

Strategic planning gained great footing in the American corporate world during the 1970s and grew in popularity throughout the 1980s. But the 1990s and 2000s were littered with the wreckage of firms that had pursued strategic leadership and strategic management without success. In the wake of these failures, strategic planning lost much of its popularity among business practitioners and many organizations dispensed with any kind of strategic management program at all. This probably happened because corporate leaders felt that strategic planning didn't deliver on the promises of greater organizational competitiveness and increased profits, and besides, it frequently was an expensive proposition to begin with.

In *Relearning Strategic Planning*, Ziegenfuss recounts four general problems with strategic planning identified by Mintzberg in *The Rise and Fall of Strategic Planning*: 1) it tends to discourage commitment, 2) it is overly conservative, 3) it engenders political activity; and 4) it is obsessed with control. In response to these potential pitfalls, Ziegenfuss suggests a redesign of traditional strategic planning processes that addresses why executives are not committed, determines whether the strategic planning process produces anything revolutionary, examines how to control politics in the organization, and avoids trying to predict future events when we simply cannot.[1]

There have been a number of excellent books published during the past ten or fifteen years examining business success and failure. Many of these include a hard look at the problems and challenges with pursuing a strategic agenda.[2] Additionally, a recent search of the Internet by googling the search words *strategic planning failure* produced over 6,800 hits, with many of the sites containing lengthy lists of what's wrong with strategic planning and prescribing correctives for getting it right.

I examined ideas from many of these books and websites about the foibles of strategic management and distilled a short list of some of the most commonly cited criticisms and observations. Earlier in this book, I postulated that many of such criticisms against strategic planning were directed more toward *strategic planning done poorly* rather than problems with strategic planning itself. This appears to be the majority view reflected in these books and websites. However, there was also a strong case made for the possibility of failure in spite of first-rate strategic leadership and management efforts.

Here is a list of twelve of the most frequently mentioned criticisms of strategic planning which addresses the overall question of why strategic leadership and strategic management sometimes fail. Following each shortcoming are suggested remedies for how to confront and overcome the problems. Many of these problem areas were covered earlier in this text and are fundamental to successful strategic leadership and management. The suggested remedies are just that . . . . suggestions . . . . and hopefully they will engage the readers' creative thinking processes as they consider how the identified shortcomings relate to specific organizations and what remedies might be most appropriate to that situation.

1. Ivory Tower Syndrome

Some organizations greatly restrict participation in the strategic planning process and only senior management participate. Typically, these senior people retire to a retreat location away from the corporate offices for days or weeks at a time and hammer out the strategic agenda for the coming year. The resulting strategic plan is top-down delivered and the rank and file of the organization are expected to support the plan. Hill and Jones refer to this as *the ivory tower approach* and suggest that working in isolation, senior leader-managers may formulate strategies that do more harm than good.[3] A top-down strategic planning process such as this is also sometimes referred to as the *black box syndrome*, in that the completed strategic plan is delivered as a fait accompli without the majority of organizational members being aware of how it was formulated.

There are a number of problems with this approach. First, there is little reason for the rank and file of an organization to buy in to such a plan since they had little or nothing to do with its creation. Second, by limiting participation in the strategic planning process to just senior management, they inhibit input from lower ranking members of the organization who are most familiar with capabilities (production), customer needs and wants (marketing and sales), and future possibilities (R&D). Third, such strategic plans are frequently poorly communicated and the rank and file never really understand the corporate vision and how they fit into it.

What's the Remedy? Include representation from the rank and file in the strategic planning process. This provides the opportunity to integrate input from those who are closest to the action in what the firm does; it tends to create much greater immediate buy-in when the plan is finally published and distributed; and it provides the possibility for better communication of the strategic agenda to members at all levels throughout the organization. In short, make strategic planning both a top-down **and** a bottom-up process.

2. Over-Emphasis on Fit

Many organizations are overly cautious and tentative about moving into an uncertain future. They seem stuck in the status quo and tend to go about change incrementally rather than going after quantum leaps of revolutionary change. These organizations tend to stay back in the pack well behind the leading edge corporations that define the direction of their industry.

These organizations focus mostly on strategic fit (operational strategies) using present resources and capabilities rather than strategic intent (developmental strategies) to guide the acquisition of new resources and capabilities in the active pursuit of visionary possibilities.[4] As a consequence, strategic planning in many organizations tends to focus more on analysis and programming rather than strategic thinking and intuitive innovation.[5] This results more in the preservation of the status quo than moving forward and adapting to stay competitive in a rapidly evolving corporate environment. Ultimately, organizations can fall further out of sync with customers and the competition, and some eventually suffer corporate decline and demise.

The saga of Blockbuster video provides a sobering example of the perils of continuing to pursue an aging business model in the face of rapid paradigm shifts in the market place. At its peak in 2009, Blockbuster had almost 60,000 employees with 840 Blockbuster stores in the United States with additional locations in 17 countries worldwide.[6] Blockbuster's business model was based on a paradigm that channeled them into seeing the video rental industry in terms of VHS tapes, DVDs and video games displayed in neighborhood brick and mortal stores. This same paradigm prevented Blockbuster from seeing video rentals in terms of online rentals through the Internet or video streaming of movies and video games. Notwithstanding Blockbuster's dominant position in the video rental marketplace, Netflix, entered the video and video game rental market with a radically different business model based on a new video rental paradigm using the Internet and unseated Blockbuster handily.[7]

As Netflix cut a huge swath through Blockbuster's market share, Blockbuster belatedly attempted to set up its own video-by-mail program but it couldn't overtake Netflix' momentum. Netflix had established too much of an early lead in the emerging video-rental—over-the-Internet industry. Blockbuster's attempt to respond with its own mail program was too little and too late to catch up.[8] Additionally, as a result of poor strategic planning and mismanagement in the face of stiff competition from Netflix, Redbox and others in the emerging video streaming and video box industries, Blockbuster suffered significant revenue losses and it finally filed for bankruptcy in September, 2010.[9] It was subsequently acquired by the satellite television provider Dish Network at auction for $233 million in April, 2011.[10]

Bottom line: Organizations need to adapt to stay competitive in a rapidly evolving corporate environment rather than merely attempting to preserve the status quo of previous success.

What's the Remedy? Fully integrate strategic thinking into the planning process. Focus less on nudging the status quo and instead attempt to envision genuine, innovative change. Work more on developmental strategies rather than merely repeating familiar operational strategies. Strategy making is the process of turning innovative ideas into action. Formulating effective strategy requires applying creative thinking to resolving problems and addressing opportunities—the more creative the thinking, the better the strategy.[11]

Osterwalder and Pigneur assert that business model innovation and strategic planning is not about looking back, because the past indicates little about what is possible in terms of future business models.[12] They also observe that strategic planning innovation should not be focused on merely following the same path as competitors, since strategic innovation is not about copying or benchmarking but about "challenging orthodoxies to design original models that meet unsatisfied, new, or hidden customer needs."[13]

3. Lack of Creative Thinking, Innovation and Learning.

Many organizational strategic planning processes are merely exercises in analytical logic and rarely reflect any creative, innovative thinking of any significance. This is partly because analysis is imbued in the corporate culture's eye on short-term goals and the quarterly bottom line.[14] Absence of creative thinking is Mintzberg's baseline argument against strategic planning.[15]

Harris identifies three issues which pose blocks to innovative thinking and planning in most organizations: 1) short-term needs (typically for profits or costs savings) tend to drive out the ability to think long-term; 2) the desire and perceived safety of copying competitors precludes real innovation; and 3) the perceived safety of protecting sunken investments and their cost advantage means risky new investments are avoided, and the safety of the well-known provides a comfort zone that stifles creativity.[16]

Harris also points out that pursuing and adopting a false sense of closure to the planning process makes it seemingly easier to deal with the uncertainty. He acknowledges that the planning process and selection of strategies indeed must come to an end so that actions can be taken. But when those moves are made, he argues that there should be a sense that there are still things that are unclear and uncertain and that the learning process remains open.[17] For Mintzberg, learning is the essence of strategy making. He argues that "strategies can develop inadvertently, without the conscious intention of senior management, often through a process of learning," and that "learning inevitably plays a, if not the, crucial role in the development of novel strategies."[18]

Here's an analogy from everyday experience that helps to illustrate this point. Most of us make detailed travel plans using maps and MapQuest when we are planning a long-distance vacation trip. We typically end up with a travel plan laid out with routes and stops and people we want to visit and sights we want to see along the way, all formatted against the calendar to fit our available vacation days. But, just as we make course corrections with the steering wheel as we drive down the freeway to compensate for unforeseen driving conditions and detours along pre-selected routes, we also must make course corrections with our strategic plan as we "drive" it into an uncertain future. That doesn't mean that the plan was bad, just that implementation of the plan constitutes a learning process and requires us to make adjustments or course corrections to the plan as we move forward.

What's the Remedy? Ensure that your strategic planning process isn't merely an exercise in financial projections and spreadsheet analysis. Look beyond short-term organizational activities and status quo and exercise creative thinking in projecting truly innovative stretch goals. Move beyond merely copying the competition and protecting sunk investment costs. Leaders and planners should think about the future in creative ways, challenging conventional wisdom, raising difficult questions, and questioning assumptions. De Geus argues that the ultimate purpose of strategic planning is to help change the mental models that leader-manager decision makers carry in their heads.[19] In other words they need to get the organization out of the status quo rut.

As a strategic plan is hammered out, recognize that it is only the starting point for moving into the future and that organizational members will have to monitor the plan closely as the future unfolds. Very little associated with the initial strategic planning process should be written in permanent marker. During implementation of the plan, replace initial assumptions with facts as they become available. Be prepared to learn and make adjustments, even significant adjustments from the original plan. It is only natural and necessary that the emergent strategic plan that is ultimately implemented should vary considerably from the original formalized plan that came out of the planning process. Systems theory prescribes that true learning organizations learn from internal and external feedback and make adjustments accordingly. Harris observes that "the only long-term sustainable advantage is to learn faster than your competitors" and that "a learning agenda should be a key output of a quality strategic plan."[20] A superb example of a learning organization has been the non-profit organization, the March of Dimes. Founded in 1938 by then-President Franklin Delano Roosevelt, the foundation funded research to develop vaccines to put an end to the polio epidemic in the United States. When that purpose was accomplished and the March of Dimes was left without an immediate cause, it redefined its vision and focus to that of preventing birth defects and infant mortality. Since 2003, the March of Dimes has also championed research into the causes of premature births.[21]

4. The Strategy-Making Process Is Too Slow.

In the past, traditional strategic planning processes typically have taken six months to a year to produce a viable strategic plan. By the time the strategic plan finally emerged as a published document, it was already an antique. Today, changes in the corporate environment can move faster than an organization's ability to develop and implement a strategic planning agenda. In the white water turbulence that most organizations are experiencing today, strategic planning may be a waste of time simply because the process can't be cycled through quickly enough for the organization to adapt to the rapidly-evolving corporate environment and the brief shelf life of a written strategic plan simply can't justify the investment in energy and time in producing it. By the time a written plan emerges from a detailed strategic planning process, organizational and environmental conditions will have evolved and moved on from the original conditions that existed when the planning process was first initiated.

What's the Remedy? Leaders need to promote faster, more responsive planning processes to overcome and eliminate excessive time lag. Moreover, organizations need to modify their mindset about strategic planning. It is not a once-and-done process. It is a continuous, ongoing process that needs to be revisited frequently as the future unfolds.[22] A thick, comprehensive strategic plan is perhaps not the best outcome from a strategic planning process. A streamlined strategic document that describes general high-level objectives, the direction the organization wants to move, and organizational commitment of resources and capabilities as to how it anticipates doing that may serve the organization better. The plan should also include brief discussions of potential contingencies and how the organization plans to respond as any particular planning scenario comes to pass.

5. Analysis Paralysis and Groupthink.

Some organizations attempt a comprehensive analysis of *all* of the factors and variables at work in the marketplace. Planners work overtime attempting to identify all of the permutations and combinations of options available to the organization. Carried to the extreme, this can result in *analysis paralysis*—a never-ending pursuit of options and the consideration of their pros and cons, and a fundamental failure to reach actionable decisions and implementing them. I once had a conversation with a senior leader of a major organization concerning the strategic meetings he attended. He lamented that in those meetings, actionable decisions were rarely reached and at the end of the meetings, the only decision that typically emerged was the decision to meet again next week to continue the discussion of options. They kept pushing the really hard decisions down the road.

Procrastination is the enemy of decision making. In the face of analysis paralysis, the decision situation remains immobilized in stasis while it is taken apart and analyzed in never-ending studies and difficult decisions are postponed. In some organizations, fact-finding and option development can be used as a stall tactic. The potential end result of such a dynamic is that, in the absence of meaningful change, the organization can be overcome by disaster without ever having really developed a strategic agenda.[23]

At the other extreme, some organizations rush the decision-making process. Anxious to move forward with actionable plans, they narrow their focus too much, considering only a limited number of factors and variables at work in the marketplace and just one or two options for moving forward. This rapid-paced dynamic is frequently the result of *groupthink*, and is characterized by an over-emphasis on organizational orthodoxy and a desire on the part of the participants in the strategic planning process to be perceived as supportive, team players. Members of the strategic planning team simply try to minimize conflict and quickly reach a consensus decision without critical evaluation of alternative ideas or viewpoints. Groupthink is a mode of thinking in which concurrence-seeking becomes so dominant in the planning in-group that it tends to override realistic appraisal of alternative courses of action.[24]

What's the Remedy? Analysis paralysis and groupthink lie at the extremes of a continuum framed by comprehensive rationality and bounded rationality decision-making approaches. Organizational planning teams must strike a balance somewhere between the two extremes, balancing the need to consider the multiplicity of variables and options that may impact decisions and their implementation with the need to reach actionable decisions in a timely manner. Good decisions are, of course, critical to success but good decisions delivered too late in the game may ultimately be worse than bad decisions or ill-thought-out decisions based upon limited information.

6. Faulty Assumptions.

To be most effective, the strategic planning process should be fact-based as much as possible. In practice, however, assumptions take the place of facts to assist planners when critical elements of information are unavailable but needed to initiate or continue planning. The faulty assumptions trap is the result of initiating a strategic planning process with incomplete information or incorrect information and then not updating the assumptions as relevant data become available. Wilson argues that faulty assumptions can corrupt planning and undermine the process if left unchecked and unresolved. He argues that faulty assumptions result in planning failure in both corporate and public sectors.[25] Ziegenfuss asserts that strategic planning problems are frequently driven by errors in assumptions and procedures.[26]

What's the Remedy? As more complete and accurate information becomes available during the planning and execution processes, initial assumptions must be updated and strategic planning decisions must be adjusted as appropriate. This is part of the learning process. Making assumptions early in the planning process allow us to get moving without having all of the facts. As we move into the future, many of these missing facts and incomplete data will present themselves. With this new, solid information, we must update the plan to reflect the new parameters. Thus the realized strategy becomes a combination between the deliberate strategy that is a product of the formalized planning process, and an emergent strategy representing an unplanned shift by top-level leader-managers, autonomous action by lower-level leader-managers, and serendipity.[27]

7. Linear Planning Processes and Simplification Schemes.

Strategic planning processes tend to be linear, reductionist, and overly simplistic while the world we live in is decidedly nonlinear and complex. A holistic approach to understanding such complex environments is critical. Ziegenfuss reminds us that early strategic planning efforts usually focused just on the financials and the processes that produced and delivered goods and services to customers because they were the easiest to measure.[28] But he argues that effective strategic planning today must include all of the social and technical aspects of the organization. It requires broader thinking including consideration for the corporate culture, organizational structure, the quality of work life, and the consideration for human resource assets.[29]

Mintzberg asserts that strategies are to organizations what blinders are to horses, keeping them moving in a straight line by impeding peripheral vision.[30] Human organizations behave in decidedly nonlinear ways and one of the more significant implications of the complexity sciences is that dynamic, nonlinear systems may exhibit surprising and counterintuitive behavior, "making prediction and control (and possibly management as it is popularly conceived) problematic."[31]

Harris observes that since planning is inherently a thinking process, at the root of poor and inadequate strategic planning is "a lack of really good thinking and stimulating ideas."[32] He concludes that in a world that is changing at a rapid rate and full of uncertainty, strategic planning must be about the organization learning its way forward.[33] Linear thinking and planning processes focused through a reductionist lens tend to be counterproductive and produce marginal results at best.

What's the Remedy? Although simplification schemes can assist leaders and planners in working through the complexities of the corporate environment, they must be careful not to oversimplify away the variables that may have significant bearing on organizational outcomes. Likewise, leaders and planners shouldn't allow consideration for the present situation and current risks to hamstring the future strategic planning agenda. Schwartz counsels that scenario building is a powerful vehicle for challenging mental models about the world and lifting the blinders that limit creativity and resourcefulness.[34] Don't focus on today's trivial and inconsequential information simply because it is easier to discern and deal with. Rather, expend the necessary effort to develop and implement a truly visionary strategy that provides an opportunity for success.

Linear thinking tends to result in once and done planning processes. Avoid that. Strategic thinking and strategic planning continue on during the implementation phase. Continue to monitor internal strengths and weaknesses and external threats and opportunities. External players in particular respond to the behavior of other actors in the organizational environment and thus it is in a constant state of flux. Linear prediction methodologies and forecasting algorithms in such a complex environment are not likely to prove effective and so the best way to move forward in an uncertain, rapidly-evolving environment is through continuous monitoring and adaptation.

8. Lack of Strategic Alignment

As the Chief Learning Officer at the Pennsylvania Department of Transportation (PennDOT) in the early 2000s, I frequently traveled around Pennsylvania visiting the district and county maintenance offices to talk about training. When visiting with PennDOT personnel at all levels in the organization, I discovered that a good indicator of the dispersion of PennDOT's corporate strategic agenda was the response to the question—"How does what you do each day support PennDOT's overall strategic objectives?" If the individual questioned could articulate the linkage between their job description and daily work activities with their organizational goals (county and district) and agency high-level objectives, then there was an excellent chance that the PennDOT's strategic agenda was well communicated and understood and that it guided the development of lower-level organizational objectives and individual work objectives. If the individual couldn't make the connection, it was a good sign that they hadn't heard about the enterprise strategic agenda at all or, if they had, they didn't understand it and probably weren't pulling in that direction.

In smooth functioning, well-run organizations, there is strong strategic alignment from top to bottom and bottom to top. Strategies developed at the lowest level support strategies at the next higher level which in turn support strategies at the next higher level and so on. Everyone in the organization is thus pulling in the same direction supporting the accomplishment of the overall enterprise strategy. Subordinate units within an organization build their strategies on the basis of strategies developed at higher levels. That is the hallmark of strategic alignment. When that alignment doesn't exist, organizational members at all levels row in different directions and the organization stalls, runs around in circles, or moves backwards.

What's the Remedy? There are no quick fixes here. Corporate leaders need to work on the corporate culture to ensure that alignment exists through the organization down to the shop floor. This is a proposition that is informed by a systems-thinking perspective. In reality, everyone in an organization from the boardroom to the shop floor is connected together in formal and informal networks. Their efforts must be coordinated and aligned so that everyone is pulling in the same direction.

When strategic alignment is achieved, employees understand what their own individual work objectives are in support of department, organizational and enterprise strategies. This can be effectively accomplished during performance appraisal time as supervisors and employees agree upon individual goals and objectives for the next time period and supervisors make sure that employees have the right combination of resources and capabilities to accomplish whatever goals are agreed upon.

As leaders meet with their direct reports and other employees, they should discuss organizational goals and objectives set at that level and ensure that they closely align with and contribute to the accomplishment of corporate strategic objectives. As all leader-managers in the organization meet with employees, they need to discuss how individual work objectives and daily work activities contribute to accomplishing those objectives. Following such a regimen over time, everyone in the organization will understand their role and organizational alignment is achieved.

9. Ineffective Leadership

In some organizations, leaders take a peripheral role in the strategy development process. They hire outside consultants to oversee the process and assume a passive position in producing even a strategic vision for the organization. Exacerbating this lack of senior leader engagement, some organizations experience high executive-turnover which jeopardizes continuity in a sound strategic leadership and strategic management culture. The poster child for executive turnover is Hewlett Packard which has had six CEOs in the past decade and four different CEOs since August 2010 alone.

Moreover, leaders must stay attuned to what's going on internally in the organization and what's going on externally in the organization's environment. Some leaders isolate themselves from the rest of the organization and the environment, holing up in their mahogany-lined offices. They rarely get out and have little communication with anyone in the organization other than their direct reports. They frequently have no direct contact with anyone else in the organization and consequently have little real understanding of precisely how the organization operates.

What's the Remedy? In the pursuit of change in a rapidly-evolving corporate environment, Kotter asserts that most organizations are over-managed and under-led.[35] Leaders must overcome organizational inertia to get the organization moving in a new direction. Leaders must actively lead strategy development and implementation in the organization. Although they ought to get input from throughout the organization, leaders are ultimately responsible for setting the organization's course into an uncertain future, including the formulation of the corporate vision and values. When they choose to utilize a facilitator to lead a strategic planning meeting, they need to remain engaged as an active participant. As the organization moves into an uncertain future through the white water turbulence of change, leaders must stay visible to their employees and project an image of confidence, modeling the way and encouraging the heart.[36] Leaders need to help organizational members to be more comfortable with the inherent messiness of change.

It is impossible to accomplish any of these imperatives of leadership comfortably ensconced in an office. Leaders need to get out among their organizational members frequently and exercise a form of leadership and management by just walking around. They need to visit with their employees face-to-face and get to know them and understand their concerns, hopes, and aspirations. During these sojourns throughout the organization, they need to make it a positive experience and project the image of a coach and mentor rather than that of an inspector. They need to ask lots of questions, expressing sincere interest in what employees are doing and even working alongside them on occasion. They need to be responsive to employee problems and concerns and share information whenever they can. Perhaps most important, they need to share their vision at every opportunity and encourage employees to focus their work effort on helping to accomplish that vision.

10. Metrics and Performance Measurement—Failure to Measure and Act

If you don't measure it, you can't manage it. Not establishing metrics is working in the dark. You have no idea whether the formulated strategic plan is achieving any degree of success in its implementation. There are generally two kinds of metrics. Performance metrics are high-level measures of what you are doing. They are externally focused and generally assess overall performance in terms of outputs, customer needs and business requirements. Diagnostic metrics are measures that ascertain why a process is not performing up to expectations. They tend to be internal in nature and are focused on system inputs and internal processes.

Organizations make several mistakes with respect to using metrics. First, they frequently focus first on diagnostic measures, measuring data concerning internal resources, capabilities, and processes, rather than beginning with an external focus on customer needs. Another common error is to establish metrics that are easy to measure but don't reflect key business information critical to the success of strategy implementation. A third mistake is to set up mechanisms to measure and report key feedback data but ignore that information in making adjustments to the strategic plan during the implementation.

What's the Remedy? In formulating the strategic agenda, be sure to clearly articulate organizational goals and objectives. Then define metrics that will help track progress toward success in achieving them. Establish up front the current status of all metrics so that there will be a point of comparison as the strategic plan passes from the formulation stage to implementation. Put in place a system to monitor and report the metrics selected. Make sure that metrics are communicated with employees so they will know how to make decisions that will improve organizational performance. Frequently review the metrics selected to be sure that, as the future unfolds, they still provide data significant to the accomplishment of the plan. Much as the original SWOT analysis revealed, metrics feedback should reflect internal strengths and weaknesses and external opportunities and threats. That information must be analyzed in the context of the strategic plan being implemented. Since the future was impossible to predict during the plan formulation stage, it is natural that there are now elements of the plan that will need to be adjusted or adapted. In extreme cases, it may be necessary to make significant changes to the plan or go back to the drawing board and develop a new plan altogether.

Defining the metrics that are most important to core business processes allows you to focus and tune out peripheral information not related to these key measurements. As a result, the implementation of the strategic plan can proceed more efficiently. Organizations that monitor metrics can spot threats and opportunities faster than organizations that don't. Metrics provide a framework for making business decisions on how to proceed into an uncertain future. Using metrics effectively can provide keen insights into what is happening internally in the organization as well as externally in the organizational environment.

Two of the most common systems for monitoring and communicating metrics are dashboards and scorecards. Dashboards are typically used at lower organizational levels to track how well goals and objectives are being met. Dashboard metrics are typically reflected on a simple chart, frequently using a color code of green for things going well, yellow for marginal performance that needs to be monitored closely, and red for issues that demand immediate attention. Much like the instrumentation warning lights on the dashboard of an automobile, dashboard metrics provide a quick visual reference for how the organization is functioning and alert on those things not going well.

Scorecards are used at higher organizational levels and typically reflect more complex high-level goals and objectives. Scorecards are similar to the scorecards kept by baseball managers to track the performance of individual players and the team as a whole. Some organizational scorecards I have seen are very detailed and reflect a considerable number of metrics. Kaplan and Norton suggest a simplified model for a balanced scorecard with fields for objectives, measures or metrics, targets, and initiatives.[37] When such scorecards for various functional areas or core processes are brought together, they provide leaders and managers with a useful tool for translating vision and strategy into actionable tasks and for tracking progress toward achieving project goals and objectives.

Effective dashboards and scorecards are not overly complex, reflect a limited number of metrics, focus on the important factors for strategic success including strategy, customers, financial management, organizational processes, and learning and development. More importantly, they assist users to relate the diverse organizational areas together in a dynamic relationship.

11. Disruptive Technologies

Much of the turbulence in today's white water marketplace is driven by new technologies—information technologies, communication technologies, and transportation technologies. Emerging technologies can either be *sustaining* or *disruptive*. Sustaining technologies generally do not create new markets or value networks but simply enhance existing ones with increased value for customers as competitors continue to compete against each other's innovations and improvements. In contrast, disruptive innovations lay the foundation for creating new markets and new value networks. Ultimately, they displace earlier successful technologies which eventually lose out and disappear from the marketplace.[38]

Christensen observes that disruptive technologies are disruptive simply because they result in a new generation of processes, products or services that are typically cheaper, simpler, smaller, more convenient to use and more attractive to the potential customer base.[39] There are many of examples of disruptive technologies that have caused significant shifts in the marketplace—the PC has replaced the typewriter, PC networks and servers have replaced much of the data processing formerly performed by mainframe computers, online news services are replacing print journalism, digital photography is replacing negative print film photography, video-teleconferencing is replacing much airline travel to attend meetings, and on-line educational degree programs are mounting strong competition for students in brick and mortar classrooms. There is no shortage of such disruptive technologies today. Christensen provides a short list of 24 matched pairs of current technologies that are being challenged by disruptive technologies.[40] There are many other examples that could have been listed.

An historic example of a business firm that didn't survive the rapid evolution of disruptive technologies was the Edison Phonograph Company.[41] Thomas Edison invented the phonograph in 1877. The Edison system recorded sound onto a tinfoil sheet wrapped around a phonograph cylinder. Alexander Graham Bell's Volta Laboratory made improvements on Edison's original design and developed wax-coated cardboard cylinders and a stylus that moved from side to side across the cylinder. In 1888, an American inventor, Emile Berliner, invented a process to record sounds on disks, a technological innovation that would soon prove disruptive for the whole emerging recorded music industry. By the beginning of the new century, the transition from phonograph cylinders to shellac-coated gramophone disc records was well underway. Gramophone records were double-sided disks with a single spiral groove running from the outer edge of the disk and tracking into the center. Edison's company had achieved great success with phonograph cylinders but he eventually realized that the market was transitioning to the new disk format technology fast and that he had better follow suit or be left behind with his now soon-to-be-antiquated technology.

Edison encountered a lot of competition in the marketplace. The Victor Talking Machine Company was founded in 1901 and quickly became the leading American producer of phonographs and phonograph records. Columbia Records was founded in 1888, evolving from the American Graphophone Company which in turn had evolved from the Volta Graphophone Company. A third major American company, Brunswick, began producing phonographs in 1916 and quickly gravitated to marketing disc records on its own record label. A fourth major record label, Vocalion, was found in 1916 by the Aeolian Piano Company as an offshoot of its organ division. It initially marketed single-sided records with a reddish-brown shellac which gave them a distinctive appearance from the more common black shellac records of the day. The Vocalion label was later acquired by Brunswick records in 1925.

These early phonograph companies were very successful in the marketplace with phonograph disk technology using a side-to-side lateral motion of the stylus in the record groove. Edison entered the market in 1912 with what he considered a greatly improved technology, the Diamond Disc phonograph. Edison's system utilized an up-and-down vertical movement of the stylus in the record groove. Unlike the Victor system, the grooves on the diamond discs were thinner and smooth with a variable depth that was translated into sound by a diaphragm and reproducer. There were other differences as well. The Victor diaphragm was located at right angles to the surface of the disc surface while the Edison diaphragm of the reproducer was located parallel to the disc. Because of these proprietary differences, the Victor system could not play Edison discs and the Edison system could not play Victor system discs. Brunswick initially used Edison's vertical cut system but it was not commercially successful. In 1920, Brunswick introduced a new line employing the lateral cut technology. Vocalion switched to dual-sided records and the lateral cut system in 1920 as well. With that transition, lateral cut technology became the standard for 78 rpm disc record technology and the Edison system became out of step with the preferred technology.

The Edison Diamond Disc records enjoyed commercial success into the early 1920s. In the tight competition with Victor, Columbia, Brunswick, and Vocalion records, the Diamond Disc's audio fidelity was considered technologically superior. But the Edison phonographs and disc records were more expensive and incompatibility with other lateral system discs made them less attractive to potential customers who already had sunk costs in established record collections. Sales began to taper off in the early 1920s and eventually, even though it demonstrated superior sound reproduction and playing time, the Edison Diamond Disc system lost out in the marketplace. As phonograph technology continued to evolve from acoustical recordings to electrical recordings, Edison was late in adopting that technology as well and sales continued to drop. By the end of the 1920s, the Edison Diamond Disc system was no longer profitable and Edison left the phonograph record business altogether in late 1929. In short, disruptive technologies can be viewed as threats to defend against or opportunities to exploit as the market continues to evolve.

What's the Remedy? The problem of disruptive technologies can only be confronted and resolved by a careful consideration of current market conditions and customer needs. In 1997, Christensen authored *The Innovator's Dilemma*, a full-length book that addresses the problem in great detail.[42] Does a disruptive technology represent an immediate threat for the organization or is it merely something that needs to be monitored for the present as the marketplace continues to evolve. The bottom line is that although it may not be necessary to take immediate action about a potentially disruptive technology, it should never be ignored. A better strategy would be to continue monitoring the disruptive technology over time to see where it seems to be leading the marketplace. When it becomes apparent that it runs the risk of totally changing current markets and value networks, then is the time to react with a well-thought-out commitment of organizational resources and capabilities. Christensen gives the contemporary example of electric cars. He acknowledges that the electric car does represent a potentially disruptive technology to the automobile industry but observes that no automobile manufacturer is making a wholesale leap into that technology at the present time. At some point in the future, however, it may be necessary for the automobile industry to pursue electric car technology with greater commitment and energy.[43]

12. The Strategy Paradox

Because of the hyper-turbulence in the marketplace today, disruptive technologies frequently result in what Raynor refers to as the *Strategy Paradox*.[44] When disruptive technologies appear to be creating genuine disruption in ongoing markets and value networks, organizations have to reevaluate their current business models and product lines to adapt to the rapidly changing environment.

According to Raynor, the Strategy Paradox represents a tradeoff in building a strategic agenda based upon specific beliefs and assumptions about an unpredictable future. **The tradeoff arises when leaders have to commit to what may become an inflexible strategy.** Changing the current business strategy typically involves creating new objectives that require new and different resources and capabilities. **An organization must make commitments to these new resources and capabilities and, once committed, do not generally have the maneuvering room they might have once had to change direction if they get it wrong.**[45]

Raynor posits that "the same behaviors and characteristics that maximize a firm's probability of notable success also maximize its probability of total failure," and suggests that "the very traits we have come to identify as determinants of high, achievement are also the ingredients of total collapse."[46] He concludes that "the opposite of success is not failure, but mediocrity," characterized by the failure to make bold commitments of resources and capabilities moving into an uncertain future.[47]

What's the Remedy? The previous eleven issues with strategic leadership and management deal fundamentally with strategic planning done wrong. Strategic Paradox deals with strategic failure when strategic planning is done well. It is the result of commitment of resources and capabilities to a given set of strategic objectives based on a set of assumptions. When the assumptions prove faulty as the future unfolds, the organization lacks flexibility in refocusing committed resources and capabilities. Raynor argues that some companies fail not because they formulate and implement bad strategies, but precisely because their strategies are great.[48] Pursuing an aggressive strategy of market leadership and domination also creates the possibility of total failure. The easy solution to the problem of strategy paradox is to see far enough into the future to make the right choices today. Failing that, you have to structure the organization so that it can adapt successfully when surprises crop up as the future unfolds.[49] Raynor acknowledges that successful planning in making the right choices will always trump strategic adaptation. However, given that predicting the future with any degree of certainty is impossible, organizations need to understand how to leverage the paradox for greatest success.

Raynor suggests that senior level executives work with longer planning horizons and therefore the strategic uncertainty they face is greater than that encountered at organizational levels.[50] According to Raynor, the ongoing debate between learning and emergent strategies over deliberate planning is a false dichotomy and that each approach is appropriate under certain conditions: a deliberate approach may be more effective under conditions of clarity and certainty and an emergent approach is more appropriate when dealing with rapidly-evolving and uncertain situations. At the end of the day, he acknowledges that each approach plays a critical role in an effective strategic leadership-strategic management program: "a deliberate strategy sets an organization on a path, and while traveling that path, the 'enacted' strategy emerges in response to the inevitable surprises and vagaries along the way."[51]

Conclusion

There is no one best way to conduct an effective strategic leadership and strategic management program. Organizational leader-managers will need to tailor their approach to the corporate culture, values, aspirations, environmental factors and business model. There are many strategic approaches and models that will help organizations move confidently and successfully into an uncertain future. But caution is advised—there are also a multiplicity of ways to get strategic leadership and strategic management wrong, either in the strategic thinking and planning phase or in the strategic implementation phase, or both. Here is a summary of some of the things to include and avoid in pursuing a strategic management process:

1. Avoid the ivory tower or black box syndrome and include members of the organization from all levels in the strategic planning and implementation. Make strategic planning both a top-down and bottom-up process.

2. Focus strategizing less on strategic fit with current resources and capabilities and more on strategic intent to guide development and acquisition of new resources and capabilities to accomplish innovative, visionary objectives in the future.

3. Ensure that strategic planning doesn't overshadow strategic thinking and hinder creativity, innovation and learning.

4. Promote a faster, leaner, more responsive strategic planning process that can keep pace with the speed of change in your organizational environment.

5. Strike a balance between the need to consider a multiplicity of factors and variables and the need to reach actionable decisions in a timely manner. Don't allow analysis paralysis or groupthink thwart your quest for an effective strategic agenda that will assist you in obtaining a competitive advantage in the marketplace.

6. Make appropriate assumptions as necessary to get moving on your strategic planning process but continue to monitor internal processes and the external environment and update those assumptions with facts as they become clear.

7. Avoid linear thinking and planning processes and simplification schemes that may obfuscate identifying key information and data to include in your decision making.

8. Establish a corporate culture that ensures strategic alignment from the shop floor to the executive offices—everyone should know how what they do at each level contributes to the overall accomplishment of the strategic agenda.

9. Be a real leader in formulating your organizational values and vision and setting your organization's course into an uncertain future. Communicate with your employees, get to know them well, and encourage the heart to help them through the throes of turbulent change.

10. Be sure that organizational vision, goals and objectives are clearly articulated and that appropriate metrics and the means to measure them are established and communicated. Take action in making adjustments to the strategic agenda based upon learning from the metrics feedback.

11. Monitor closely potential disruptive technologies and take appropriate action to ensure that they don't undermine organizational competitiveness.

12. If your organizational aim is market leadership and domination in your field, go for it and commit the necessary resources and capabilities to accomplish your purposes. Balance deliberate planning with strategic learning and emergent strategies. Identify future scenarios and contingency plans in your strategic planning to be prepared for whatever happens. Stay agile and be prepared to recommit resources and capabilities in other directions as necessary if the future doesn't unfold according to your planning assumptions.

In brief, strategic planning doesn't' guarantee organizational success, however, when done well, it will generally position organizations well for achieving success as they move into an uncertain future.

Conclusion

In order to deal effectively with white-water turbulence and chaos in today's organizational environment, organizations must first move from a hierarchical, industrial-age, command-and-control governance style to a more participative leadership-management approach. Organizational structures must become flatter which necessitates the need for knowledge and skills to be widely dispersed throughout the organization secured by the motivation of either shared success or failure. This change requires a high degree of organizational trust because information and knowledge must be shared throughout the organization—they can no longer be commodities reserved for the highest levels of the organization.

Freed from the chains of industrial-age emphasis on command and control, organizations can leverage new approaches and new tools to develop and deploy strategies that will be more effective. The approaches and models presented in this book suggest ways to unlock the latent creativity of leader-managers in an effort to develop and execute more dynamic plans and to be able to adapt effectively to evolving organizational environments.

Whenever people are first hired into an organization following academic degree completion or professional technical training, it is generally because of the technical skill sets they possess. Initially, they spend almost all of their time exercising those technical skills in completing the requirements of their job tasks. However, over time, they spend less time on their technical skill area as they begin to exercise basic leadership and management skills in supervisory roles. As they are promoted into higher positions of responsibility, they eventually are spending at least half of their time in leader-manager responsibilities. Some eventually end up spending most of their time on their leader-manager responsibilities and have little time in which to practice their technical skills.

Significantly, leadership and management are distinct yet complementary skill sets. Leader-managers in today's flatter organizations generally wear both hats. The manager's role is to ensure that all the work gets done in a timely and efficient manner consistent with all aspects of organizational policy. Management typically engages in problem solving to keep organizational systems operational and functioning. Management focuses on the delivery of goods and services in the present context. Management focuses on operational systems and thrives in stability.

The leader's role is to envision the future, share that vision, and help people move through the turbulence of change. Leadership focuses on the continued competitiveness and survivability of the organization in a future context. Leadership typically engages in decision making to make adjustments and affect changes to help move the organization into an uncertain future. Leadership focuses on people and thrives in turbulence.

There is an unfortunate, pervasive notion that although management can be learned, leadership cannot. Many believe that people are either born leaders or they are not. This is patently untrue. Although the study of leadership may not be approached in the same analytical, formulaic manner as traditional management studies, leadership can be learned. It involves practicing innovative thinking to create and communicate the organizational vision and developing a sincere concern and caring for people in discomfort as they move into a turbulent and uncertain future.

Leader-managers are responsible for developing strategies that balance organizational objectives with organizational resources and capabilities. A complete strategy is represented by the formula:

Strategy = Ends   +   Ways   + Means
or
Strategy = Objectives + Capabilities + Resources

Operational strategies are developed based upon current resources and capabilities and can be immediately implemented. As ambitious, stretch goals are envisioned, it requires a developmental strategy to acquire additional resources and capabilities to reach beyond present constraints.

An effective strategic leadership and management program should occur seamlessly through five phases which cycle back on each other: analysis, planning, implementation, measurement, and adjustment. Although strategic thinking and strategic planning are two distinct activities in this process, they do not need to be adversarial or incompatible; they can and should be complementary and mutually reinforcing. Although strategic planning initiatives are generally conducted on an annual or biannual basis, they are not once-and-done events. Strategic planning is a dynamic, never-ending process, not a static event.

Effective strategic leadership and management programs begin with internal and external scans which are then conducted continually thereafter as the organization responds and adjusts to feedback from internal and external sources. Written strategic plans that emerge from the planning process are not inviolate. The strategic planning process should include envisioning possible future scenarios and corresponding contingency planning. Plans must be constantly reviewed and adjusted as the future unfolds in unanticipated ways.

The mission statement describes the fundamental purpose of an organization. It is present-oriented and articulated using present tense verbs. It provides employees with a clear understanding of precisely what the organization does now and reveals how their daily work effort contributes to its accomplishment. A vision statement is a picture of the organization set in the future. It is generally articulated using future tense verbs. The vision statement should provide employees and stakeholders with a clear picture of the direction the organization is taking into the future.

Once the strategic plan is completed, implemented and adjusted for unanticipated factors, metrics should be set in place to track progress towards accomplishing organizational objectives. Dashboards and scorecards are useful graphical tools to provide leaders and managers critical performance information at a glance as they are intuitive snapshots of strategic and operational data. Although the terms are sometimes used interchangeably, there are important distinctions between them. Dashboards are typically used to monitor and display data about lower level operational processes while scorecards track higher level strategic goals and objectives in much greater detail.

In addition to setting the strategic vision, one of the most important tasks of strategic leadership is assisting organizational members through the psychological trauma of turbulence and change. This can be most effectively accomplished by demonstrating genuine caring and concern for employee welfare, modeling behavior, and establishing a visible presence in the workplace. Implementing a program of leadership and management by walking around can be a very effective way for helping employees through the turbulence of change.

Traditional problem solving and decision-making models suffer from two major shortcomings: first, they use linear approaches for what is in actuality a highly complex, interactive, nonlinear reality; and second, they employ various simplification strategies that distort the nature of the problem arena and ignore information that could prove key to problem resolution.

As our understanding of the implications of complexity expands, we must correspondingly adjust our understanding of the role of rationality and comprehensiveness in decision and policymaking. Today's leader-managers must reexamine traditional, classical approaches to decision making and problem solving processes in the light of emerging insights from the complexity sciences. The images created by visually graphing complex relationships suggest that when analyzed from an open-system, complexity perspective, there may be a rich wealth of additional information on trends, change, and dynamic structure hidden by ostensibly well-understood, linear, theoretical models.

For most organizational environments, complexity approaches offer a more comprehensive set of tools and strategies for accurately assessing real world systems and can produce more robust decisions, fewer unintended consequences, and problem resolutions more acceptable to a broader set of stakeholders. The transition to a systems-thinking approach to understanding organizations and the use of insights from the complexity sciences to reexamine traditional ideas about leadership and management are not minor tasks. They require focus and a good deal of energy. In pursuing these tasks, students and practitioners alike will develop a set of conceptual tools that will assist them in not only understanding the nature of our rapidly changing organizational environments but in actually enjoying and thriving in the white-water organizational turbulence of today.

Strategic failure is most typically the outcome of flawed strategic planning processes or errors made in the implementation of the resulting strategic agenda. Occasionally, strategic failure may result simply from the bold commitment of resources and capabilities based upon assumption that don't play out as the uncertain future unfolds. Whatever the reason, organizations will generally do better moving into an uncertain future by integrating strategic thinking into a strategic planning exercise and then adapting the resulting deliberate strategic plan with emergent strategies as unanticipated events occur. By retaining a certain degree of flexibility in reassigning critical resources and capabilities should planning assumptions not play out as expected, organizations will better position themselves for the turbulent change and the hyper-competition characteristic of our organizational world today.

End Notes

Introduction

[1] Maxwell, John C. *Developing the Leader Within You.* Thomas Nelson, 1993.

[2] Hock, Lee. *Birth of the Chaordic Age.* Berrett-Koehler Publishers, 2000.

[3] Taylor, Frederick Winslow. The *Principles of Scientific Management.* Mineola, NY: Dover Publications, Inc., 1998; Fayol, Henri. *General and Industrial Management.* translated by Irwin Gray. Ieee., Rev Sub edition, 1984; Weber, Max, *Economy and Society: An Outline of Interpretive Sociology*, University of California Press, 1978; Gulick, Luther, and Lyndall Urwick, eds. *Papers on the Science of Administration.* New York: Institute of Public Administration, 1937.

[4] Porter, Michael E. *Competitive Strategy.* The Free Press, 1980. In Charles Hill and Gareth Jones, *Strategic Management: An Integrated Approach*, Houghton-Mifflin Company, 8th Edition, 2008, 64-65, the authors point out that the Five Forces Model breaks down in the highly turbulent, rapidly changing business environments of today. Building on the concept of punctuated equilibrium, Porter argues in *The Competitive Advantage of Nations*, Free Press, 1990, that following periods of hyper-turbulence triggered by innovation and change, industry environments settle down once again into more stable, predictable patterns, and the Five Forces Model once again becomes useful in the corporate environment. Richard D'Avani in *Hypercompetition*, Free Press, 1994, argues against the punctuated equilibrium proposal pointing out that many industries today are engaged in permanent innovation and competitive change.

[5] Kotter, John. *Leading Change.* Harvard Business School Press, 1996, 29.

[6] Mintzberg, Henry. *The Rise and Fall of Strategic Planning.* The Free Press, 1994.

[7] Ibid.

[8] In Mintzberg, Henry, Ahlstrand, Bruce, and Lampel, Joseph. *Strategy Bites Back: It is Far More and Less, Than You Ever Imagined.* Pearson Prentice Hall, 2005, 30.

Chapter One, "Theory, Models, Metaphor and Paradigms"

[1] See Max A. Eckstein, "The Comparative Mind: Metaphor in Comparative Education," *Comparative Education Review* 27, 1983: 311-323. Eckstein distinguishes between theories, metaphors, models, and paradigms in this way: *Metaphor* is the figure of speech in which a name or a descriptive term is transferred to an object different from, but analogous to, the one to which it is properly applicable. A *paradigm* is a pattern or exemplar. A *theory* is a scheme or system of ideas held to explain or account for a set of facts or phenomena, or a statement of what are held to be general laws, principles, or causes. A *model* refers to a representation of a theory in some kind of structural form; here the phenomena are related to one another in terms of the set of ideas composing the theory. Eckstein concludes that ". . . any theory, model, or paradigm is likely to comprise a major metaphor (or set of metaphors); alternatively, any metaphor suggests or assumes a theory, model, or paradigm." (p. 322)

[2] Nagel, Ernest. *The Structure of Science: Problems in the Logic of Scientific Explanation.* New York: Harcourt Brace, 108.

[3] Kuhn, Thomas S. *The Structure of Scientific Revolutions.* Chicago: University of Chicago Press, 1970, 184.

[4] Eckstein, 311.

[5] Kuhn, Ibid.

[6] Frankfort-Nachmias, Chava, and Nachmias, David. *Research Methods in the Social Sciences.* New York: St. Martin's Press, 1992. The authors suggest that in its broadest sense, any conceptualization, as opposed to mere observation, is theory. In a narrower sense, theory is a logical-deductive system consisting of a set of interrelated concepts from which testable propositions or hypotheses can be deductively derived.

[7] The model of four distinct levels of theory—classification systems; taxonomies; conceptual frameworks; and theoretical systems—is adapted from Parson, Talcott, and Shils, Edward A. *Toward a General Theory of Action.* New York: Harper & Row, 1962.

[8] Although not generally scientifically valid, pollsters frequently conduct polling place exit interviews in an attempt to overall predict voter preferences and election outcomes.

[9] Leadership-Management theorists frequently differentiate between the outcomes of their ideas in the context of the three major types of organizations where they might be applied—business corporations, public government agencies, and non-profit organizations.

[10] de Bono, Edward. *Six Thinking Hats: An Essential Approach to Business Management.* Little, Brown, & Company, 1985.

[11] McGregor, Douglas. *The Human Side of Enterprise.* New York, McGraw-Hill. 1960. Douglas McGregor of MIT Sloan School of Management described Theory X and Theory Y in the early 1960s. They are contrasting models of workforce motivation. Theory X assumes that employees are inherently lazy and will try to shirk work when possible. They inherently dislike work and will avoid responsibility. As a result, managers need to closely supervise employees and develop comprehensive systems of controls. Theory Y assumes that employees may be self-motivated and enjoy mental and physical work. Given the right support and encouragement, they will exercise self-direction and self-control in accomplishing tasks and objectives to which they are committed.

[12] Lewin, Kurt. *Field Theory in Social Science; Selected Theoretical Papers.* D. Cartwright (Ed.). New York: Harper & Row, 1951.

[13] Christensen, Clayton M., Anthony, Scott D., and Roth, Erik A. *Seeing What's Next: Using the Theories of Innovation to Predict Industry Change.* Harvard Business School Press, 2004, vii.

[14] Christensen, Clayton M., and Raynor, Michael E. *The Innovator's Solution: Creating and Sustaining Successful Growth.* Harvard Business School Press,

2003. In *See What's Next: Using Theories of Innovation to predict Industry Change*, Harvard Business School Press, 2004, Christensen makes a strong statement about the usefulness of theory for business practitioners: "Using theory in a meticulous, rigorous fashion can shine a light where darkness once prevailed. It can thankfully bring an end to an era when hucksters and augurs made their livings selling splendid tales to desperate disciples who needed something, anything, to help guide their decision-making processes. Using theory allows us to see the future more clearly and act more confidently to shape our destiny."

[15] Ibid.

[16] Ibid.

[17] Verne, Jules. *Journey to the Center of the Earth*. Malleson translation; Ward, Lock & Co., 1877.

[18] Collins, Jim. *How the Mighty Fall and Why Come Companies Never Give In*. HarperCollins, Publisher, Inc. 2009, 20.

[19] Box, George E. P., and Draper, Norman R. *Empirical Model-Building and Response Surfaces*, Wiley, 1987, 424.

[20] The Bonini Paradox was suggested by Stanford business professor Charles Bonini in Bonini, Charles P. *Simulation of Information and Decision Systems in the Firm*. Prentice-Hall, 1963.

[21] Gaddis, John Lewis. *The Landscape of History: How Historians Map the Past*. Oxford University Press, 2002, 32-34.

[22] Ibid. Gaddis discusses this idea using the metaphor of maps, a graphical model of the topography of the earth. He suggests that cartographic verification is entirely relative—"it depends upon how well the mapmaker achieves a fit between the landscape that's being mapped and the requirements of those for whom the map is being made."

[23] Eckstein.

[24] Wirth, Ross A. Lewin/Schein's Change Theory. 2004. URL: http://www.entarga.com/orgchange/lewinschein.pdf

[25] Kotter, John. *Leading Change*. Boston, MA: Harvard Business School Press, 1996.

[26] Collins, 20.

[27] Ibid.

[28] Osterwalder, Alexander, and Pigneur, Yves. *Business Model Generation: A Handbook for Visionaries, Game Changers, and Challengers*. Wiley, 2010, 3.

[29] Johnson, Mark W., Christensen, Clayton M., and Kagermann, Henning. "Reinventing your Business Model," in *HBR's 10 Must Reads on Strategy*. Harvard Business Review Press, 2011, 103-122, 122. Originally published in *Harvard Business Review*, September, 1996.

[30] Ibid., 106.

[31] Morgan, Gareth. *Images of Organization*. Thousand Oaks, CA: Sage Publications, 1996.

[32] Ibid.

[33] Ibid.

[34] Ibid. Gaddis suggests that theory sometimes begins with metaphors, 68.

[35] Ibid.

[36] Gaddis, 128.

[37] Kuhn, Thomas S. *The Structure of Scientific Revolutions*. Chicago: The University of Chicago Press, 1962. For a review and analysis of Kuhn's proposals concerning paradigms and paradigm shifts, see also Lisa J. "Thomas Kuhn's *The Structure of Scientific Revolutions*." *ETC: A Review of General Semantics*, Spring, 2000, Vol. 57, Issue 1, 59-75.

[38] Ibid.

[39] Ibid.

[40] Ibid.

[41] Ibid.

[42] Luvaas, Jay. *The Legacy of the Civil War: The European Inheritance.* University of Chicago Press, 1959; see also Russell F. Weigley, *The American Way of War: A History of United States Military Strategy and Policy.* Bloomington: Indiana University Press, 1973, Chapter 6, "Napoleonic Strategy: R.E. Lee and the Confederacy."

[43] Kuhn.

Additional Reading

Cohen Jon. "The March of Paradigms." *Science*, 1999, 26 March, Vol. 283, Issue 5410.

Raymo, Chet. "A New Paradigm for Thomas Kuhn." *Scientific American*, September, 2000, Vol. 283 Issue 3, 104-106.

Chapter Two, "A Systems Thinking Approach to Understanding Organizations"

[1] Meadows, Donella H. "Places to Intervene in a System." *Whole Earth*, 1997, Winter, Issue 91, 78-84 and Meadows, Donella H. "Dancing with Systems." *Whole Earth*, 2001, Winter, Issue 106: 58-63.

[2] Bertanlannfy, Ludwig von. "The History and Status of General Systems Theory." *Academy of Management Journal*, 1972, Vol. 15, Issue 4.

[3] Arnold, Darrell. "Hegel and Ecologically Oriented System Theory." *Journal of Philosophy: A Cross Disciplinary Inquiry*, 2011, Vol. 7, Issue 16, 53-64.

[4] Wiener, Norbert. *Cybernetics: Or Control and Communication in the Animal and the Machine.* John Wiley & Sons, 1949. See also Conway, Flo, and Siegelman, Jim. *Dark Hero of the Information Age: In Search of Norbert Wiener, The Father of Cybernetics.* Basic Books. 2006.

[5] Bertalanffy, Ludwig von. *General System Theory: Foundations, Development, Application.* New York: G. Braziller, 1968.

[6] Bertalanffy included a sixth element of an open system—the system boundary. Bertalanffy posited that open systems have porous boundaries through which useful feedback can readily be exchanged and closed systems have hard boundaries through which little information is exchanged. Organizations that try to operate as closed systems (Bureaucracies, monopolies and stagnating systems) have impermeable boundaries that create unhealthy outcomes. In today's highly turbulent, rapidly evolving environments, system boundaries can be very difficult to identify since they are constantly evolving and changing as well.

[7] Gaddis, John Lewis. *The Landscape of History: How Historians Map the Past.* Oxford University Press, 2002, 22. Gaddis makes a similar comment about the facility with which historians can change the scale of analysis to selectively emphasize those historical elements which they deem most important to describing and explaining an historical incident or event.

[8] Argyris, Chris., and Schön, Donald A. *Organizational Learning: A Theory of Action Perspective.* Reading, Addison Wesley, 1978.

[9] Senge, Peter M. *The Fifth Discipline.* Doubleday, 1990.

[10] Argyris and Schön.

[11] Weick, Karl E. *Sensemaking in Organizations.* Sage Publications, 1995.

[12] Aronson suggested that an organization is like an organism, each of whose cells contains a particular, partial, changing image if itself in relation to the whole. An organization's activities and practice stem from those very images. Organization is an artifact of individual ways of representing

organization. Aronson, Daniel. "Introduction to Systems Thinking." 1998, *Thinking Page*. Retrieved December 5, 2008, from http://www.thinking.net

[13] *Merriam-Webster's Collegiate Dictionary*, 11th Edition, Merriam-Webster Inc., 2008.

[14] Aronson.

[15] Bellinger, Gene. *Systems Thinking: A Disciplined Approach*, 2005. Retrieved December 5, 2008, from http://www.systems-thinking.org/stada/stada.htm.

[16] Meadows, Donella H. *Thinking in Systems*. White River Junction, VT: Chelsea Green Publishing, 2008.

Additional Reading

Argyris, Chris. *Behind the Front Page*. San Francisco: Jossey Bass, 1974.

Checkland, Peter. "Systems Theory and Management Thinking." *American Behavioral Scientist*, 1994, September/October, Vol. 38, Issue 1, 75-91.

Emery, Fred E. (ed.) *Systems Thinking: Selected Readings*. Penguin, 1969.

Gharajedaghi, Jamshid. *Systems Thinking: Managing Chaos and Complexity*. Butterworth-Heinemann, 2005.

Haines, Stephen G. *The Manager's Pocket Guide to Systems Thinking and Learning*. HRD Press, 1998.

Kast, Fremont E., and Rosenweig, James E. *Organization and Management: A Systems Approach*. McGraw Hill, 1970.

Kast, Fremont E., and Rosenweig, James E. "General Systems Theory: Applications for Organization and Management." *Academy of Management Journal*, 1972, 447-465.

Scott, W. Richard. *Organizations: Rational, Natural, and Open Systems*. 4th Ed. Prentice Hall, 1998.

Weinberg, Gerald M. *An Introduction to General Systems Thinking*. Dorset House Publishing, 1975.

Chapter Three, "The Basics of Strategy: What Does It Mean and Where Does It Come From?"

[1] Builder, Carl H. *The Army in the Strategic Planning Process*. Santa Monica, CA: The Rand Corporation, 1989, 5.

[2] Wylie, Joseph C. *Military Strategy: A General Theory of Power Control*. Annapolis: Naval Institute Press, 1989. To Wylie, *control* was the essence of strategy.: "The primary aim of the strategist in the conduct of war is some selected degree of control of the enemy for the strategist's own purpose; this is achieved by control of the pattern of war; and this control of the pattern of war is had by manipulation of the center of gravity of war to the advantage of the strategist and the disadvantage of the opponent."

[3] Lykke, Arthur F., Jr. "Defining Military Strategy."1997. Reprint from *Military Review*, 1989, Vol. 77, No. 1, Jan.-Feb., 183-186. It is interesting to note that Lykke's strategy model of resources, capabilities, and objectives roughly correlates to Christensen's organizational capabilities framework model of resources, processes, and values—three classes of factors which Christensen asserts affect what an organization can and cannot do. See Christensen, Clayton M. *The Innovator's Dilemma: The Revolutionary Book That Will Change the Way You Do Business*. Harper Business, 1997, 186.

[4] Hamel, Gary, and Prahalad, C. K. *Competing for the Future*. New York: Free Press, 1989.

[5] Ibid.

[6] Yarger, H. Richard. *Towards a Theory of Strategy: Art Lykke and the Army War College Strategy Model*. U.S. Army War College, Carlisle Barracks, Carlisle, PA, 1997.

[7] See Liddell, Henry, and George, Robert Scott, *A Greek-English Lexicon*, on Perseus Digital Library, for a comprehensive etymology of the term *strategy*.

[8] Fuller, J.F.C. *The Generalship of Alexander the Great.* New York: De Capo Press, 1960.

[9] Clausewitz, Carl von. *On War.* Indexed Edition. Edited and translated by Michael Howard and Peter Paret. Princeton, NJ: Princeton University Press, 1976.

[10] Jomini, Baron Antoine Henri de. *The Art of War.* Mechanicsburg, PA: Stackpole Books, 1992.

[11] Clausewitz.

[12] Quoted in Paret, Peter, Craig, Gordon A., and Gilbert, Felix. Eds. *Makers of Modern Strategy from Machiavelli to the Nuclear Age.* Princeton, NJ: Princeton University Press, 1986, 190.

[13] Ibid.

[14] Jomini.

[15] Sun Tzu, and Sun Pin. *The Complete Art of War.* Translated by Ralph D. Sawyer. Boulder, CO: Westview Press, 1996. In this excellent translation, Sawyer also provides a detailed commentary and analysis of Sun Tzu's approach to strategy.

[16] Musashi, Miyamoto. *A Book of Five Rings: The Classic Guide to Strategy.* Translated by Victor Harris. Woodstock, NY: The Overlook Press, 1974.

[17] Ibid.

[18] Ibid.

[19] Clausewitz.

[20] Drucker, Peter F. *The Practice of Management.* New York: Harper & Row, 1956.

[21] Selznick, Philip. *Leadership in Administration: A Sociological Interpretation.* New York: Harper & Row, 1957.

[22] Chandler, Alfred. *Strategy and Structure: Chapters in the History of Industrial Enterprise*. New York: Doubleday, 1962.

[23] Ansoff, H. Igor. *Corporate Strategy: An Analytic Approach to Business Policy for Growth and Expansion*. New York: McGraw-Hill, 1965. Ansoff later collaborated with DeClerck and Hayes in describing the evolution from strategic planning to strategic management in Ansoff, H. Igor, DeClerck, R.P., and Hayes, R.L. Eds. *From Strategic Planning to Strategic Management*. New York: John Wiley & Sons, 1976.

[24] Ackoff, Russell L. *A Concept of Corporate Planning*. John Wiley & Sons, Inc., 1970.

[25] Ackoff, Russell L., and Emery, Frederick E. *On Purposeful Systems: An Interdisciplinary Analysis of Individual and Social Behavior as a System of Purposeful Events*. Chicago: Aldine-Atherton, 1972.

[26] Steiner, George. *Strategic Planning: What Every Manager Must Know*. New York: Free Press, 1979.

[27] Porter, Michael. *Competitive Strategy: Techniques for Analyzing Industries and Competitors*. New York: The Free Press, 1980.

[28] Ghyczy, Tiha von, Bolko, Oetinger von, and Bassford, Christopher. *Clausewitz on Strategy, Inspiration and Insight from a Master Strategist*. New York: John Wiley & Sons, Inc, 2001.

[29] Ibid.

[30] McNeilly, Mark R. *Sun Tzu and the Art of Business: Six Strategic Principles for Managers*. Revised Edition. Oxford University Press, 2011; Krause, Donald G. *The Art of War for Executives: Ancient Knowledge for Today's Business Professional*. Perigee Trade, 2007.

Additional Reading

An early example of the development and application of political strategy can be found in Machiavelli, Niccolo. *The Art of War*. Revised Edition. New York: Da Capo Press, 1965.

Two excellent edited works on the development and evolution of military strategy are Paret, Peter, ed., *Makers of Modern Strategy from Machiavelli to the Nuclear Age.* Princeton, NJ: Princeton University Press, 1986; and Murray, Williamson, Knox, MacGregor, and Bernstein, Alvin. *The Making of Strategy: Rulers, States, and War.* New York: Cambridge University Press, 1994.

Chapter Four, "The Relationship between Organizational Environment and Strategy"

[1] Emery, Fred E., and Trist, Eric L. "The Causal Texture of Organizational Environments." *Human Organization*, 1965, Vol. 18, 21-32.

[2] Stacey, Ralph. "Management and the Science of Complexity: If Organizational Life is Nonlinear, Can Business Strategies Prevail?" *Research Technology Management*, 1996, May/June, Vol. 39, Issue 3, 8-10.

[3] Schumpeter, J. A. "The Historical Approach to the Analysis of Business Cycles," in *Essays: On Entrepreneurs, Innovations, Business Cycles, and the Evolution of Capitalism.* New Brunswick, N.J. and London: Transaction, 1949.

[4] Lindberg, Curt, et al. "Life at the Edge of Chaos." *Physician Executive*, January/February, 1998, Vol. 24, Issue 1, 6-20.

[5] Emery and Trist.

[6] For a more detailed account of Deming's and Juran's philosophy on quality, see Landesberg, Phil. "In the Beginning, There Were Deming and Juran." *Journal for Quality & Participation*, November/December, Vol. 22, Issue 6, 1999, 59-61.

[7] 238 companies that made the 1989 Fortune 500 list were gone from the 1999 list. Collins and Porras observe that only 71 of the original 1955 Fortune 500 list were still there forty years later, in Collins, James C., and Porras, Jerry. *Built to Last: Successful Habits of Visionary Companies.* HarperBusiness, 1994.

Additional Reading

Anderson, Philip. "Complexity Theory and Organization Science." *Organization Science: A Journal of the Institute of Management Sciences*, 1999, May/June, Vol. 10, Issue 3, 216-232.

Begun, James W. "Chaos and Complexity: Frontiers of Organization Science." *Journal of Management Inquiry*, 1994, December, Vol. 3, Issue 4, 329-335.

Crossan, Mary M., et al. "The Improvising Organization: Where Planning Meets Opportunity." *Organizational Dynamics*, 1996, Spring, Vol. 24, Issue 4, 20-35.

Deming, W. Edwards. *Out of the Crisis*. Massachusetts Institute of Technology, 1982.

Hamel, Gary, and Prahalad, C.K. *Competing for the Future*. Boston: Harvard Business School Press, 1994.

Juran, Joseph M. *Juran's Quality Handbook*. Mcgraw Hill Professional; 5th Edition, 2000.

Kiel, L. Douglas. *Managing Chaos and Complexity in Government: A New Paradigm for Managing Change, Innovation, and Organizational Renewal*. San Francisco: Jossey Bass, 1994.

Senge, Peter M. *The Fifth Discipline: The Art and Practice of the Learning Organization*. New York: Doubleday, 1990.

Zohar, Danah. "What Would A Quantum Organization Look Like?" *Management Review*, 1998, March, Vol. 87, Issue 3, 56-58.

Chapter 5—"Understanding Leadership and Management"

[1] Founded in 1881 at the University of Pennsylvania, the Wharton School was the world's first collegiate business school. Founded in 1898, The University of Chicago Booth School of Business was the first U.S. business

school to offer a PhD program. The College of Commerce was founded at the University of California, Berkeley, in 1898. Later renamed the Haas School of Business, it was the first business school founded at a public university. The Tuck School of Business, founded in 1900 at Dartmouth College, was the first graduate school of business in the U.S. to offer a master's degree in business administration entitled "Master of Commercial Science" (MCS). Founded in 1908, Harvard Business School was the first school to offer a degree called the Master of Business Administration (MBA) in 1910.

[2] Taylor, Frederick Winslow. *Shop Management.* New York, NY: American Society of Mechanical Engineers, 1903. It began as a speech by Taylor to a meeting of the ASME, which published it in pamphlet form which was later republished by Harper and Brothers in 1912. Taylor's more complete treatise on Scientific Management was published in Taylor, Frederick Winslow. *The Principles of Scientific Management.* New York: Harper & Brothers, 1911.

[3] Calas, Marta and Smircich, Linda. "Reading Leadership as a Form of Cultural Analysis," in *Emerging Leadership Vistas.* James G. Hunt, B. Rajaram Baliga, H. Peter Dachler and Chester A. Schriesheim, Eds. Lanham, MD: Lexington Books, 1988.

[4] Bass, Bernard M. *Bass & Stogdill's Handbook of Leadership,* 3rd Edition. New York: The Free Press, 1990.

[5] Rost, Joseph. *Leadership for the Twenty-First Century.* New York: Praeger, 1991.

[6] Daft, Richard L. *The Leadership Experience.* Mason, OH: South Western, 2008.

[7] Maxwell, John C. *Developing the Leader Within You.* Nashville, TN: Thomas Nelson, 1993.

[8] Rost. This inability to precisely label and characterize it was a primary contributing factor to leadership not being included in the early school of management programs of instruction.

[9] Ciulla, Joanne B. "Leadership Ethics: Mapping the Territory." *Business Ethics Quarterly*, 1995, Vol. 5, Issue 1, 5-28.

[10] Kotter, John. *Leading Change*. Boston, MA: Harvard Business School Press, 1996.

[11] Kouzes, James M. and Posner, Barry Z. *The Leadership Challenge*. San Francisco: Jossey-Bass, 1995.

[12] Burns, James MacGregor. *Leadership*. New York: Harper & Row, 1979.

[13] Each of these monographs on leadership are excellent and highly recommended by this author: Welter, Bill, and Egmon, Jean. *The Prepared Mind of a Leader: Eight Skills Leaders Use to Innovate, Make Decisions, and Solve Problems*. San Francisco: Jossey-Bass, 2006; Lencioni, Patrick. *The Five Dysfunctions of a Team: A Leadership Fable*. San Francisco: Jossey-Bass, 2002; Covey, Stephen R. *The 7 Habits of Highly Effective People*. New York: Fireside, Simon and Schuster, 1989; Maxwell, John C. *The 21 Irrefutable Laws of Leadership*. Nashville, TN: Thomas Nelson, 1998; Goldstein, Jefrfrey, Hazy, James K., and Lichtenstein, Benyamin B. *Complexity and the Nexus of Leadership: Leveraging Nonlinear Science to Create Ecologies of Innovation*, Palgrave MacMillan, 2010.

[14] Hill, Charles W.L. and Jones, Gareth R. *Strategic Management: An Integrated Approach*. 8th Edition. Boston: Houghton Mifflin Company, 2008.

[15] Ibid.

[15] Kotter.

[16] Ibid.

[17] Ibid. Kotter further identifies four potential situations and their consequences. When neither leadership nor management functions are in place, the change transformation is doomed to failure from the beginning. If only one or the other is working well, the change transition is in doubt but will probably suffer from short-term or long-term challenges. But if both leadership and management functions are working well in concert with

each other, the change initiative will likely go well and achieve successful short-term and long-term results.

Additional Reading

Bridges, William. *Managing Transitions: Making the Most of Change.* 2nd Edition. Cambridge, MA: De Capo Press, 2003.

Greenleaf, Robert K. *Servant Leadership.* Mahwah, NJ: Paulist Press, 1977.

Lewin, Kurt. "Action Research and Minority Problems." *Journal of Social Issues.* 1946, Vol. 2, Issue 4: 34-46.

Vaill, Peter. *Managing as a Performing Art: New Ideas for a World of Chaotic Change.* San Francisco: Jossey Bass, 1991.

Chapter 6—"Organizational Change Models"

[1] Leana, Carrie R. "Stability and Change as Simultaneous Experiences in Organizational Life." *Academy of Management Review*, 2000, October, Vol. 25 Issue 4, 753-759.

[2] Adapted from Leana, Ibid.

[3] Lawrence, Paul R. and Lorsch, Jay W. *Organization and Environment: Managing Differentiation and Integration.* Boston: Graduate School of Business Administration, Harvard University, 1967.

[4] Bertalanffy, Ludwig von. *General System Theory: Foundations, Development, Application.* New York: G. Braziller, 1968.

[5] Lawrence, Paul R. and Lorsch, Jay W. "Differentiation and Integration in Complex Organizations." *Administrative Science Quarterly*, 1967, Vol. 12, 1-30.

[6] Burns, Tom, and Stalker, George M. *The Management of Innovation.* Chicago: Quadrangle Books, 1961.

[7] Katz, Daniel, and Kahn, Robert L. *The Social Psychology of Organizations*. 2nd Edition. New York: John Wiley, 1978. (Note: 1st ed., 1966.)

[8] Hannan, Michael T. and Freeman John. *Organizational Ecology*. Cambridge, MA, Harvard University Press, 1989.

[9] Trist, Eric L. "The Evolution of Sociotechical Systems as a Conceptual Framework and as an Action Research Program" in *Perspectives on Organization Design and Behavior*. Edited by A. H. Van de Ven and W. F. Joyce. New York: Wiley—Interscience, 1975. One of the most important outcomes of socio-tech research was the notion that the development of semi-autonomous work groups within an organization can lead to much greater organizational productivity and effectiveness in the face of a rapidly-changing, organizational environment.

[10] Huber, George P., and Glick, William H., Eds. *Organizational Change and Redesign: Ideas and Insights for Improving Performance*. New York: Oxford University Press, Inc., 1993.

[11] Lawrence and Lorsch described the proliferation of areas in which man was exploring the unknown and "pushing back the frontiers of knowledge." Their model of the development of knowledge reflects the expanding body of knowledge and complexity confronting organizations and the resultant rapidly accelerating pace of change.

[12] These four strategies are adapted from Huber and Glick. The fourth strategy refers to loose couplings and slack resources. From a systems-thinking perspective, everything in the system environment is interrelated, interconnected and interdependent. The term "loose couplings" refers to the notion that this interconnectivity is more relaxed and thus affords greater flexibility. "Slack resources" are resources that are not constrained and likewise provide greater flexibility in strategy making in an environment of turbulence and uncertainty.

[13] Kurt Lewin theorized a three-stage model of change that has come to be known as the unfreeze-move-refreeze model. Edgar Schein provided further detail for a more comprehensive model of change calling this approach "cognitive redefinition." See: Wirth, Ross A. (2004). Lewin/

Schein's Change Theory. URL: http://www.entarga.com/orgchange/lewinschein.pdf.

[14] Kotter, John. *Leading Change*. Boston, MA: Harvard Business School Press, 1996.

[15] Wyman, O. "Discontinuous Change: The Unique Challenges of Radical Transformation." *Delta Organization and Leadership*. Marsh, Mercer & Kroll, 2003. http://www.oliverwyman.com/ow/pdf_files/Discontinuous_Change_POV.pdf

Additional Reading

Argyris, Chris, and Schon, Donald. *Organizational Learning: A Theory of Action Perspective*. Reading, MA: Addison-Wesley, 1978.

Carr, Adrian. "The Learning Organization New Lessons/ Thinking for the Management of Change and Management Development." *Journal of Management Development*, 1997, Vol. 16, Issue 4, 224-231.

Dannemiller, Kathleen D., and Jacobs, Robert W. "Changing the Way Organizations Change: A Revolution of Common Sense." *Journal of Applied Behavioral Science*, 1992, December, Vol. 28, Issue 4, 480-498.

Gladwell, Malcolm. *The Tipping Point: How Little Things Can Make a Big Difference*. New York: Little, Brown, and Company, 2000.

Goldstein, Jeffrey. *The Unshackled Organization: Facing the Challenge of Unpredictability Through Spontaneous Reorganization*. Portland, OR: Productivity Press, 1994.

Kast, Fremont E., and Rosenweig, James E. *Organization and Management: A Systems Approach*. New York: McGraw Hill, 1970.

Kast, Fremont E., and Rosenweig, James E. "General Systems Theory: Applications for Organization and Management." *Academy of Management Journal*, 1972, 447-465.

Morel, Benoit, and Ramanujam, Rangaraj. "Through the Looking Glass of Complexity: The Dynamics of Organizations as Adaptive and Evolving." *Organization Science: A Journal of the Institute of Management Sciences*, 1999, May/June, Vol. 10, Issue 3, 278-293.

Newman, Karen L. "Organizational Transformation during Institutional Upheaval." *Academy of Management Review*, 2000, July, Vol. 25, Issue 3, 602-619.

Peters, Tom. *The Tom Peters Seminar: Crazy Times Call for Crazy Organizations.* London: Macmillan, 1994.

Chapter 7—"Strategic Leadership and Strategic Management: Thinking and Planning Strategically"

[1] Welter, Bill, and Egmon, Jean. *The Prepared Mind of a Leader.* San Francisco: Jossey-Bass, 2006.

[2] Grove, Andy. *Only the Paranoid Survive.* New York: Currency Doubleday, 1996.

[3] Quoted by Kevin Nourse, "Tackling 21st Century Challenges through Strategic Leadership", AAPA Annual Convention, New Orleans, September 12, 2006. Ansel Adams, the famed photographer, once made a profound observation in a similar vein: "There is nothing worse than a sharp picture of a fuzzy concept."

[4] Wooton, Simon, & Horne, Terry. *Strategic Thinking: A Step-by-Step Approach to Strategy.* Second Edition. Sterling, VA: Kogan Page Ltd., 2002.

[5] Mintzberg, Henry. "The Fall and Rise of Strategic Planning." *Harvard Business Review*, 1994, January/February, Vol. 72, Issue 1, 107-114.

[6] Welter and Egmon, 2006.

[7] Lykke, Arthur F., Jr. "Defining Military Strategy." *Military Review*, 1989, Vol. 77, No. 1, Jan.-Feb., 1989, 183-186.

[8] Paret, Peter, Craig, Gordon A., and Gilbert, Felix., Eds. *Makers of Modern Strategy from Machiavelli to the Nuclear Age*. Princeton, NJ: Princeton University Press, 1986.

[9] Drucker, Peter. *The Age of Discontinuity*. New York: Harper & Row, 1968.

[10] Graetz, F. "Strategic Thinking versus Strategic Planning: Towards Understanding the Complementarities." *Management Decision*, 2002, Vol. 40, Issue 5/6, 456-462.

[11] Ibid.

[12] Mintzberg, Henry. *The Rise and Fall of Strategic Planning: Reconceiving Roles for Planning, Plans, Planners*. New York: The Free Press, 1994.

[13] Ibid.

[14] Ibid. In a similar vein, in "Places to Intervene in a System," Meadows comments that numbers are the least powerful of all leverage points in changing an organization: "Numbers are last on my list of leverage points. Diddling with details, arranging the deck chairs on the *Titanic*. Probably ninety-five percent of our attention goes to numbers, but there's not a lot of power in them." Meadows, Donella H., "Places to Intervene in a System." *Whole Earth*, Winter, 1997, Issue 91, 78-84.

[15] Adapted from *Performance Measurement Concepts and Techniques*, American Society for Public Administration (ASPA) Center for Accountability and Performance (CAP).

[16] Emery, Fred E., and Trist, Eric L. "The Causal Texture of Organizational Environments." *Human Organization*, 1965, Vol. 18, 21-32.

[17] Kotter, John. *Leading Change*. Boston, MA: Harvard Business School Press, 1996.

[18] The term *Big Hairy Audacious Goal* (BHAG) was introduced by James Collins and Jerry Porras in "Building Your Company's Vision." *Harvard Business Review*, 1996, Sep-Oct. A BHAG encourages companies to define

visionary goals that are more strategic and emotionally compelling. In the article, the authors define a BHAG as a form of vision statement, " . . . an audacious 10-to-30-year goal to progress towards an envisioned future."

[19] Quoted in Nixon, Richard. *Six Crises.* Doubleday Publishing, 1962.

[20] Kaplan, Robert S., and Norton, David P. "Using the Balanced Scorecard as a Strategic Management System." *Harvard Business Review,* 1996, January-February, 75-85.

[21] Ibid.

[22] Ibid.

[23] Senge, Peter M. *The Fifth Discipline.* Doubleday, 1990.

Additional Reading

Bamford, Charles E., and West, G. Page, III. *Strategic Management: Value Creation, Sustainability, and Performance.* Mason, OH: South-Western Cenage Learning, 2010.

Birnbaum, Bill. *Strategic Thinking: A Four-Piece Puzzle.* Central Oregon: Douglas Mountain Publishing, 2004.

Bradford, Robert W., and Duncan, J. Peter, with Tarcy, Brian. *Simplified Strategic Planning: A No-Nonsense Guide for Busy People Who Want Results Fast.* Worcester, MA: Chandler House Press, 2000.

Brown, Mark Graham. "Improving Your Organization's Vision." *Journal for Quality & Participation,* 1998, Sep/ Oct, Vol. 21, Issue 5, 18-21.

Clark, Scott. "Sealed with a SWOT: Initial Steps Toward Needed Strategic Planning." *Houston Business Journal,* 1999, Vol. 30, Issue 15, 28.

Dalton, Jim. "In Search of Strategy." *Association Management,* 2001, June, Vol. 53, Issue 6, 70-74.

DeGeus, A. P. "Planning as Learning." Boston: MA: *Harvard Business Review*, 1988, March/April, 70-74.

Eisenhardt, Kathleen M. and Sull, Donald N. "Strategy as Simple Rules." Boston, MA: *Harvard Business Review*, 2001, January, Vol. 79, Issue 1, 106-116.

Eisenhardt, Kathleen M. "Strategy as Strategic Decision Making." *Sloan Management Review*, 1999, Spring, Vol. 40, Issue 3, 65-72.

Fitzroy, Peter, and Hulbert, James. *Strategic Management: Creating Value in Turbulent Times*. Danvers, MA: John Wiley and Sons, 2005.

Joy, Earl R. "Make the Future Happen: A Model for Strategic Planning." *Economic Development Review*, 1999, Vol. 16, Issue 2, 33-34.

Kolzow, David. "A Perspective on Strategic Planning: What's Your Vision? *Economic Development Review*, 1999, Vol. 16, Issue 2, 5-9.

Liedtka, J. M. "Linking Strategic Thinking with Strategic Planning." *Strategy and Leadership*, 1998, Vol. 26, Issue 4, 30-35.

Mintzberg, H, Ahlstrand, B., and Lampel, J. *Strategy bites back: It is far more and less, than you ever imagined*. Pearson Prentice Hall, 2005.

Morrison, James L. "From Strategic Planning to Strategic Thinking." *On the Horizon*, 1994, Vol. 2, Issue 3, 3-4.

Poister, Theodore H. and Streib, Gregory D. "Strategic Management in the Public Sector." *Public Productivity & Management Review*, 1999, March, Vol. 22, Issue 3, 308-325.

Porter, Michael E. "What is Strategy?" *Harvard Business Review*, November/December, 1996, Vol. 74, Issue 6, 61-78.

Robert, Michael. *The New Strategic Thinking, Pure and Simple*. New York: McGraw-Hill, 2006.

Stahl, Michael J. and Grigsby, David W. *Strategic Management: Total Quality and Global Competition.* Cambridge, MA: Blackwell Business, 1997.

Thakur, Manab, and Calingo, Luis Ma. R. "Strategic Thinking Is Hip, But Does It Make A Difference?" *Business Horizons*, 1992, September/October, Vol. 35, Issue 5, 47-54.

Zuckerman, Alan M. "Is Strategic Planning Relevant Anymore?" *Trustee*, 2000, April, Vol. 53, Issue 4, 26-27.

Chapter 8—"Leading Employees through the Psychological Challenges of Change"

[1] Zemke, Ron, Raines, Claire, and Filipczak, Bob. *Generations at Work: Managing the Clash of Veterans, Boomers, Xers, and Nexters in Your Workplace,* Amacom, 2000.

[2] Bennis, Warren G. and Thomas, Robert J. *Geeks and Geezers: How Era, Values, and Defining Moments Shape Leaders.* Harvard Business School Press, 2002.

[3] Welter, Bill, and Egmon, Jean. *The Prepared Mind of a Leader: Eight Skills Leaders Use to Innovate, Make Decisions, and Solve Problems.* San Francisco: Jossey-Bass, 2006.

[4] Foster, Charles A. "Navigating Organization Change: Leading the Way during Turbulent Times." In Huber, Nancy S. and Wren, J. Thomas., Eds., *Leadership Bridges*, College Park, MD: International Leadership Association, 62-69, 2004.

[5] Kouzes, James M. and Posner, Barry Z. *The Leadership Challenge.* San Francisco: Jossey-Bass, 1995.

[6] Bridges, William. *Managing Transitions: Making the Most of Change.* 2nd Edition, Cambridge, MA: De Capo Press, 2003.

[7] Ibid.

[8] Kotter, John. *Leading Change.* Harvard Business School Press, 1996.

Additional Reading

Burns, James MacGregor. *Leadership*. New York: Harper & Row, 1979.

Covey, Stephen R. *The 7 Habits of Highly Effective People*. New York: Simon & Schuster, 1989.

Maxwell, John C. *Developing the Leader Within You*. Nashville, TN: Thomas Nelson, 2005.

Chapter 9—"Leading and Managing Change on the Edge of Chaos"

[1] Stein, Daniel L. "Focusing on Complexity and Those Who Study It." *Physics Today*, 1992, December, Vol. 45, Issue 12, 83-85.

[2] Newton, Isaac. *The Principia: Mathematical Principles of Natural Philosophy*. Translated by I. Bernard Cohen and Anne Whitman. University of California Press, 1st Edition, 1999.

[3] Descartes, Rene. *Discourse on Method and Meditations on First Philosophy*. translated by Donald Cress. Hacket Pub Co, 4th Edition, 1999.

[4] Smith, Adam. *An Inquiry into the Nature and Causes of the Wealth of Nations*. translated by Edwin Cannan. London: Methuen and Col., Ltd., 5th Edition, 1904.

[5] Taylor, Frederick Winslow. The *Principles of Scientific Management*. Mineola, NY: Dover Publications, Inc., 1998.

[6] Descartes, *Discourse*.

[7] Ibid.

[8] Ibid.

[9] Ibid.

10 Ibid.

11 Newton, *Principia.*

12 Smith, *Wealth of Nations.*

13 Ibid.

14 Ibid.

15 Taylor, *Principles of Scientific Management.*

16 An early example of Follet's work was published in 1927: Follett, Mary P. *Dynamic Administration.* 1927 which was later reprinted in 1942: New York: Harper & Brothers Publishers. An interesting review of Follet's influence on the development of American management theory is: Graham, Pauline (Editor). *Mary Parker Follett: Prophet of Management.* Beard Books Incorporated, 2003.

17 Based on his experimental work at the Hawthorne Works Western Electric Plant Mayo later published: *The Human Problems of an Industrial Civilization.* New York: MacMillan, 1933. The Hawthorne Effect refers to Mayo's observation that people modify their behavior being experimentally measured in simple response to their awareness that they are being observed or studied and not necessarily in response to any particular experimental parameters.

18 Fayol, Henri. *General and Industrial Management.* Translated by Irwin Gray. Ieee., Rev. Sub. edition, 1984.

19 Weber, Max. *Economy and Society: An Outline of Interpretive Sociology.* University of California Press, 1978.

20 Gulick, Luther, and Urwick L., Editors. *Papers on the Science of Administration.* New York: Institute of Public Administration, 1937. This work includes articles by Gulick and Urwick, as well as James D. Mooney, Henri Fayol, Henry S. Dennison, L. J. Henderson, T. N. Whitehead, Elton Mayo, Mary Parker Follett, John Lee, and V. A. Graicunas.

21 Simon, Herbert. *Administrative Behavior: A Study of Decision-Making Processes in Administrative Organizations.* 1947. 4th Edition, The Free Press, 1997. See also Simon, Herbert. "Bounded Rationality and Organizational Learning." *Organization Science*, 1991, Vol. 2, Issue 1, 125-134.

22 Waldo, Dwight. *The Administrative State: A Study of the Political Theory of American Public Administration.* 1948, 2nd Edition, New York: Holmes and Meier Publishers, 1984.

23 Shafritz, Jay M. and Ott, J. Steven. *Classics of Organization Theory.* 3rd Edition. Pacific Grove, CA: Brooks/Cole Publishing Company, 1992.

24 Lissack, Michael R. "Complexity: The Science, Its Vocabulary, and Its Relation to Organizations." *Emergence*, 1999, Vol. 1, Issue 1, 110-26; Horgan, John. "Trends in Complexity Studies: From Complexity to Perplexity." *Scientific American*, 1995, 272:74-9; Wheatley, Margaret. *Leadership and the New Science: Discovering Order in a Chaotic World.* 3rd Edition, San Francisco: Berrett-Koehler Publishers, Inc., 2006.

25 Poincaré, Henri. *Methods of Celestial Mechanics* (Méthodes nouvelles de la mécanique céleste). Edited and introduced by Daniel L. Goroff. Woodbury, NY: American Institute of Physics, 1993.

26 Einstein, Albert. (with commentary by Roger Penrose, Robert Geroch, and David Cassidy. *Relativity: The Special and General Theory.* Pi Press, The Masterpiece Science Edition, 2005.

27 Heller, Eric J. and Tomsovic, Steven. "Postmodern Quantum Mechanics." *Physics Today*, 1993, July, Vol. 46, Issue 7, 38-46.

28 Zohar, Danah. "What Would A Quantum Organization Look Like?" *Management Review*, 1998, March, Vol. 87, Issue 3, 56-58.

29 Lorenz, Edward. *The Essence of Chaos.* CRC Press, The Jessie and John Danz Lecture Series, 1995.

30 Ibid.

[31] Ibid.

[32] Mandelbrot, Benoit B. *The Fractal Geometry of Nature*. W.H. Freeman, 1982.

[33] See Prigogine, Ilya. *The End of Certainty*. Free Press, 1997.

[34] Prigogine, Ilya. *Order Out of Chaos*. Shambhala, 1984.

[35] Gleick, James. *Chaos: Making a New Science*. New York: Penguin, 1987.

[36] Horgan discusses the initial resistance to the application of insights from the new sciences in Horgan, John. "From Complexity to Perplexity." *Scientific American*, 1995, June, Vol. 272, Issue 6, 104-109.

[37] Gleick.

[38] See Overman, E. Sam. "The New Science of Management: Chaos and Quantum Theory and Method." *Journal of Public Administration Research & Theory*, January, 1996, Vol. 6, Issue 1, 75-89, and Overman, E. Sam. "The New Sciences of Administration: Chaos and Quantum Theory." *Public Administration Review*, 1996, September/October, 1996, Vol. 56, Issue 5, 487-491.

[39] Gleick.

[40] Geisert, Paul, and Futrell, Mynga. "Free Will: A Human, Fuzzy, Chaotic Process." *Humanist*, 1996, May/Jun, Vol. 56, Issue 3, 26-29.

[41] Coveney, P, and Highfield, R. *Frontiers of Complexity: The Search for Order in a Chaotic World*. New York: Fawcett, 1995.

[42] Whitesides, George M., and Ismagilov, Rustem F. "Complexity in Chemistry." *Science*, 1999, Vol. 284, Issue 5411, 89-92.

[43] Zadeh, Lofti. "Fuzzy Sets." *Information and Control*, 1965, Vol. 8, 338-353.

[44] Geisert and Futrell.

[45] Treadwell, William A. "Fuzzy Set Theory Movement in the Social Sciences." *Public Administration Review*, 1995, January/February, Vol. 55, Issue 1, 91-98.

[44] Kiel, L. Douglas. "Nonlinear Dynamical Analysis: Assessing Systems Concepts in a Government Agency." *Public Administration Review*, 1993, March/April, Vol. 53, Issue 2, 143-153.

[45] Stacey, Ralph D. *Complexity and Creativity in Organizations*. San Francisco: Berrett-Koehler Publishers, 1996.

[46] Zadeh.

[47] Kiel, L. Douglas. *Managing Chaos and Complexity in Government: A New Paradigm for Managing Change, Innovation and Organizational Renewal*. San Francisco, CA: Jossey-Bass, 1995.

[48] Stacy.

[49] Overman.

[50] Heller, Eric J. and Tomsovic, Steven. "Postmodern Quantum Mechanics." *Physics Today*, 1993, July, Vol. 46, Issue 7, 38-46.

[51] Ibid.

[52] Begun, James W. "Chaos and Complexity: Frontiers of Organization Science." *Journal of Management Inquiry*, 1994, December, Vol. 3, Issue 4, 329-335.

[53] Ibid. These three observations are already well underway today.

[54] Stewart, Ian. *Does God Play Dice? The Mathematics of Chaos*. Cambridge, MA: Blackwell, 1989.

[55] Begun.

[56] Ibid.

[57] Hamel, Gary, and Prahalad, C.K. *Competing for the Future.* Boston, MA: Harvard Business School Press, 1994.

[58] Laszlo, Ervin. *Vision 2020: Reordering Chaos for Global Survival.* Langhorne, PA: Gordon and Breach Science Publishers S.A, 1994.

[59] Cohen, Michael. "Commentary on the Organization Science Special "Issue on Complexity." *Organization Science: A Journal of the Institute of Management Sciences*, 1999, May/June, Vol. 10, Issue 3, 373-376.

Additional Reading

Anderson, Philip. "Complexity Theory and Organization Science." *Organization Science: A Journal of the Institute of Management Sciences*, 1999, May/June, Vol. 10, Issue 3, 216-232.

Axelrod, Robert, and Cohen, Michael E. *Harnessing Complexity: Organizational Implications of a Scientific Frontier.* New York: Free Press, 2000.

Bak, Per. *How Nature Works: The Science of Self-Organized Criticality.* New York: Springer-Verlag, 1996.

Beinhocker, Eric D. "Strategy at the Edge of Chaos." *McKinsey Quarterly*, 1997, Issue 1, 24-39.

Bertalanffy, Ludwig von. "General Systems Theory." *General Systems. Yearbook of the Society for the Advancement of General System Theory*, 1956, Vol. 1, 1-10.

Bertalanffy, Ludwig von. *General System Theory: Foundations, Development, Application.* 1968, New York: G. Braziller, 2nd Ed., 1980.

Brown Shona L., and Eisenhardt, Kathleen. "The Art of Continuous Change: Linking Complexity Theory and Time-Paced Evolution in Relentlessly Shifting Organizations." *Administrative Science Quarterly*, 1997, March, Vol. 42, Issue 1, 1-34.

Brown, Shona L., and Eisenhardt, Kathleen M. *Competing on the Edge: Strategy as Structured Chaos.* Boston, MA: Harvard Business School Press, 1998.

Comfort, Louse K. "Self-Organization in Complex Systems." *Journal of Public Administration Research & Theory*, 1994, July, Vol. 4, Issue 3, 393-410.

Comfort, Louise K. "Toward a Theory of Transition in Complex Systems: Reflections on the Process of Change." *American Behavioral Scientist*, 1997, January, Vol. 40, Issue 3, 375-383.

Contractor, Noshir S. "Self-Organizing Systems Research in the Social Sciences: Reconciling the Metaphors and Models." *Management Communication Quarterly*, 1999, August, Vol. 13, Issue 1, 154-166.

Dennard, Linda F. "Neo-Darwinism and Simon's Bureaucratic Antihero." *Administration & Society*, 1995, February, Vol. 26, Issue 4, 464-487.

Hock, Dee. "The Chaordic Organization: Out of Control and Into Order." *World Business Perspectives*, 1995, Vol. 9, No. 1, 5-18.

Kast, Fremont E., and Rosenweig, James E. *Organization and Management: A Systems Approach*. New York: McGraw Hill, 1970.

Katz, Daniel, and Kahn, Robert L. *The Social Psychology of Organizations*. New York: John Wiley & Sons, 1978.

Kauffman, Stuart A. *The Origins of Order: Self Organization and Selection In Evolution*. New York: Oxford University Press, 1993.

Kauffman, Stuart A. *At Home in the Universe: The Search for Laws of Self-Organization and Complexity*. New York: Oxford University Press, 1995.

Lawrence, Paul R. and Lorsch, Jay W. "Differentiation and Integration in Complex Organizations." *Administrative Science Quarterly*, 1967, Vol. 12, 1-30.

Treadwell, William A. "Fuzzy Set Theory Movement in the Social Sciences." *Public Administration Review*, 1995, January/February, Vol. 55, Issue 1, 91-98.

Waldrop, M. Mitchell. *Complexity: The Emerging Science at the Edge of Order and Chaos*. New York: Simon & Schuster, 1992.

Weick, Karl E. *Sensemaking in Organizations.* Thousand Oaks, CA: Sage Publications, 1995.

Chapter 10—"A Complexity Approach to Decision Making and Problem Solving"

[1] Morçöl, Goktug. "A Framework for a Complexity Theory for Policy Analysis." Paper presented at the PAT-Net Conference, May, Harrisburg, PA, 2007.

[2] Richardson, K. A. "Complex Systems Thinking and Its Implications for Policy Analysis." In G. Morçöl, (Ed.), *Handbook of Decision Making,* Boca Raton, FL: CRC Press, Taylor and Francis Group, 2006, 189-221.

[3] Morçöl, 2007.

[4] Axelrod, Robert. and Cohen, Michael. D. *Harnessing Complexity: Organizational Implications of a Scientific Frontier.* New York: The Free Press, 1999.

[5] Kauffman, Stuart A. *At Home in the Universe: The Search for Laws of Self-Organization and Complexity.* New York: Oxford University Press, 1995.

[6] Axelrod and Cohen.

[7] Ibid.

[8] Richardson, 2006.

[9] Sabatier, Paul A. "The Need for Better Theories." In Paul A. Sabatier (Ed.) *Theories of the Policy Process,* Boulder, CO: Westview, 1999, 3-17; Sharkansky, Ira. *Politics and Policy Making: In Search of Simplicity.* London: Lynne Rienner Publishers, 2002.

[10] Sharkansky in Morçöl, 2007.

[11] Boisot, Max, and Child, John. "Organizations as Adaptive Systems in Complex Environments: The Case of China." *Organization Science,* 1999, Vol. 10, Issue 3, 237-252. See also Stringham, Shand H. "A Complexity

Approach to Decision Making and Problem Solving Models." A paper presented at the PAT-Net Conference, Harrisburg, PA, May 26-27, 2007.

[12] Perrow, Charles. *Normal Accidents: Living with High-Risk Technologies.* New York: Basic Books, Inc., Publishers, 1984.

[13] Ibid.

[14] Ibid.

[15] Smith, Adam. *An Inquiry into the Nature and Causes of the Wealth of Nations.* Translated by Edwin Cannan. London: Methuen and Col., Ltd., 5th Edition, 1904.

[16] Simon, Herbert. A. *Administrative Behavior.* New York: Macmillan, 1945.

[17] Lindblom, Charles E. "The Science of Muddling Through." *Public Administration Review,* Spring, 1959, Vol. 19, Issue 2, 79-88.

[18] Stone, Deborah. *Policy Paradox: The Art of Political Decision Making.* W.W. Norton & Company, 3rd Edition, 2001.

[19] Janis, Irving L. *Victims of Groupthink.* Boston, MA: Houghton Mifflin Company, 1972; see also Janis, Irving L. *Groupthink: Psychological Studies of Policy Decisions and Fiascos.* 2nd Edition. Boston: Houghton Mifflin Company, 1982.

[20] See Holloway, Charles A. *Decisionmaking Under Uncertainty: Models and Choices.* Englewood Cliffs, New Jersey: Prentice-Hall, Inc., 1979.

[21] Lindblom.

[22] Morçöl, 2007.

[23] Simon.

[24] Dunn, William N. "Probing the Boundaries of Ignorance in Policy Analysis." *American Behavioral Scientist,* 1997, January, Vol. 40, Issue 3, 277-299.

[25] Lindblom.

[26] Dunn.

[27] Lindblom.

[28] Etzioni, Amitai. "Mixed Scanning: A Third Approach to Decision Making." *Public Administration Review*, 1967, December, Vol. 27, Issue 12, 385-92.

[29] Rittel, Horst, and Webber, Melvin M. "Dilemmas in a General Theory of Planning." *Policy Sciences*, 1973, Vol. 4, 155-169.

[30] Bryson, John M. *Strategic Planning For Public and Nonprofit Organizations. A Guide to Strengthening and Sustaining Organizational Achievement*. San Francisco: Jossey-Bass Publishers, 1995.

[31] Arrow, Kenneth J. *Social Choice and Individual Values*. New York: John Wiley & Sons, Inc., 2nd Edition, 1963.

[32] Rittel and Webber.

[33] Stone, Deborah. *Policy Paradox: The Art of Political Decision Making*. New York: W.W. Norton, 1997.

[34] Edwards, George C., III, and Sharkansky, Ira. *The Policy Predicament: Making and Implementing Public Policy*. San Francisco: W.H. Freeman and Company, 1978.

[35] Huber, George P. *Managerial Decision Making*. Glenview, IL: Scott, Foresman, 1980.

[36] Stewart, Ian. *Does God Play Dice? The New Mathematics of Chaos*. Penguin Books, 1989.

[37] Begun, James W. "Chaos and Complexity: Frontiers of Organization Science." *Journal of Management Inquiry*, 1994, December, Vol. 3, Issue 4, 329-335.

[38] Strogatz, Steven H. *Nonlinear Dynamics and Chaos: with Applications to Physics, Biology Chemistry and Engineering.* Addison Wesley, 1994.

[39] Begun.

[40] Morçöl.

[41] Harmon Michael M., and Meyer, Richard T. *Organization Theory for Public Administration.* Burke, VA: Chatalaine Press, 1986.

[42] See Pegis, Anton C., (Translator) *Basic Writings of St. Thomas Aquinas.* New York: Random House, 1945, 129.

[43] Ariew, Roger. *Ockham's Razor: A Historical and Philosophical Analysis of Ockham's Principle of Parsimony.* Champaign-Urbana, IL: University of Illinois, 1976.

[44] Ibid.

[45] Stacey, Ralph D. *Complexity and Creativity in Organizations.* San Francisco: Berrett-Koehler Publishers, 1996.

[46] For a more detailed history and analysis of the Aswan Dam project, see Dougherty, James E. "The Aswan Decision in Perspective," *Political Science Quarterly*, 1959, Vol. 74, No. 1, March, 21-45.

[47] Associated Press April 10, 2007.

[48] Associated Press, February 18, 2007.

[49] Acker, Fabian (2009-03-02). "Taming the Yangtze." *IET magazine.* 2 Mar 09. http://kn.theiet.org/magazine/issues/0904/taming-the-yangtze-0904. cfm#.

[50] See: Lin Yang. "China's Three Gorges Dam Under Fire." *Time.* 12 Dec 07, http://www.time.com/time/world/article/0,8599,1671000,00.html. Retrieved 28 Mar 09; Laris, Michael. "Untamed Waterways Kill Thousands Yearly". *Washington Post.* 17 Aug 08, http://www.washingtonpost.com/ wp-srv/inatl/longterm/china/stories/death081798.htm. Retrieved 28 Mar

09; "Global Challenges: Ecological and Technological Advances Around the World". CNN. http://edition.cnn.com/TRANSCRIPTS/0506/18/gc.01. html. Retrieved March 28 2009; Topping, Audrey Ronning. Environmental controversy over the Three Gorges Dam. Earth Times News Service.

[51] Qing, Dai. *The River Dragon Has Come: The Three Gorges Dam and the Fate of China's Yangtze River and Its People.* New York: M.E. Sharpe, 1997.

[52] Winchester, Simon *The River at the Center of the World.* New York: Henry Holt & Co., 1998, 228.

[53] *The Wall Street Journal.* 28 Aug 07. http://chinese.wsj.com/gb/20070829/ chw110745.asp?source=baidu. Retrieved August 16 2009.

[54] Yang, Sung. "No Casualties in Three Gorges Dam Landslide"". *Xinhua News Network.* CRIEnglish.com. http://english.cri. cn/6909/2009/05/19/45s485830.htm. Retrieved June 3, 2009.

[55] Richard Jones, Michael Sheridan. "Chinese dam causes quakes and landslides"". *The Times* (London). 30 May 10. http://www.timesonline. co.uk/tol/news/environment/article7140217.ece. Retrieved January 25, 2011.

[56] Kiel, L. Douglas, and Elliott, Euel. "Long-Wave Economic Cycles, Techno-Economic Paradigms, and the Pattern of Reform in American Public Administration." *Administration & Society*, 1999, January, Vol. 30, Issue 6, 616-639.

[57] See Wheatley, Margaret J. *Leadership and the New Science: Learning About Organization from an Orderly Universe.* San Francisco: Berrett-Koehler Publishers, 1992; and Mandelbrot, Benoit. "Towards a Second Stage of Indeterminism in Science." *Interdisciplinary Science Review*, 1987, Vol. 12, 117-127.

[58] Brodnick, Robert J., Jr., and Krafft, Larry J. "Chaos and Complexity Theory: Implications for Research and Planning in Higher Education." Contributed Paper, *Association for Institutional Research, Thirty-Seventh Annual Forum*, May 18-21, 1997.

URL: http://basie.irp.udel.edu/air/airforum.97/TRACK5/37-518/
BRODNICK.RTF.

[59] Mathews, K. Michael., White, Michael C., and Long, Rebecca G. "Why Study the Complexity Sciences in the Social Sciences?" *Human Relations*, 1999, April, Vol. 52, Issue 4, 439-462.

[60] Kiel, L. Douglas. "Nonlinear Dynamical Analysis: Assessing Systems Concepts in a Government Agency." *Public Administration Review*, 1993, March/April, Vol. 53, Issue 22, 143-153.

[61] See Overman, E. Sam. "The New Sciences of Administration: Chaos and Quantum Theory." *Public Administration Review*, 1996, September/October, Vol. 56, Issue 5, 487-491; and Overman, E. Sam. "The New Science of Management: Chaos and Quantum Theory and Method." *Journal of Public Administration Research & Theory*, 1996, January, Vol. 6, Issue 1, 75-89.

[62] Comfort, Louise K. "Toward a Theory of Transition in Complex Systems." *American Behavioral Scientist*, 1997, January, Vol. 40, Issue 3, 375-383.

[63] Sanders, T. Irene. *Strategic Thinking and the New Science*. New York: Free Press, 1998.

[64] Lazslo, Ervin. *The Systems View of the World: A Holistic Vision for Our Time (Advances in Systems Theory, Complexity, and the Human Sciences)*. Cresskill, NJ: Hampton Press, 1996.

[65] Tasaka, Hiroshi. "Twenty-First Century Management and the Complexity Paradigm." *Emergence*, 1999, Vol. 1, Issue 4, 115-123.

[66] Ibid.

[67] Lorenz, Edward. "Deterministic Nonperiodic Flow." *Journal of the Atmospheric Sciences*, 1963, Vol. 20, 130-141.

[68] Christensen, Clayton M., Anthony, Scott D., and Roth, Erik A. *Seeing What's Next: Using the Theories of Innovation to Predict Industry Change*. Harvard Business School Press, 2004, viii.

[69] Sanders.

[70] Campbell, David K. and Mayer-Kress, Gottfried. "Chaos and Politics: Applications of Nonlinear Dynamics to Socio-Political Issues." In Grebogi, Celso, and Yorke, James A., Eds. *The Impact of Chaos on Science and Society.* New York: United Nations University Press, 1997.

[71] Sanders.

[72] Elliott and Kiel.

[73] Durlauf, Steven N. "What Should Policymakers Know About Economic Complexity?" *Washington Quarterly*, 1998, Winter, Vol. 21, Issue 1, 157-165.

[74] Sanders.

[75] Warren, Keith, Franklin, Cynthia, and Streeter, Calvin L. "New Directions in Systems Theory: Chaos and Complexity." *Social Work*, 1998, July, Vol. 43, Issue 4, 357-372.

[76] Mathews, K. M., White, M. C., & Long, R. G. "Why Study the Complexity Sciences in the Social Sciences." *Human Relations*, 1999, Vol. 52, Issue 4, 439.

[77] Cartwright, T. J. "Planning and Chaos Theory." *APA Journal*, 1991, Vol. 57, Issue 1, 44-56.

[78] Bendor, J. and T. H. Hammond. "Rethinking Allison's Models." *American Political Science Review*, 1992, Vol. 86, No. 2, 301-322.

[79] Ibid. See also Allison, Graham. T. "Conceptual Models and the Cuban Missile Crisis." *The American Political Science Review*, 1969, Vol. 63, No. 3, 689-718.

[80] Campbell and Meyer-Kress.

[81] Saperstein, Alvin M. "Chaos and National Security Policy: Metaphors or Tools?" In Alberts, David S., and Cserwinski, Thomas J., Eds. *Complexity,*

Global Politics, and National Security. Washington, D.C.: National Defense University, 1996. http://www.ndu.edu/ndu/inss/books/complexity/index.html.

[82] Brook-Shepherd, Gordon. *Royal Sunset: The European Dynasties and the Great War*. Doubleday, 1987, 139; Marshall, S.L.A. *World War I*. Mariner Books, 2001, 1; Keegan, John. *The First World War*. Vintage, 2000, 48.

[83] Jervis, Robert. "Complex Systems: The Role of Interactions." In Alberts, David S., and Cserwinski, Thomas J., Eds. *Complexity, Global Politics, and National Security*. Washington, D.C.: National Defense University, 1996.

[84] Ibid.

[85] Marion, Russ, and Bacon, Josh. "Organizational Extinction and Complex Systems." *Emergence*, 2000, Vol. 1, Issue 4, 71-96.

[86] Ibid.

[87] Holland.

[88] Durlauf.

[89] Sanders.

[90] Wheatley.

[91] Brodnick, and Krafft.

[92] Zadeh, L. A. "Fuzzy Sets." In R. Yager, S. Ovchinnikov, R. Tong, and H Nguyen, Eds., *Fuzzy Sets and Applications: Selected Papers by L. A. Zadah*. New York: John Wiley and Sons, 1987.

[93] Kosko, Bart. *Fuzzy Thinking: The New Science of Fuzzy Logic*. Hyperion, 1994.

[94] Ibid.

[95] Ibid.

[96] Treadwell, William A. "Fuzzy Set Theory Movement in the Social Sciences." *Public Administration Review*, 1995, January, Vol. 55, Issue 1, 91-98.

[97] Kosko.

[98] Dimitrov, Vladimir. "Decision Emergence Out of Complexity and Chaos: Manifesto of Emergence." 2001. URL: http://members.tripod.com/~Vlad_3_6_7/Decision-Making-in-Complexity.html

[99] Shewart, Walter. *A. Statistical Method for the Viewpoint of Quality Control*. New York: Dover, 1939; Deming, W. Edward. *Out of the Crisis*. MIT Center for Advanced Engineering Study, 1986.

Additional Reading

Cohen, Michael D., Marsh, James G., and Olsen, Johan P. "A Garbage Can Model of Organizational Choice." *Administrative Science Quarterly*, 1972, March, Vol. 17, Issue 1, 1-25.

Comfort, Lousie K. "Nonlinear Dynamics in Disaster Response: The Northride, California Earthquake, January 17, 1994." In Elliot, Euel, and Kiel, L. Douglas, Eds. *Nonlinear Dynamics, Complexity and Public Policy*. Commack, NY: Nova Science Publishers, Inc., 1999.

DeGrace, Peter, and Stahl, Leslie H. *Wicked Problems, Righteous Solutions-A Catalogue of Modern Software Engineering Paradigms*. Englewood Cliffs, NJ: Yourdon Press, 1990.

Dutton, John M., and Starbuck, William H. *Computer Simulation of Human Behavior*. New York: Wiley, 1971.

Eisenhardt, Kathleen M. "Speed and Strategic Choice: How Managers Accelerate Decision Making," In David A. Kolb, Joyce S. Osland, and Irwin M. Rubin, Eds., *The Organizational Behavior Reader*. 6th Edition. Englewood Cliffs, NJ: Prentice Hall, 1995.

Eoyang, Glenda H., Yellowthunder, Lois, and Ward, Victor. "A Complex Adaptive Systems (CAS) Approach to Public Policy Decision Making." *Society for Chaos Theory in Psychology in the Life Sciences*, 1998, August, 1-19.

Fernandes, Ronald, and Simon, Herbert A. "A Study of How Individuals Solve Complex and Ill-Structured Problems." *Policy Sciences*, 1999, Vol. 32, 225-245.

Greenberg, George D. et al. "Developing Public Policy Theory: Perspectives from Empirical Research." *American Political Science Review*, December, 1977, Vol. 71, 1532-1543.

Kiel, L. Douglas, Eds. *Nonlinear Dynamics, Complexity and Public Policy.* Commack, NY: Nova Science Publishers, Inc., 1999.

Morçöl, Goktug. *A New Mind for Policy Analysis: Toward a Post-Newtonian and Postpositivist Epistemology and Methodology.* Westport, CT: Praeger, 2002.

Morçöl, Goktug, Ed. *Handbook of Decision Making.* Boca Raton, FL: CRC Press, Taylor and Francis Group, 2006.

Morgan, Gareth. *Images of Organization.* 2nd Edition. Thousand Oaks, CA: Sage Publications, 1997.

Taylor, Mark C. *The Moment of Complexity: Emerging Network Culture.* Chicago: The University of Chicago Press, 2001.

Chapter 11 References

[1] Ziegenfuss, James T., Jr. *Relearning Strategic Planning: Lessons of Philosophy and Procedure.* Allen Press, 1996; Mintzberg, Henry. *The Rise and Fall of Strategic Planning.* Free Press, 1994.

[2] Here is a sampling of some of the more important books of the past twenty years that, in part, take a hard analytical look at strategic planning: Stacey, Ralph D. *Managing the Unknowable: Strategic Boundaries between Order and Chaos in Organizations.* Jossey-Bass Publishers, 1992; Mintzberg, Henry. *The Rise and Fall of Strategic Planning Reconceiving Roles for Planning, Plans, Planners.* The Free Press, 1994; Bryson, John M. *Strategic Planning for Public and*

Nonprofit Organizations: A Guide to Strengthening and Sustaining Organizational Achievement. Revised Edition, Jossey-Bass Publishers, 1995; Weick, Karl. E., and Sutcliffe, Kathleen. M. *Managing the Unexpected: Resilient Performance in an Age of Uncertainty.* San Francisco: Jossey-Bass, 2001; Mintzberg, Henry, Ahlstrand, Bruce, and Lampel, Joseph. *Strategy Bites Back: It Is Far More and Less, Than You Ever Imagined.* Pearson, Prentice Hall, 2005; Raynor, Michael E. *The Strategy Paradox: Why Committing to Success Leads to Failure [And What To Do About It].* Currency Doubleday, 2007; Collins, Jim. *How the Mighty Fall and Why Some Companies Never Give In.* Harper Collins Publishers, 2009.

3   Hill, Charles W. L., and Jones, Gareth R. *Strategic Management Theory.* 10th Edition, South-Western Cenage Learning, 2012, 27.

4   Hamel, Gary, and Prahalad, C. K. *Competing for the Future.* New York: Free Press, 1989.

5   This is Mintzberg's primary argument against strategic planning. Mintzberg, Henry. *The Rise and Fall of Strategic Planning: Reconceiving Roles for Planning, Plans, Planners.* The Free Press, 1994.

6   Rick Newman (February 6, 2009). "15 Companies That Might Not Survive 2009" ". US News. http://money.usnews.com/money/blogs/flowchart/2009/2/6/15-companies-that-might-not-survive-2009.html. Retrieved September 20, 2012. See also "The Making of a Blockbuster". Bloomberg Businessweek. Retrieved July 23, 2011 http://www.businessweek.com/chapter/chap0009.htm.

7   Martinex-Moncada. "How Netflix Destroyed Blockbuster." Infographic, May 23, 2011. Retrieved September 29, 2012. http://dailyinfographic.com/how-netflix-destroyed-blockbuster-infographic

8   Payton, Susan. "Netflix: The Nimblest Company Wins the Race. *Growth University,* June 3, 2011. Retrieved September 29, 2012. http://www.futuresimple.com/blog/netflix-the-nimblest-company-wins-the-race/

9   "Blockbuster Reaches Agreement on Plan to Recapitalize Balance Sheet and Substantially Reduce its Indebtedness." Blockbuster Press Release.

September 9, 2010. Retrieved September 28, 2010. http://blockbuster. mediaroom.com/index.php?s=119&item=929.

[10] "DISH Network Completes Acquisition of Blockbuster Assets—April 26, 2011." Dishnetwork.mediaroom.com. Retrieved July 23, 2012. http:// dishnetwork.mediaroom.com/index.php?s=8778&item=33969.

[11] Harris, Gerald. *The Art of Quantum Planning: Lessons from Quantum Physics for Breakthrough Strategy, Innovation, and Leadership.* Berrett-Koehler, 2009, 16.

[12] Osterwalder, Alexander, and Pigneur, Yves. *Business Model Generation.* John Wiley & Sons, Inc. 2010.

[13] Ibid.

[14] Schwartz, Peter. *The Art of the Long View: Planning for the Future in an Uncertain World.* Currency Doubleday, 1991.

[15] Mintzberg.

[16] Harris, 10.

[17] Ibid, 50.

[18] Mintzberg.

[19] De Geus, Arie. "Planning As Learning." *Harvard Business Review*, 1988, Vol. 66, Issue 4, 70-74.

[20] Harris, 17.

[21] March of Dimes website, History. Retrieved October 7, 2012 from http://. www.marchofdimes.com/mission/history.html.

[22] Hill and Jones, 21.

[23] Wilson, G.I. "Abundance of Planning Failures, Webster University. Retrieved August 16, 2012, from http://www.projectwhitehorse.com/pdfs/Planning%20-%20Wilson.pdf

[24] Janis, Irving L. "Groupthink." *Psychology Today*, 1971, November, Volume 5, Issue 6, 43-46, 74-76.

[25] Wilson.

[26] Ziegenfuss, 9.

[27] Hill and Jones, adapted from Mintzberg, H., and McGugh, A., *Administrative Science Quarterly*, 1985, Vol. 30, No. 2, June.

[28] Ziegenfuss, 20-21.

[29] Ibid.

[30] Mintzberg, Henry. "The Fall and Rise of Strategic Planning." *Harvard Business Review*, 1994, January-February. 107-114.

[31] Mathews, K. M., White, M. C., & Long, R. G. "Why Study the Complexity Sciences in the Social Sciences." *Human Relations*, 1999, Vol. 52, Issue 4, 439.

[32] Harris, 22.

[33] Ibid., 19.

[34] Schwartz, Peter. *The Art of the Long View*. Currency Doubleday, 1991.

[35] Kotter, John. *Leading Change*. Harvard Business School Press, 1996, 29.

[36] Kouzes and Posner suggested a leadership model of five key practices: challenging the process, inspiring a shared vision, enabling others to act, modeling the way, and encouraging the heart. Kouzes, James M., and Posner, Barry Z. *The Leadership Challenge: How to Keep Getting Extraordinary Things Done in Organizations*. Jossey-Bass Publishers, 1995.

[37] Kaplan Robert S. and Norton, David P. "Using the Balanced Scorecard as a Strategic Management System," *Harvard Business Review*, January-February, 1996, 75-85.

[38] Christensen, Clayton M. *The Innovator's Dilemma: The Revolutionary Book That Will Change the Way You Do Business*. Harper Business, 2011, xviii.

[39] Ibid.

[40] Ibid., xxix.

[41] Stross, Randall E. *The Wizard of Menlo Park: How Thomas Alva Edison Invented the Modern World*. Broadway, 2008.

[42] Christensen.Clayton M. *The Innovator's Dilemma: The Revolutionary Book that Will Change the Way You Do Business*. Harper Business, 1997; See also Christensen, Clayton. *The Innovator's Solution: Creating and Sustaining Successful Growth*. Harvard Business School Press, 2003.

[43] Ibid.

[44] Raynor, Michael E. *The Strategy Paradox: Why Committing to Success Leads to Failure [And What to Do About It]*. Currency Books, 2007.

[45] Ibid.

[46] Ibid., 1.

[47] Ibid.

[48] Ibid.

[49] Ibid., 270.

[50] Ibid.

[51] Ibid.

Additional Reading

Mitchell, Helen. M. "Avoiding Strategic Planning Failure." A presentation delivered at the Association Strategic Planning National Conference, Long Beach, CA, March 27, 2007. Retrieved August 15, 2007, from http://mediaserver.prweb.com/pdfdownload/513802/pr.pdf

Schultz, Norman. "Uncertainty." in *Beyond Intractability*. Eds. Burgess, Guy, and Burgess, Heidi. Conflict Information Consortium, University of Colorado, Boulder. Posted: January 2004, retrieved August 16, 2012. http://www.beyondintractability.org/bi-essay/fact-finding-limits.
Davis, Paul K. and Hillestad, Richard. *Exploratory Analysis for Strategy Problems With Massive Uncertainty*, RAND, Santa Monica, CA, 2000.

Bibliography

Acker, Fabian (2009-03-02). "Taming the Yangtze." *IET magazine*. 2 Mar 09. http://kn.theiet.org/magazine/issues/0904/taming-the-yangtze-0904. cfm#.

Ackoff, Russell L. *A Concept of Corporate Planning*. John Wiley & Sons, Inc., 1970.

Ackoff, Russell L., and Emery, Frederick E. *On Purposeful Systems: An Interdisciplinary Analysis of Individual and Social Behavior as a System of Purposeful Events*. Chicago: Aldine-Atherton, 1972.

Allison, Graham. T. "Conceptual Models and the Cuban Missile Crisis." *The American Political Science Review*, 1969, Vol. 63, No. 3, 689-718.

Anderson, Philip. "Complexity Theory and Organization Science." *Organization Science: A Journal of the Institute of Management Sciences*, 1999, May/June, Vol. 10, Issue 3, 216-232.

Ansoff, H. Igor. *Corporate Strategy: An Analytic Approach to Business Policy for Growth and Expansion*. New York: McGraw-Hill, 1965.

Ansoff, H. Igor, DeClerck, R.P., and Hayes, R.L. Eds. *From Strategic Planning to Strategic Management*. New York: John Wiley & Sons, 1976.

Argyris, Chris. *Behind the Front Page*. San Francisco: Jossey Bass, 1974.

Argyris, Chris., and Schön, Donald A. *Organizational Learning: A Theory of Action Perspective*. Reading, Addison Wesley, 1978.

Ariew, Roger. *Ockham's Razor: A Historical and Philosophical Analysis of Ockham's Principle of Parsimony*. Champaign-Urbana, IL: University of Illinois, 1976.

Aronson, Daniel. "Introduction to Systems Thinking." 1998, *Thinking Page*. Retrieved December 5, 2008, from http://www.thinking.net

Arrow, Kenneth J. *Social Choice and Individual Values*. New York: John Wiley & Sons, Inc., 2nd Edition, 1963.

Axelrod, Robert, and Cohen, Michael E. *Harnessing Complexity: Organizational Implications of a Scientific Frontier*. New York: Free Press, 2000.

Bak, Per. *How Nature Works: The Science of Self-Organized Criticality*. New York: Springer-Verlag, 1996.

Bamford, Charles E., and West, G. Page, III. *Strategic Management: Value Creation, Sustainability, and Performance*. Mason, OH: South-Western Cenage Learning, 2010.

Bass, Bernard M. *Bass & Stogdill's Handbook of Leadership*, 3rd Edition. New York: The Free Press, 1990.

Begun, James W. "Chaos and Complexity: Frontiers of Organization Science." *Journal of Management Inquiry*, 1994, December, Vol. 3, Issue 4, 329-335.

Beinhocker, Eric D. "Strategy at the Edge of Chaos." *McKinsey Quarterly*, 1997, Issue 1, 24-39.

Bellinger, Gene. *Systems Thinking: A Disciplined Approach*, 2005. Retrieved December 5, 2008, from http://www.systems-thinking.org/stada/stada.htm.

Bendor, J. and T. H. Hammond. "Rethinking Allison's Models." *American Political Science Review*, 1992, Vol. 86, No. 2, 301-322.

Bertalanffy, Ludwig von. "General Systems Theory." *General Systems. Yearbook of the Society for the Advancement of General System Theory*, 1956, Vol. 1, 1-10.

Bertalanffy, Ludwig von. *General System Theory: Foundations, Development, Application*. New York: G. Braziller, 1968.

Birnbaum, Bill. *Strategic Thinking: A Four-Piece Puzzle*. Central Oregon: Douglas Mountain Publishing, 2004.

"Blockbuster Reaches Agreement on Plan to Recapitalize Balance Sheet and Substantially Reduce its Indebtedness." Blockbuster Press Release. September 9, 2010. Retrieved September 28, 2010. http://blockbuster.mediaroom.com/index.php?s=119&item=929.

Boisot, Max, and Child, John. "Organizations as Adaptive Systems in Complex Environments: The Case of China." *Organization Science*, 1999, Vol. 10, Issue 3, 237-252.

Bonini, Charles P. *Simulation of Information and Decision Systems in the Firm.* Prentice-Hall, 1963.

Box, George E. P., and Draper, Norman R. *Empirical Model-Building and Response Surfaces*, Wiley, 1987.

Bradford, Robert W., and Duncan, J. Peter, with Tarcy, Brian. *Simplified Strategic Planning: A No-Nonsense Guide for Busy People Who Want Results Fast.* Worcester, MA: Chandler House Press, 2000.

Bridges, William. *Managing Transitions: Making the Most of Change.* 2nd Edition. Cambridge, MA: De Capo Press, 2003.

Brodnick, Robert J., Jr., and Krafft, Larry J. "Chaos and Complexity Theory: Implications for Research and Planning in Higher Education." Contributed Paper, *Association for Institutional Research, Thirty-Seventh Annual Forum*, May 18-21, 1997.
URL: http://basie.irp.udel.edu/air/airforum.97/TRACK5/37-518/ BROD NICK.RTF.

Brook-Shepherd, Gordon. *Royal Sunset: The European Dynasties and the Great War.* Doubleday, 1987, 139; Marshall, S.L.A. *World War I.* Mariner Books, 2001, 1; Keegan, John. *The First World War.* Vintage, 2000, 48.

Brown Shona L., and Eisenhardt, Kathleen. "The Art of Continuous Change: Linking Complexity Theory and Time-Paced Evolution in Relentlessly Shifting Organizations." *Administrative Science Quarterly*, 1997, March, Vol. 42, Issue 1, 1-34.

Brown, Shona L., and Eisenhardt, Kathleen M. *Competing on the Edge: Strategy as Structured Chaos*. Boston, MA: Harvard Business School Press, 1998.

Brown, Mark Graham. "Improving Your Organization's Vision." *Journal for Quality & Participation*, 1998, Sep/ Oct, Vol. 21, Issue 5, 18-21.

Bryson, John M. *Strategic Planning For Public and Nonprofit Organizations. A Guide to Strengthening and Sustaining Organizational Achievement*. San Francisco: Jossey-Bass Publishers, 1995.

Builder, Carl H. *The Army in the Strategic Planning Process*. Santa Monica, CA: The Rand Corporation, 1989.

Burns, Tom, and Stalker, George M. *The Management of Innovation*. Chicago: Quadrangle Books, 1961.

Burns, James MacGregor. *Leadership*. New York: Harper & Row, 1979.

Calas, Marta and Smircich, Linda. "Reading Leadership as a Form of Cultural Analysis," in *Emerging Leadership Vistas*. James G. Hunt, B. Rajaram Baliga, H. Peter Dachler and Chester A. Schriesheim, Eds. Lanham, MD: Lexington Books, 1988.

Campbell, David K. and Mayer-Kress, Gottfried. "Chaos and Politics: Applications of Nonlinear Dynamics to Socio-Political Issues." In Grebogi, Celso, and Yorke, James A., Eds. *The Impact of Chaos on Science and Society*. New York: United Nations University Press, 1997.

Carr, Adrian. "The Learning Organization New Lessons/ Thinking for the Management of Change and Management Development." *Journal of Management Development*, 1997, Vol. 16, Issue 4, 224-231.

Cartwright, T. J. "Planning and Chaos Theory." *APA Journal*, 1991, Vol. 57, Issue 1, 44-56.

Chandler, Alfred. *Strategy and Structure: Chapters in the History of Industrial Enterprise*. New York: Doubleday, 1962.

Checkland, Peter. "Systems Theory and Management Thinking." *American Behavioral Scientist*, 1994, September/October, Vol. 38, Issue 1, 75-91.

Christensen, Clayton M. *The Innovator's Dilemma: The Revolutionary Book That Will Change the Way You Do Business*. Harper Business, 1997, 186.

Christensen, Clayton M., and Raynor, Michael E. *The Innovator's Solution: Creating and Sustaining Successful Growth*. Harvard Business School Press, 2003.

Christensen, Clayton M., and Raynor, Michael E. *What's Next: Using Theories of Innovation to predict Industry Change*, Harvard Business School Press, 2004

Christensen, Clayton M., Anthony, Scott D., and Roth, Erik A. *Seeing What's Next: Using the Theories of Innovation to Predict Industry Change*. Harvard Business School Press, 2004.

Ciulla, Joanne B. "Leadership Ethics: Mapping the Territory." *Business Ethics Quarterly*, 1995, Vol. 5, Issue 1, 5-28.

Clark, Scott. "Sealed with a SWOT: Initial Steps Toward Needed Strategic Planning." *Houston Business Journal*, 1999, Vol. 30, Issue 15, 28.

Clausewitz, Carl von. *On War*. Indexed Edition. Edited and translated by Michael Howard and Peter Paret. Princeton, NJ: Princeton University Press, 1976.

Cohen Jon. "The March of Paradigms." *Science*, 1999, 26 March, Vol. 283, Issue 5410.

Cohen, Michael. "Commentary on the Organization Science Special "Issue on Complexity." *Organization Science: A Journal of the Institute of Management Sciences*, 1999, May/June, Vol. 10, Issue 3, 373-376.

Cohen, Michael D., Marsh, James G., and Olsen, Johan P. "A Garbage Can Model of Organizational Choice." *Administrative Science Quarterly*, 1972, March, Vol. 17, Issue 1, 1-25.

Collins, James C., and Porras, Jerry. *Built to Last: Successful Habits of Visionary Companies*. HarperBusiness, 1994.

Collins, James C. and Porras, Jerry. "Building Your Company's Vision." *Harvard Business Review*, 1996, Sep-Oct.

Collins, Jim. *How the Mighty Fall and Why Come Companies Never Give In*. HarperCollins, Publisher, Inc. 2009.

Comfort, Louse K. "Self-Organization in Complex Systems." *Journal of Public Administration Research & Theory*, 1994, July, Vol. 4, Issue 3, 393-410.

Comfort, Louise K. "Toward a Theory of Transition in Complex Systems: Reflections on the Process of Change." *American Behavioral Scientist*, 1997, January, Vol. 40, Issue 3, 375-383.

Comfort, Lousie K. "Nonlinear Dynamics in Disaster Response: The Northride, California Earthquake, January 17, 1994." In Elliot, Euel, and Kiel, L. Douglas, Eds. *Nonlinear Dynamics, Complexity and Public Policy*. Commack, NY: Nova Science Publishers, Inc., 1999.

Contractor, Noshir S. "Self-Organizing Systems Research in the Social Sciences: Reconciling the Metaphors and Models." *Management Communication Quarterly*, 1999, August, Vol. 13, Issue 1, 154-166.

Coveney, P, and Highfield, R. *Frontiers of Complexity: The Search for Order in a Chaotic World*. New York: Fawcett, 1995.

Covey, Stephen R. *The 7 Habits of Highly Effective People*. New York: Fireside, Simon and Schuster, 1989.

Crossan, Mary M., et al. "The Improvising Organization: Where Planning Meets Opportunity." *Organizational Dynamics*, 1996, Spring, Vol. 24, Issue 4, 20-35.

Daft, Richard L. *The Leadership Experience*. Mason, OH: South Western, 2008.

Dalton, Jim. "In Search of Strategy." *Association Management*, 2001, June, Vol. 53, Issue 6, 70-74.

Dannemiller, Kathleen D., and Jacobs, Robert W. "Changing the Way Organizations Change: A Revolution of Common Sense." *Journal of Applied Behavioral Science*, 1992, December, Vol. 28, Issue 4, 480-498.

D'Avani, Richard. *Hypercompetition*, The Free Press, 1994.

Davis, Paul K. and Hillestad, Richard. *Exploratory Analysis for Strategy Problems With Massive Uncertainty*, RAND, Santa Monica, CA, 2000.

de Bono, Edward. *Six Thinking Hats: An Essential Approach to Business Management.* Little, Brown, & Company, 1985.

DeGeus, A. P. "Planning as Learning." Boston: MA: *Harvard Business Review,* 1988, March/April, 70-74.

DeGrace, Peter, and Stahl, Leslie H. *Wicked Problems, Righteous Solutions-A Catalogue of Modern Software Engineering Paradigms.* Englewood Cliffs, NJ: Yourdon Press, 1990.

Deming, W. Edwards. *Out of the Crisis.* Massachusetts Institute of Technology, 1982.

Dennard, Linda F. "Neo-Darwinism and Simon's Bureaucratic Antihero." *Administration & Society*, 1995, February, Vol. 26, Issue 4, 464-487.

Descartes, Rene. *Discourse on Method and Meditations on First Philosophy.* translated by Donald Cress. Hacket Pub Co, 4th Edition, 1999.

Dimitrov, Vladimir. "Decision Emergence Out of Complexity and Chaos: Manifesto of Emergence." 2001. URL: http://members.tripod.com/~Vlad_3_6_7/Decision-Making-in-Complexity.html

"DISH Network Completes Acquisition of Blockbuster Assets—April 26, 2011." Dishnetwork.mediaroom.com. Retrieved July 23, 2012. http://dishnetwork.mediaroom.com/index.php?s=8778&item=33969.

Dougherty, James E. "The Aswan Decision in Perspective," *Political Science Quarterly*, 1959, Vol. 74, No. 1, March, 21-45.

Drucker, Peter F. *The Practice of Management*. New York: Harper & Row, 1956.

Drucker, Peter. *The Age of Discontinuity*. New York: Harper & Row, 1968.

Dunn, William N. "Probing the Boundaries of Ignorance in Policy Analysis." *American Behavioral Scientist*, 1997, January, Vol. 40, Issue 3, 277-299.

Durlauf, Steven N. "What Should Policymakers Know About Economic Complexity?" *Washington Quarterly*, 1998, Winter, Vol. 21, Issue 1, 157-165.

Dutton, John M., and Starbuck, William H. *Computer Simulation of Human Behavior*. New York: Wiley, 1971.

Eckstein, Max A. "The Comparative Mind: Metaphor in Comparative Education," *Comparative Education Review* 27, 1983: 311-323.

Edwards, George C., III, and Sharkansky, Ira. *The Policy Predicament: Making and Implementing Public Policy*. San Francisco: W.H. Freeman and Company, 1978.

Einstein, Albert. (with commentary by Roger Penrose, Robert Geroch, and David Cassidy. *Relativity: The Special and General Theory*. Pi Press, The Masterpiece Science Edition, 2005.

Eisenhardt, Kathleen M. and Sull, Donald N. "Strategy as Simple Rules." Boston, MA: *Harvard Business Review*, 2001, January, Vol. 79, Issue 1, 106-116.

Eisenhardt, Kathleen M. "Speed and Strategic Choice: How Managers Accelerate Decision Making," In David A. Kolb, Joyce S. Osland, and Irwin M. Rubin, Eds., *The Organizational Behavior Reader*. 6th Edition. Englewood Cliffs, NJ: Prentice Hall, 1995.

Eisenhardt, Kathleen M. "Strategy as Strategic Decision Making." *Sloan Management Review*, 1999, Spring, Vol. 40, Issue 3, 65-72.

Emery, Fred E. (ed.) *Systems Thinking: Selected Readings*. Penguin, 1969.

Emery, Fred E., and Trist, Eric L. "The Causal Texture of Organizational Environments." *Human Organization*, 1965, Vol. 18, 21-32.

Eoyang, Glenda H., Yellowthunder, Lois, and Ward, Victor. "A Complex Adaptive Systems (CAS) Approach to Public Policy Decision Making." *Society for Chaos Theory in Psychology in the Life Sciences*, 1998, August, 1-19.

Etzioni, Amitai. "Mixed Scanning: A Third Approach to Decision Making." *Public Administration Review*, 1967, December, Vol. 27, Issue 12, 385-92.

Fayol, Henri. *General and Industrial Management*. translated by Irwin Gray. Ieee., Rev Sub edition, 1984.

Fernandes, Ronald, and Simon, Herbert A. "A Study of How Individuals Solve Complex and Ill-Structured Problems." *Policy Sciences*, 1999, Vol. 32, 225-245.

Fitzroy, Peter, and Hulbert, James. *Strategic Management: Creating Value in Turbulent Times*. Danvers, MA: John Wiley and Sons, 2005.

Follett, Mary P. *Dynamic Administration*.: New York: Harper & Brothers Publishers, 1942. (Originally published in 1927.)

Foster, Charles A. "Navigating Organization Change: Leading the Way during Turbulent Times." In Huber, Nancy S. and Wren, J. Thomas., Eds., *Leadership Bridges*, College Park, MD: International Leadership Association, 62-69, 2004.

Frankfort-Nachmias, Chava, and Nachmias, David. *Research Methods in the Social Sciences*. New York: St. Martin's Press, 1992.

Fuller, J.F.C. *The Generalship of Alexander the Great*. New York: De Capo Press, 1960.

Gaddis, John Lewis. *The Landscape of History: How Historians Map the Past*. Oxford University Press, 2002.

Geisert, Paul, and Futrell, Mynga. "Free Will: A Human, Fuzzy, Chaotic Process." *Humanist*, 1996, May/Jun, Vol. 56, Issue 3, 26-29.

Gharajedaghi, Jamshid. *Systems Thinking: Managing Chaos and Complexity.* Butterworth-Heinemann, 2005.

Ghyczy, Tiha von, Bolko, Oetinger von, and Bassford, Christopher. *Clausewitz on Strategy, Inspiration and Insight from a Master Strategist.* New York: John Wiley & Sons, Inc, 2001.

Gladwell, Malcolm. *The Tipping Point: How Little Things Can Make a Big Difference.* New York: Little, Brown, and Company, 2000.

Gleick, James. *Chaos: Making a New Science.* New York: Penguin, 1987.

"Global Challenges: Ecological and Technological Advances Around the World". CNN. http://edition.cnn.com/TRANSCRIPTS/0506/18/gc.01. html. Retrieved March 28 2009.

Goldstein, Jeffrey. *The Unshackled Organization: Facing the Challenge of Unpredictability Through Spontaneous Reorganization.* Portland, OR: Productivity Press, 1994.

Graetz, Fiona. "Strategic Thinking versus Strategic Planning: Towards Understanding the Complementarities." *Management Decision*, 2002, Vol. 40, Issue 5/6, 456-462.

Greenberg, George D. et al. "Developing Public Policy Theory: Perspectives from Empirical Research." *American Political Science Review*, December, 1977, Vol. 71, 1532-1543.

Greenleaf, Robert K. *Servant Leadership.* Mahwah, NJ: Paulist Press, 1977.

Grove, Andy. *Only the Paranoid Survive.* New York: Currency Doubleday, 1996.

Gulick, Luther, and Lyndall Urwick, eds. *Papers on the Science of Administration.* New York: Institute of Public Administration, 1937.

Haines, Stephen G. *The Manager's Pocket Guide to Systems Thinking and Learning.* HRD Press, 1998.

Hamel, Gary, and Prahalad, C. K. *Competing for the Future.* New York: Free Press, 1989.

Hannan, Michael T. and Freeman John. *Organizational Ecology.* Cambridge, MA, Harvard University Press, 1989.

Harmon Michael M., and Meyer, Richard T. *Organization Theory for Public Administration.* Burke, VA: Chatalaine Press, 1986.

Harris, Gerald. *The Art of Quantum Planning: Lessons from Quantum Physics for Breakthrough Strategy, Innovation, and Leadership.* Berrett-Koehler, 2009, 16.

Heller, Eric J. and Tomsovic, Steven. "Postmodern Quantum Mechanics." *Physics Today,* 1993, July, Vol. 46, Issue 7, 38-46.

Hill, Charles W. L., and Jones, Gareth R. *Strategic Management Theory.* 10th Edition, South-Western Cenage Learning, 2012.

Hock, Lee. *Birth of the Chaordic Age.* Berrett-Koehler Publishers, 2000.

Holloway, Charles A. *Decisionmaking Under Uncertainty: Models and Choices.* Englewood Cliffs, New Jersey: Prentice-Hall, Inc., 1979.

Horgan, John. "Trends in Complexity Studies: From Complexity to Perplexity." *Scientific American,* 1995, Vol. 272:74-9.

Huber, George P., and Glick, William H., Eds. *Organizational Change and Redesign: Ideas and Insights for Improving Performance.* New York: Oxford University Press, Inc., 1993.

Janis, Irving L. "Groupthink." *Psychology Today,* 1971, November, Volume 5, Issue 6, 43-46, 74-76.

Janis, Irving L. *Victims of Groupthink.* Boston, MA: Houghton Mifflin Company, 1972.

Janis, Irving L. *Groupthink: Psychological Studies of Policy Decisions and Fiascos.* 2nd Edition. Boston: Houghton Mifflin Company, 1982.

Jervis, Robert. "Complex Systems: The Role of Interactions." In Alberts, David S., and Cserwinski, Thomas J., Eds. *Complexity, Global Politics, and National Security.* Washington, D.C.: National Defense University, 1996.

Johnson, Mark W., Christensen, Clayton M., and Kagermann, Henning. "Reinventing your Business Model," in *HBR's 10 Must Reads on Strategy.* Harvard Business Review Press, 2011, 103-122, 122. Originally published in Harvard Business Review, September, 1996.

Jomini, Baron Antoine Henri de. *The Art of War.* Mechanicsburg, PA: Stackpole Books, 1992.

Jones, Richard, and Sheridan, Michael. "Chinese dam causes quakes and landslides"". *The Times* (London). 30 May 10. http://www.timesonline.co.uk/ tol/news/environment/article7140217.ece. Retrieved January 25, 2011.

Joy, Earl R. "Make the Future Happen: A Model for Strategic Planning." *Economic Development Review,* 1999, Vol. 16, Issue 2, 33-34.

Juran, Joseph M. *Juran's Quality Handbook.* Mcgraw Hill Professional; 5th Edition, 2000.

Kaplan, Robert S., and Norton, David P. "Using the Balanced Scorecard as a Strategic Management System." *Harvard Business Review,* 1996, January-February, 75-85.

Kast, Fremont E., and Rosenweig, James E. *Organization and Management: A Systems Approach.* McGraw Hill, 1970.

Kast, Fremont E., and Rosenweig, James E. "General Systems Theory: Applications for Organization and Management." *Academy of Management Journal,* 1972, 447-465.

Katz, Daniel, and Kahn, Robert L. *The Social Psychology of Organizations.* 2nd Edition. New York: John Wiley, 1978. (Note: 1st ed., 1966.)

Kauffman, Stuart A. *The Origins of Order: Self Organization and Selection In Evolution.* New York: Oxford University Press, 1993.

Kauffman, Stuart A. *At Home in the Universe: The Search for Laws of Self-Organization and Complexity.* New York: Oxford University Press, 1995.

Kiel, L. Douglas. "Nonlinear Dynamical Analysis: Assessing Systems Concepts in a Government Agency." *Public Administration Review*, 1993, March/April, Vol. 53, Issue 2, 143-153.

Kiel, L. Douglas. *Managing Chaos and Complexity in Government: A New Paradigm for Managing Change, Innovation, and Organizational Renewal.* San Francisco: Jossey Bass, 1994.

Kiel, L. Douglas, and Elliott, Euel. "Long-Wave Economic Cycles, Techno-Economic Paradigms, and the Pattern of Reform in American Public Administration." *Administration & Society*, 1999, January, Vol. 30, Issue 6, 616-639.

Kolzow, David. "A Perspective on Strategic Planning: What's Your Vision? *Economic Development Review*, 1999, Vol. 16, Issue 2, 5-9.

Kosko, Bart. *Fuzzy Thinking: The New Science of Fuzzy Logic.* Hyperion, 1994.

Kotter, John. *Leading Change.* Harvard Business School Press, 1996.

Kouzes, James M. and Posner, Barry Z. *The Leadership Challenge.* San Francisco: Jossey-Bass, 1995.

Krause, Donald G. *The Art of War for Executives: Ancient Knowledge for Today's Business Professional.* Perigee Trade, 2007.

Kuhn, Thomas S. *The Structure of Scientific Revolutions.* Chicago: University of Chicago Press, 1970.

Landesberg, Phil. "In the Beginning, There Were Deming and Juran." *Journal for Quality & Participation*, 1999, November/December, Vol. 22, Issue 6, 59-61.

Laris, Michael. "Untamed Waterways Kill Thousands Yearly". *Washington Post*. 17 Aug 08, http://www.washingtonpost.com/wp-srv/inatl/longterm/china/stories/death081798.htm. Retrieved 28 Mar 09.

Laszlo, Ervin. *Vision 2020: Reordering Chaos for Global Survival*. Langhorne, PA: Gordon and Breach Science Publishers S.A, 1994.

Lazslo, Ervin. *The Systems View of the World: A Holistic Vision for Our Time (Advances in Systems Theory, Complexity, and the Human Sciences)*. Cresskill, NJ: Hampton Press, 1996.

Lawrence, Paul R. and Lorsch, Jay W. *Organization and Environment: Managing Differentiation and Integration*. Boston: Graduate School of Business Administration, Harvard University, 1967.

Lawrence, Paul R. and Lorsch, Jay W. "Differentiation and Integration in Complex Organizations." *Administrative Science Quarterly*, 1967, Vol. 12, 1-30.

Leana, Carrie R. "Stability and Change as Simultaneous Experiences in Organizational Life." *Academy of Management Review*, 2000, October, Vol. 25 Issue 4, 753-759.

Lencioni, Patrick. *The Five Dysfunctions of a Team: A Leadership Fable*. San Francisco: Jossey-Bass, 2002.

Lewin, Kurt. *Field Theory in Social Science; Selected Theoretical Papers*. D. Cartwright (Ed.). New York: Harper & Row, 1951.

Lewin, Kurt. "Action Research and Minority Problems." *Journal of Social Issues*. 1946, Vol. 2, Issue 4: 34-46.

Liddell, Henry, and George, Robert Scott, *A Greek-English Lexicon*, on Perseus Digital Library.

Liedtka, J. M. "Linking Strategic Thinking with Strategic Planning." *Strategy and Leadership*, 1998, Vol. 26, Issue 4, 30-35.

Lin Yang. "China's Three Gorges Dam Under Fire." *Time*. 12 Dec 07, http://www.time.com/time/world/article/0,8599,1671000,00.html. Retrieved 28 Mar 09.

Lindberg, Curt, et al. "Life at the Edge of Chaos." *Physician Executive*, January/February, 1998, Vol. 24, Issue 1, 6-20.

Lindblom, Charles E. "The Science of Muddling Through." *Public Administration Review*, Spring, 1959, Vol. 19, Issue 2, 79-88.

Lissack, Michael R. "Complexity: The Science, Its Vocabulary, and Its Relation to Organizations." *Emergence*, 1999, Vol. 1, Issue 1, 110-26.

Lorenz, Edward. "Deterministic Nonperiodic Flow." *Journal of the Atmospheric Sciences*, 1963, Vol. 20, 130-141.

Lorenz, Edward. *The Essence of Chaos*. CRC Press, The Jessie and John Danz Lecture Series, 1995.

Luvaas, Jay. *The Legacy of the Civil War: The European Inheritance*. University of Chicago Press, 1959.

Lykke, Arthur F., Jr. "Defining Military Strategy."1997. Reprint from *Military Review*, 1989, Vol. 77, No. 1, Jan.-Feb., 183-186.

Machiavelli, Niccolo. *The Art of War*. Revised Edition. New York: Da Capo Press, 1965.

Mandelbrot, Benoit B. *The Fractal Geometry of Nature*. W.H. Freeman, 1982.

Mandelbrot, Benoit. "Towards a Second Stage of Indeterminism in Science." *Interdisciplinary Science Review*, 1987, Vol. 12, 117-127.

Marion, Russ, and Bacon, Josh. "Organizational Extinction and Complex Systems." *Emergence*, 2000, Vol. 1, Issue 4, 71-96.

Martinex-Moncada. "How Netflix Destroyed Blockbuster." Infographic, May 23, 2011. Retrieved September 29, 2012. http://dailyinfographic.com/how-netflix-destroyed-blockbuster-infographic

Mathews, K. Michael., White, Michael C., and Long, Rebecca G. "Why Study the Complexity Sciences in the Social Sciences?" *Human Relations*, 1999, April, Vol. 52, Issue 4, 439-462.

Maxwell, John C. *Developing the Leader Within You*. Thomas Nelson, 1993.

Maxwell, John C. *The 21 Irrefutable Laws of Leadership*. Nashville, TN: Thomas Nelson, 1998.

Mayo, Elton. *The Human Problems of an Industrial Civilization*. New York: MacMillan, 1933.

McGregor, Douglas. *The Human Side of Enterprise*. New York, McGraw-Hill. 1960.

McNeilly, Mark R. *Sun Tzu and the Art of Business: Six Strategic Principles for Managers*. Revised Edition. Oxford University Press, 2011.

Meadows, Donella H. "Places to Intervene in a System." *Whole Earth*, 1997, Winter, Issue 91, 78-84.

Meadows, Donella H. "Dancing with Systems." *Whole Earth*, 2001, Winter, Issue 106: 58-63.

Meadows, Donella H. *Thinking in Systems*. White River Junction, VT: Chelsea Green Publishing, 2008.

Mintzberg, Henry. *The Rise and Fall of Strategic Planning*. The Free Press, 1994.

Mintzberg, Henry. "The Fall and Rise of Strategic Planning." *Harvard Business Review*, 1994, January/February, Vol. 72, Issue 1, 107-114.

Mintzberg, Henry, Ahlstrand, Bruce, and Lampel, Joseph. *Strategy Bites Back: It is Far More and Less, Than You Ever Imagined*. Pearson Prentice Hall, 2005.

Mitchell, Helen. M. "Avoiding Strategic Planning Failure." A presentation delivered at the Association Strategic Planning National Conference, Long Beach, CA, March 27, 2007. Retrieved August 15, 2007, from http://mediaserver.prweb.com/pdfdownload/513802/pr.pdf.

Morçöl, Goktug. *A New Mind for Policy Analysis: Toward a Post-Newtonian and Postpositivist Epistemology and Methodology.* Westport, CT: Praeger, 2002.

Morçöl, Goktug, Ed. *Handbook of Decision Making.* Boca Raton, FL: CRC Press, Taylor and Francis Group, 2006.

Morçöl, Goktug. "A Framework for a Complexity Theory for Policy Analysis." Paper presented at the PAT-Net Conference, May, Harrisburg, PA, 2007.

Morel, Benoit, and Ramanujam, Rangaraj. "Through the Looking Glass of Complexity: The Dynamics of Organizations as Adaptive and Evolving." *Organization Science: A Journal of the Institute of Management Sciences*, 1999, May/June, Vol. 10, Issue 3, 278-293.

Morgan, Gareth. *Images of Organization.* Thousand Oaks, CA: Sage Publications, 1996.

Morrison, James L. "From Strategic Planning to Strategic Thinking." *On the Horizon*, 1994, Vol. 2, Issue 3, 3-4.

Murray, Williamson, Knox, MacGregor, and Bernstein, Alvin. *The Making of Strategy: Rulers, States, and War.* New York: Cambridge University Press, 1994.

Musashi, Miyamoto. *A Book of Five Rings: The Classic Guide to Strategy.* Translated by Victor Harris. Woodstock, NY: The Overlook Press, 1974.

Nagel, Ernest. *The Structure of Science: Problems in the Logic of Scientific Explanation.* New York: Harcourt Brace, 108.

Newman, Karen L. "Organizational Transformation during Institutional Upheaval." *Academy of Management Review*, 2000, July, Vol. 25, Issue 3, 602-619.

Newman, Rick. (February 6, 2009). "15 Companies That Might Not Survive 2009" ". US News. http://money.usnews.com/money/blogs/flowchart/2009/2/6/15-companies-that-might-not-survive-2009.html. Retrieved September 20, 2012.

Newton, Isaac. *The Principia: Mathematical Principles of Natural Philosophy.* Translated by I. Bernard Cohen and Anne Whitman. University of California Press, 1st Edition, 1999.

Nixon, Richard. *Six Crises.* Doubleday Publishing, 1962.

Osterwalder, Alexander, and Pigneur, Yves. *Business Model Generation: A Handbook for Visionaries, Game Changers, and Challengers.* Wiley, 2010.

Overman, E. Sam. "The New Science of Management: Chaos and Quantum Theory and Method.*" Journal of Public Administration Research & Theory*, 1996, January, Vol. 6, Issue 1, 75-89.

Overman, E. Sam. "The New Sciences of Administration: Chaos and Quantum Theory." *Public Administration Review*, 1996, September/October, Vol. 56, Issue 5, 487-491.

Paret, Peter, ed., *Makers of Modern Strategy from Machiavelli to the Nuclear Age.* Princeton, NJ: Princeton University Press, 1986.

Parson, Talcott, and Shils, Edward A. *Toward a General Theory of Action.* New York: Harper & Row, 1962.

Payton, Susan. "Netflix: The Nimblest Company Wins the Race. *Growth University*, June 3, 2011. Retrieved September 29, 2012. http://www.futuresimple.com/blog/netflix-the-nimblest-company-wins-the-race/

Pegis, Anton C., (Translator) *Basic Writings of St. Thomas Aquinas.* New York: Random House, 1945, 129.

Perrow, Charles. *Normal Accidents: Living with High-Risk Technologies.* New York: Basic Books, Inc., Publishers, 1984.

Peters, Tom. *The Tom Peters Seminar: Crazy Times Call for Crazy Organizations.* London: Macmillan, 1994.

Poincaré, Henri. *Methods of Celestial Mechanics* (Méthodes nouvelles de la mécanique céleste). Edited and introduced by Daniel L. Goroff. Woodbury, NY: American Institute of Physics, 1993.

Poister, Theodore H. and Streib, Gregory D. "Strategic Management in the Public Sector." *Public Productivity & Management Review,* 1999, March, Vol. 22, Issue 3, 308-325.

Porter, Michael E. *Competitive Strategy.* The Free Press, 1980.

Porter, Michael E. *The Competitive Advantage of Nations,* The Free Press, 1990.

Porter, Michael E. "What is Strategy?" *Harvard Business Review,* November/ December, 1996, Vol. 74, Issue 6, 61-78.

Prigogine, Ilya. *Order Out of Chaos.* Shambhala, 1984.

Prigogine, Ilya. *The End of Certainty.* Free Press, 1997.

Qing, Dai. *The River Dragon Has Come: The Three Gorges Dam and the Fate of China's Yangtze River and Its People.* New York: M.E. Sharpe, 1997.

Raymo, Chet. "A New Paradigm for Thomas Kuhn." *Scientific American,* September, 2000, Vol. 283 Issue 3, 104-106.

Raynor, Michael E. *The Strategy Paradox: Why Committing to Success Leads to Failure [And What To Do About It].* Currency Doubleday, 2007.

Richardson, K. A. "Complex Systems Thinking and Its Implications for Policy Analysis." In G. Morçöl, (Ed.), *Handbook of Decision Making,* Boca Raton, FL: CRC Press, Taylor and Francis Group, 2006, 189-221.

Rittel, Horst, and Webber, Melvin M. "Dilemmas in a General Theory of Planning." *Policy Sciences,* 1973, Vol. 4, 155-169.

Robert, Michael. *The New Strategic Thinking, Pure and Simple*. New York: McGraw-Hill, 2006.

Rost, Joseph. *Leadership for the Twenty-First Century*. New York: Praeger, 1991.

Sabatier, Paul A. "The Need for Better Theories." In Paul A. Sabatier (Ed.) *Theories of the Policy Process*, Boulder, CO: Westview, 1999, 3-17.

Sanders, T. Irene. *Strategic Thinking and the New Science*. New York: Free Press, 1998.

Saperstein, Alvin M. "Chaos and National Security Policy: Metaphors or Tools?" In Alberts, David S., and Cserwinski, Thomas J., Eds. *Complexity, Global Politics, and National Security*. Washington, D.C.: National Defense University, 1996. http://www.ndu.edu/ndu/inss/books/complexity/index.html.

Schultz, Norman. "Uncertainty." in *Beyond Intractability*. Eds. Burgess, Guy, and Burgess, Heidi. Conflict Information Consortium, University of Colorado, Boulder. Posted: January 2004, retrieved August 16, 2012. http://www.beyondintractability.org/bi-essay/fact-finding-limits.

Schumpeter, J. A. "The Historical Approach to the Analysis of Business Cycles," in *Essays: On Entrepreneurs, Innovations, Business Cycles, and the Evolution of Capitalism*. New Brunswick, N.J. and London: Transaction, 1949.

Schwartz, Peter. *The Art of the Long View: Planning for the Future in an Uncertain World*. Currency Doubleday, 1991.

Scott, W. Richard. *Organizations: Rational, Natural, and Open Systems*. 4th Ed. Prentice Hall, 1998.

Selznick, Philip. *Leadership in Administration: A Sociological Interpretation*. New York: Harper & Row, 1957.

Senge, Peter M. *The Fifth Discipline*. Doubleday, 1990.

Shafritz, Jay M. and Ott, J. Steven. *Classics of Organization Theory*. 3rd Edition. Pacific Grove, CA: Brooks/Cole Publishing Company, 1992.

Sharkansky, Ira. *Politics and Policy Making: In Search of Simplicity*. London: Lynne Rienner Publishers, 2002.

Shewart, Walter. *A. Statistical Method for the Viewpoint of Quality Control*. New York: Dover, 1939; Deming, W. Edward. *Out of the Crisis*. MIT Center for Advanced Engineering Study, 1986.

Simon, Herbert. *Administrative Behavior: A Study of Decision-Making Processes in Administrative Organizations*. 1947. 4th Edition, The Free Press, 1997.

Simon, Herbert. "Bounded Rationality and Organizational Learning." *Organization Science*, 1991, Vol. 2, Issue 1, 125-134.

Smith, Adam. *An Inquiry into the Nature and Causes of the Wealth of Nations*. translated by Edwin Cannan. London: Methuen and Col., Ltd., 5th Edition, 1904.

Stacey, Ralph. "Management and the Science of Complexity: If Organizational Life is Nonlinear, Can Business Strategies Prevail?" *Research Technology Management*, 1996, May/June, Vol. 39, Issue 3, 8-10.

Stacey, Ralph D. *Complexity and Creativity in Organizations*. San Francisco: Berrett-Koehler Publishers, 1996.

Stahl, Michael J. and Grigsby, David W. *Strategic Management: Total Quality and Global Competition*. Cambridge, MA: Blackwell Business, 1997.

Stein, Daniel L. "Focusing on Complexity and Those Who Study It." *Physics Today*, 1992, December, Vol. 45, Issue 12, 83-85.

Steiner, George. *Strategic Planning: What Every Manager Must Know*. New York: Free Press, 1979.

Stewart, Ian. *Does God Play Dice? The Mathematics of Chaos*. Cambridge, MA: Blackwell, 1989.

Stone, Deborah. *Policy Paradox: The Art of Political Decision Making.* W.W. Norton & Company, 3rd Edition, 2001.

Stringham, Shand H. "A Complexity Approach to Decision Making and Problem Solving Models." A paper presented at the PAT-Net Conference, Harrisburg, PA, May 26-27, 2007.

Strogatz, Steven H. *Nonlinear Dynamics and Chaos: with Applications to Physics, Biology Chemistry and Engineering.* Addison Wesley, 1994.

Stross, Randall E. *The Wizard of Menlo Park: How Thomas Alva Edison Invented the Modern World.* Broadway, 2008.

Sun Tzu, and Sun Pin. *The Complete Art of War.* Translated by Ralph D. Sawyer. Boulder, CO: Westview Press, 1996.

Tasaka, Hiroshi. "Twenty-First Century Management and the Complexity Paradigm." *Emergence*, 1999, Vol. 1, Issue 4, 115-123.

Taylor, Frederick Winslow. *Shop Management.* New York, NY: American Society of Mechanical Engineers, 1903.

Taylor, Frederick Winslow. *The Principles of Scientific Management.* New York: Harper & Brothers, 1911.

Taylor, Mark C. *The Moment of Complexity: Emerging Network Culture.* Chicago: The University of Chicago Press, 2001.

Thakur, Manab, and Calingo, Luis Ma. R. "Strategic Thinking Is Hip, But Does It Make A Difference?" *Business Horizons*, 1992, September/October, Vol. 35, Issue 5, 47-54.

"The Making of a Blockbuster". Bloomberg Businessweek. Retrieved July 23, 2011, http://www.businessweek.com/chapter/chap0009.htm.
Topping, Audrey Ronning. Environmental controversy over the Three Gorges Dam. Earth Times News Service, 12 May 1998.

Treadwell, William A. "Fuzzy Set Theory Movement in the Social Sciences." *Public Administration Review*, 1995, January/February, Vol. 55, Issue 1, 91-98.

Trist, Eric L. "The Evolution of Sociotechical Systems as a Conceptual Framework and as an Action Research Program" in *Perspectives on Organization Design and Behavior*. Edited by A. H. Van de Ven and W. F. Joyce. New York: Wiley—Interscience, 1975.

Verne, Jules. *Journey to the Center of the Earth*. Malleson translation; Ward, Lock & Co., 1877.

Vaill, Peter. *Managing as a Performing Art: New Ideas for a World of Chaotic Change*. San Francisco: Jossey Bass, 1991.

Waldo, Dwight. *The Administrative State: A Study of the Political Theory of American Public Administration*. (1st Edition, 1948), 2nd Edition, New York: Holmes and Meier Publishers, 1984.

Waldrop, M. Mitchell. *Complexity: The Emerging Science at the Edge of Order and Chaos*. New York: Simon & Schuster, 1992.

Warren, Keith, Franklin, Cynthia, and Streeter, Calvin L. "New Directions in Systems Theory: Chaos and Complexity." *Social Work*, 1998, July, Vol. 43, Issue 4, 357-372.

Weber, Max, *Economy and Society: An Outline of Interpretive Sociology*, University of California Press, 1978.

Weick, Karl E. *Sensemaking in Organizations*. Thousand Oaks, CA: Sage Publications, 1995.

Weick, Karl. E., and Sutcliffe, Kathleen. M. *Managing the Unexpected: Resilient Performance in an Age of Uncertainty*. San Francisco: Jossey-Bass, 2001.

Weigley, Russell F. *The American Way of War: A History of United States Military Strategy and Policy*. Bloomington: Indiana University Press, 1973.

Weinberg, Gerald M. *An Introduction to General Systems Thinking*. Dorset House Publishing, 1975.

Welter, Bill, and Egmon, Jean. *The Prepared Mind of a Leader: Eight Skills Leaders Use to Innovate, Make Decisions, and Solve Problems*. San Francisco: Jossey-Bass, 2006.

Wheatley, Margaret. *Leadership and the New Science: Discovering Order in a Chaotic World*. 3rd Edition, San Francisco: Berrett-Koehler Publishers, Inc., 2006.

Whitesides, George M., and Ismagilov, Rustem F. "Complexity in Chemistry." *Science*, 1999, Vol. 284, Issue 5411, 89-92.

Wilson, G.I. "Abundance of Planning Failures, Webster University. Retrieved August 16, 2012, from http://www.projectwhitehorse.com/pdfs/Planning%20-%20Wilson.pdf

Winchester, Simon *The River at the Center of the World*. New York: Henry Holt & Co., 1998.

Wirth, Ross A. Lewin/Schein's Change Theory. 2004. URL: http://www.entarga.com/orgchange/lewinschein.pdf

Wooton, Simon, & Horne, Terry. *Strategic Thinking: A Step-by-Step Approach to Strategy*. Second Edition. Sterling, VA: Kogan Page Ltd., 2002.

Wylie, Joseph C. *Military Strategy: A General Theory of Power Control*. Annapolis: Naval Institute Press, 1989.

Wyman, O. "Discontinuous Change: The Unique Challenges of Radical Transformation." *Delta Organization and Leadership*. Marsh, Mercer & Kroll, 2003. http://www.oliverwyman.com/ow/pdf_files/Discontinuous_Change_POV.pdf

Yang, Sung. "No Casualties in Three Gorges Dam Landslide"". *Xinhua News Network*. CRIEnglish.com. http://english.cri.cn/6909/2009/05/19/45s485830.htm. Retrieved June 3, 2009.

Yarger, H. Richard. *Towards a Theory of Strategy: Art Lykke and the Army War College Strategy Model.* U.S. Army War College, Carlisle Barracks, Carlisle, PA, 1997.

Zadeh, Lofti. "Fuzzy Sets." *Information and Control,* 1965, Vol. 8, 338-353.

Zadeh, L. A. "Fuzzy Sets." In R. Yager, S. Ovchinnikov, R. Tong, and H Nguyen, Eds., *Fuzzy Sets and Applications: Selected Papers by L. A. Zadah.* New York: John Wiley and Sons, 1987.

Ziegenfuss, James T., Jr. *Relearning Strategic Planning: Lessons of Philosophy and Procedure.* Allen Press, 1996.

Zohar, Danah. "What Would A Quantum Organization Look Like?" *Management Review,* 1998, March, Vol. 87, Issue 3, 56-58.

Zuckerman, Alan M. "Is Strategic Planning Relevant Anymore?" *Trustee,* 2000, April, Vol. 53, Issue 4, 26-27.